THE BIRTH OF THE CHURCH

AD 33–200

THE CHURCH IN HISTORY SERIES of St Vladimir's Seminary Press balances the approaches of the abundance of church histories written from a Western Christian point of view. Series authors—in the unique position of being Orthodox scholars conversant with Western scholarship—have taken on the task of analyzing complicated primary sources and thoroughly critiquing modern scholarly literature to guide readers through the maze of centuries of church formation and life. Through fresh eyes, they chronicle the past with fairness, objectivity, and sympathy, and add equilibrium to the annals of Christendom.

Series Editor
ANDREW LOUTH

Previous Series Editors
JOHN MEYENDORFF (†1992), JOHN H. ERICKSON

volume I
Formation and Struggles: The Church AD 33–450
Part I: The Birth of the Church AD 33–200
by Veselin Kesich

volume II
Imperial Unity and Christian Divisions: The Church AD 450–680
by John Meyendorff

volume III
Greek East and Latin West: The Church AD 681–1071
by Andrew Louth

volume IV
The Christian East and the Rise of the Papacy: The Church AD 1071–1453
by Aristeides Papadakis

THE CHURCH IN HISTORY, VOLUME I

FORMATION AND STRUGGLES
THE CHURCH AD 33–450

PART I

The Birth
of the Church

AD 33–200

VESELIN KESICH

ST VLADIMIR'S SEMINARY PRESS
CRESTWOOD, NEW YORK
2007

Library of Congress Cataloging-in-Publication Data

Kesich, Veselin. 1921–.
    Formation and struggles : the church, A.D. 33–450 / by Veselin Kesich
    p. cm. – (The church in history)
    Includes bibliographical references and index.
    ISBN 978-0-88141-319-9 (alk. paper)
    1. Church history–Primitive and early church, ca. 30–600. I. Title.

BR162.5.K47 2007
270.1–dc22

                                        2007029373

ST VLADIMIR'S SEMINARY PRESS
575 Scarsdale Road, Crestwood, NY 10707
1–800–204–2665
www.svspress.com

ISBN 978-0-88141-319-9
ISSN 1938-8306

PRINTED IN THE UNITED STATES OF AMERICA

To the memory of

Lydia,

beloved wife, wonderful mother, generous "Grandma L."

*She contributed to the shape of this book and
eagerly transcribed my handwritten text.*

CONTENTS

ILLUSTRATIONS

1. Veneranda and Saint Petronilla. Location: Catacomb of S. Domitilla, Rome, Italy. Photo Credit: Scala/Art Resource, NY.

2. General view with Corinthian Columns. Location: Asklepion, Kos, Greece. Photo Credit: Vanni/Art Resource, NY.

3. Scale model of Jerusalem and the second temple at the time of King Herod the Great (ca 20 BCE). The picture shows the temple compound. Location: Holy Land Hotel, Jerusalem, Israel. Photo Credit: Erich Lessing/Art Resource, NY.

4. Silver shekel of the Second Jewish Revolt from Rome. Jewish, AD 133–35. From Judaea (modern Israel). CM 1908,0110.776. On the obverse (front) of this coin can be seen a representation of the façade of the Temple at Jerusalem. On the reverse is depicted the ritual "Lulav," a palm-branch tied together with willow and myrtle branches. Location: British Museum, London, Great Britain. Photo Credit: © British Museum/Art Resource, NY.

5. Interdiction for non-Jews to enter the Inner Sanctum of the temple in Jerusalem. Greek inscription from the outer wall of the temple. Saint Paul was falsely accused of having introduced a former pagan into the precinct. Plaster cast. 3rd BCE–IST CE. Location: Museo della Civilta Romana, Rome, Italy. Photo Credit: Erich Lessing/Art Resource, NY.

6. The theatre of Ephesus, built under Lysimachos. View towards the audience. The theatre was reconstructed during IST BCE and IST CE. Saint Paul preached here. Location: Ephesus, Turkey. Photo Credit : Erich Lessing/Art Resource, NY.

7. The victorious army of Titus with the spoils from Jerusalem. c. 90 CE. Marble. 204 x 380 cm. Location: Arch of Titus, Rome, Italy. Photo Credit: Alinari/Art Resource, NY.

8. Gerasa (Jerash) in the north of Jordan, was a Hellenistic-Roman town which became rich as a safe trading post for Nabataean, Jewish and Roman merchants. Columns of the propylaeum of the Artemis-Temple on a hill above the cardo (main street). Photo Credit: Erich Lessing/Art Resource, NY.

9. Arrest of Saint Paul. Detail from the "Travellers sarcophagus." Early Christian. Location: St. Victor Basilica, Marseille, France. Photo Credit: Erich Lessing/Art Resource, NY.

FOREWORD

In the 1980s, Father John Meyendorff planned a six-volume history of the Church, written by Orthodox scholars, to be called *The Church in History*, which was to be published by St Vladimir's Seminary Press. In 1989, his own volume was the first to appear, *Imperial Unity and Christian Divisions: The Church AD 450–680*, numbered as the second volume in the series. In 1994, volume 4 in the series appeared, *The Christian East and the Rise of the Papacy: The Church AD 1071–1453*, written by Aristeides Papadakis, with Father John himself having contributed the chapters on the Slav world. At the time of publication, Father John was dead; he had died prematurely in 1992. Thereafter the project lost steam, and most of those whom Father John had approached to contribute to the other four volumes thought that, in the absence of Father John's leadership, the project had fallen by the wayside. Professor Veselin Kesich, however, who had been Father John's colleague on the faculty of St Vladimir's Seminary, had not given up hope, and completed the first part of volume 1, *Formation and Struggles: The Church AD 33–450*, which covers the first two centuries of Christian history and is entitled, *The Birth of the Church AD 33–200*. The second part of volume 1, covering the period AD 200–450, is to appear later as a separate half-volume.

It has been my distinct honour and pleasure to follow Father Meyendorff as series editor, and to author the third volume, *Greek East and Latin West: The Church AD 681–1071*. Upon publication of planned volumes 5 and 6 respectively, *The Crisis of Tradition: The Church AD 1453–1782* and *The Orthodox Church and the Modern World: The Church AD 1782–the Present*, the completed series, I sincerely hope, will be a fitting tribute to Father John's scholarship and vision.

–Andrew Louth
General Editor

PREFACE

I wish to express my thanks to Professor Andrew Louth, general editor of The Church in History series, for providing me with some bibliographical data, comments, and valuable suggestions.

I am particularly grateful to Deborah Belonick, editor at St Vladimir's Seminary Press, for her close reading of the text and editorial work. Her many queries brought clarity where there was ambiguity.

Needless to say, I am responsible for any error or misinterpretation of the views of others expressed in the text.

—Veselin Kesich, Professor of New Testament Emeritus,
St Vladimir's Orthodox Theological Seminary

ABBREVIATIONS

A.H. = *Against the Heresies [Adversus haeresies]*, Irenaeus of Lyons

A.J. = *Apocryphon of John*

A.N. = *To the Nations [Ad Nationes]*, Tertullian

Ann. = *Annales*, Tacitus

Ant. = *Antiquities of the Jews*, Josephus

I Apol. = *First Apology*, Justin Martyr

II Apol. = *Second Apology*, Justin Martyr

BAR = *Biblical Archeological Review*

Barn. = *Letter of Barnabas*

Bib = *Biblica*. Rome, Italy. v.1 (1920)-

BR = *Biblical Review*

C.C. = *Against Celsus [Contra Celsum]*, Origen

Claud. = *The Life of Claudius [De Vita Caesarum: Divus Claudius]*, Suetonius

1–2 Clem. = *1–2 Clement*, Clement of Rome

De Anima = *On the Soul [De Anima]*, Tertullian

Dial. = *Dialogue with Trypho*, Justin Martyr

Did. = *The Teaching [Didache]*

Ep. Tra. = *Epistulae ad Trajanum*, Pliny the Younger

Gos. Thom. = *Gospel of Thomas*

H.E. = *Ecclesiastical History [Historia Ecclesiastica}*, Eusebius

Herm. Mand. = *Mandate(s)*, Shepherd of Hermas

Herm. Sim. = *Similitude(s)*, Shepherd of Hermas

Herm. Vis. = Vision(s), Shepherd of Hermas

HTR = Harvard Theological Review

Ign. *Eph. = To the Ephesians*, Ignatius

Ign. *Magn. = To the Magnesians*, Ignatius

Ign. *Phld. = To the Philadelphians*, Ignatius

Ign. *Pol. = To Polycarp*, Ignatius

Ign. *Rom. = To the Romans*, Ignatius

Ign. *Smyrn. = To the Smyrnaeans*, Ignatius

Ign. *Trall. = To the Trallians*, Ignatius

JBL = Journal of Biblical Literature

J.W. = The Jewish War, Josephus

Mart. Pol. = Martyrdom of Polycarp

Nero = Nero

NJBC = New Jerome Biblical Commentary

NTS = New Testament Studies

Numen = Numen: International Review for the History of Religion

Plea = A Plea Regarding Christians, Athenagorus

Pol. *Phil. = Letter to the Philippians*, Polycarp

Praescr. = De praescriptione haereticorum [On the prescription of heretics], Tertullian

Protr. = Protrepticus [Exhortation to the Greeks], Clement of Alexandria

Ps.-Clem. = Homilies and *Recognitions*, Pseudo-Clementine

SBT = Studies in Biblical Theology

Strom. = Stromata [Miscellanies], Clement of Alexandria

SVTQ = St Vladimir's Theological Quarterly (formerly *SVSQ = St Vladimir's Seminary Quarterly*)

INTRODUCTION

T his book is intended for the general reader who is interested in the formation of the earliest Christian community and its first Christological
reflections and convictions. It is a short history of Christian origins, covering
some of the most important events from the public ministry of Jesus, the
founder of Christianity, up to the church father, Irenaeus, who sums up second-century development.

In 1947, Hebrew and Aramaic scrolls were discovered at Qumran, near the
Dead Sea. Most scholars regard these scrolls as expressions of the views of the
Essenes, a pre-Christian Jewish group. When the finds were identified, many
began searching them for clues to Jesus, his world, and his times. The search
has been fruitless, however. "There's nothing in the scrolls about Jesus,"
declared Emanuel Tov, chief editor of the Scrolls, in an interview (*Biblical
Archeological Review,* May/June 2002); but, Tov concluded that what we did
find here is something of the language and background of the New Testament, though nothing about Jesus or John the Baptist.

Two years earlier, in 1945, Coptic codices (books) were unearthed at Nag
Hammadi, Egypt. Many of these treatises were of a Gnostic character. Of
them all, the Gospel of Thomas is generally considered the most significant.
This title is misleading, however, as this "gospel" is clearly different from the
four New Testament Gospels. It is a collection of sayings attributed to Jesus.
We are not given his historical portrait or data on his ministry. For this we
must turn to the New Testament Gospels, which "emanate" from the histor-
ical Jesus, whom "they reflect from the post-Easter standpoint," as the noted
New Testament scholar Rudolf Schnackenburg observed in *Jesus in the Gospels:
A Biblical Christology* (1995).

The rise of Christianity began with the formation of the earliest Christian
community in Jerusalem, led by Jesus' disciples. They had witnessed to his
death and resurrection and participated in the daily life and affairs of the
church. Under such leadership, the Jerusalem community could never deny
or minimize the importance of knowledge of the historical Jesus.

Before the Apostle Paul's call and conversion, the church already had its message, liturgical life, and Christological convictions. Paul was not the founder of Christianity, nor did he "invent" the Christian message. He suffered martyrdom as Jesus' ambassador. His letters to the churches reveal the life of Christians, their struggle, faith, and hope in the age of religious syncretism. Later embraced by Gnostics, although he was not a Gnostic, Paul was attacked by some Jewish Christian sects for his failure to convert the Jews. Some of Paul's opponents even denied his Jewish heritage, reproaching him for being a Gentile, not a Jew.

Following the martyrdom of the apostles James, Peter, and Paul, and, above all, after the destruction of the temple in AD 70, the partition between Christians and Jews became noticeable as the followers of Jesus were expelled from the synagogues. The disastrous Second Jewish-Roman War (AD 132–135) intensified what had been a "family quarrel." The break between Christians and Jews exposed the Christians to the eventual persecution by Roman authorities. Unlike the Jews, the Christians now appeared to them to be a new religious group, without old roots and traditions. They were suspected of secret activities and therefore considered a danger to Roman society.

Christianity did not rebel against Roman society, but rejected the cult of the emperor. They prayed *for* the emperor, but refused to pray *to* the emperor. Sporadic outbreaks against Christians followed. Martyrs witnessing to the historical and resurrected Jesus argued against their accusers, evidently a new experience for the Romans. These "Apologists" pointed out the differences between Christianity and Platonism, expanding the field of theological reflection with their "Logos" Christology. The best known of them is Justin the Philosopher, also fittingly called "Justin Martyr."

Nevertheless, an even greater danger to the church than Roman persecution came from within Christian communities, from those who did not deliver what they received from the apostles but substituted their own speculations. The first main controversy centered on the Incarnation. The so-called Docetics and Gnostics denied that the "heavenly Christ" could become flesh: he only appeared to be human, but was not so in reality. For the most part, Docetics and Gnostics did not have their own congregations, but grew in the midst of the Christian churches. Nevertheless, Gnostics within the Christian communities, as well as Gnostic groups outside the boundary lines of the church, practiced their own rituals; a member of the group would lead their cultic celebrations. So, whether within or outside of the Christian churches, Gnostics presented a serious challenge to the apostolic church. Through the decades, as the Christian church spread, three new Christian centers appeared: Rome, Antioch, and Alexandria; Gnostics and Docetics were involved in all these communities. Starting with the historical Jesus, we shall conclude our narrative of the formative Christian period with Irenaeus and the church's struggle against Gnosticism.

CHAPTER ONE

JESUS OF NAZARETH:
THE FOUNDER

Over the cross of Jesus, Pontius Pilate, the Roman Prefect, ordered the
title: "Jesus of Nazareth, King of the Jews" in "Hebrew, in Latin, and
in Greek" (John 19:19f). The three languages stood for the three distinct and
intersecting worlds in which Jesus lived and conducted his mission.

For centuries, the Jewish people had lived under foreign domination,
often brutal. In 538 BC the Persians under Cyrus, founder of the empire, ended
the Babylonian captivity of the Jews, returning them to Jerusalem. Now, by
538 BC, they could restore Solomon's temple, which the Babylonians had
destroyed.

Alexander the Great (333–323 BC) ended Persian rule there, replacing Persian with Greek dominance. Alexander and his successors forced the Hellenization of Palestine. After the conqueror's death and wars of succession,
around 200 BC, Palestine finally passed to the rule of the Seleucids, successors of Alexander's general Seleucus. They strove more forcefully to bring the
people of Palestine into the world of Greek culture and language. Some aris-
tocratic families were susceptible to the pressure of the Seleucids, but most
Jews resisted. Clashes between pious Jews and the agents of Hellenism
became more frequent under Antiochus IV (175–164 BC) when he added the
title "Epiphanes" ["Zeus is manifested"] to his name. By trying to bring all
the diverse peoples of his empire under the protection of Zeus, he directly
confronted Jewish practice. He even forbade celebration of the Sabbath and
circumcision and installed an altar to Zeus in the temple. Jews were ordered
to offer sacrifices to Greek gods. Antiochus appointed inspectors to enforce
his order of 167 BC.

Conflict started immediately. Judas Maccabeus (his name probably means
"the hammer") led a successful revolt. King Antiochus V, the successor of

Antiochus IV, restored Jewish worship and allowed the Jews to follow practices according to the Torah. The Jews had fought for their identity in the
world of Hellenism and were victorious. To safeguard their achievement, they
began building "fences" around the Torah. Nevertheless, Jewish unity forged
in the victorious war disintegrated soon after the triumph. Three religious
groups evolved from the Hasidim, the "pious ones" of the Maccabean
period: the Essenes, the Sadducees, and the Pharisees. The political and religious ambitions of the Maccabees provoked divisions among the Jews.
Jonathan, a member of the Maccabean family, was appointed high priest (AD
152–143) by a Syrian Hellenistic successor to Antiochus IV; but he was not of
the high priestly family of Zadok, and traditional Jews rejected him. In protest
against the ascension of the Maccabees to the high priesthood, some Jews
under the leadership of a Zadokite priest, known to us from the Dead Sea
Scrolls as the Teacher of Righteousness, withdrew into the wilderness and
founded their own sect (probably the Essenes). They settled at Qumran, produced the Dead Sea Scrolls, and called themselves the sons of Zadok. Some
of them spread to a section of Jerusalem, where Jesus may have met them.
Although there are no direct references to them in the Gospels, some material in Jesus' parables suggests that he was aware of their teaching.

Shortly afterward, the parties of the Pharisees and Sadducees emerged.
The Pharisees ["those who are separated"], like Essenes, descended from the
supporters of the Maccabees and their goals, but could not tolerate the mis-
use of religion as a tool "through which all inhabitants of the country could
be made loyal to Jerusalem, where the ruler was at the same time the high
priest."[1] Remaining in Jerusalem, the Pharisees opposed the religious policies
of the Maccabees. Finally they came into conflict with the ruling family and
were severely persecuted by Alexander Janneus (104–76 BC). About eight hundred were crucified. When the Pharisees regained their influence after the
death of Alexander Janneus, they reacted against the Sadducees, former advi-
sors to the now-deceased king, and they "repaid them like for like."[2]

The Sadducees ["Zadokites"] were mentioned first in the second century
BC, when the Pharisees also appeared as a group. In contrast to them, they orig-

---

[1]Helmut Koester, *History, Culture, and Religion of the Hellenistic Age* (vol. 1 of *Introduction to the New Testament;* English translation; Philadelphia, PA: Fortress Press, 1982), p. 218.

[2]Martin Hengel, *Crucifixion in the Ancient World and the Folly of the Message of the Cross* (Philadelphia, PA: Fortress Press, 1977), p. 60ff.

inated with the wealthy families, who had profited from trade in the land. Their religious interest was in the temple and its cult. They accepted the first five books of Moses and interpreted them literally. They regarded the prophets as disturbers of the peace. When the king assumed the duties of high priest, the Sadducees had no objection and some served as priests in the temple.

These three groups, appearing in the second century BC, had one thing in common: all were preoccupied with the law and its demands. The Essenes broke with Jerusalem, protesting that the law was not fully observed there. Their leader, the Teacher of Righteousness, was an interpreter of Scripture, especially of the law. The Pharisees, as described by the first-century Jewish historian Josephus, were "considered the most accurate interpreters of the laws." They tried to extend the observance of the laws of ritual purity outside the temple, to all aspects of life. Their messianic expectation was inseparable from the fulfillment of the law. In contrast, the Sadducees did not trust in a messiah and were inflexible in their literal attitude toward the law. Jesus attacked this literal-mindedness, accusing the Sadducees of knowing neither the Scripture nor the power of God (Matt 22:23–33 and paral.).

In the time of forced Hellenization, the Jews in the struggle for their identity emphasized the law. As a consequence, they discouraged criticism of the law and the temple, so that prophetic criticism "could no longer develop freely within Judaism"; and, both Jesus' and the Apostle Paul's attitudes toward the law would be considered "intolerable."[3] The New Testament indicates that the Pharisees and Sadducees reacted occasionally with violence against the Christian leaders because of their attitude toward the law and the temple. Indeed there were Jewish sages who could not be confined within the legalistic piety of these groups, and they would speak in accord with Jesus and Paul.[4]

By 63 BC, Rome conquered Palestine. The struggle over the succession to the high priesthood had led to the disintegration of the ruling dynasty in Jerusalem. Pharisees, Sadducees, and others took an active part in the dynastic struggle and appealed to the Romans to help them to solve the problem of succession. Pompey responded, intervening to terminate Hasmonean [Maccabean] rule.[5]

---

[3]Martin Hengel, *Judaism and Hellenism: Studies in Their Encounter in Palestine During the Early Hellenistic Period* (Eugene, OR: Wipf & Stock Publishers, 2003), p. 308.

[4]Ibid., p. 77.

[5]"Hasmonean" comes from Hasmon, the family name of Mattathian, whose son Judas (166–60 BC) took the surname "Maccabeus."

Pompey entered the temple without destroying it or taking its treasure and was surprised that the temple was without images. He allowed the Jews to continue temple sacrifices and other observances. From the time of the conquest, Palestine would remain under the domination of the Roman rulers, either Eastern or Western, for about seven centuries.

Following the conquest of Palestine, the Romans supported the claim of Herod, a friend of Rome, to be king of Judea. Herod was of Idumean origin and kept close contact with the Roman authorities, to whom he gave his unflinching support. He viewed the Romans as the victors and took their side. True, he had erred in supporting Mark Antony against Augustus, but quickly shifted support to him. The Romans rewarded Herod for his loyalty. He was King of the Jews from 37–4 BC. To honor Augustus, he rebuilt the ancient city of Samaria into a Hellenistic city, naming it Sebaste [Greek for Augustus]. As a Hellenizer and a tyrant, Herod imposed peace upon his subjects. Some of the population became involved in trade and commerce and enjoyed prosperity, but many of his people remembered Herod for murdering his wife and others. The nativity story in the Gospel of Matthew reflects Herod's ruthlessness.

Resented by the Jews, Herod tried to earn their trust and loyalty by rebuilding the temple. The work started in 20 BC and was completed long after Herod's death, just before the new temple was destroyed by the Romans in AD 70.[6] The grandeur of Herod's temple is known to us from archeological excavations. This was the temple that Jesus knew, and the earliest disciples visited it for prayer. Still, Herod was not a born Jew but an Idumean, of the tribe that had been forcefully converted to Judaism by the Hasmoneans; and the aggressive measures the Maccabeans had used to convert the people of the areas they conquered during their wars of liberation had earned their distrust.

The death of a strong ruler was often followed by disputes among his followers, who fought to succeed him. After Herod's death the Romans had to intervene to reconcile his three quarreling sons by dividing the kingdom he had built into three parts, but they did not grant the title of King to any of them. Herod Archelaus (4 BC–AD 6, mentioned in Matt 2:22) became ethnarch over half of Judea, Samaria, and Idumea. He was a cruel and incompetent ruler whom Rome removed, appointing a Roman procurator, or

---

[6]For his preparation for the new temple, see Veselin and Lydia Kesich, *Treasures of the Holy Land* (Crestwood, NY: St Vladimir's Seminary Press, 1985), p. 53f.

governor, in his place. One of these Roman governors was Pontius Pilate (AD 26–37). Herod Antipas, whose name is frequently mentioned in the Gospels, became Tetrarch of Galilee and Perea (4 BC–AD 39), the ruler of about a quarter of Herod's original territory. Jesus referred to him as "that fox" (Luke 13:31–32). According to Luke, he was involved in the trial of Jesus (Luke 23:6–16; Acts 4:27). To honor the Roman Emperor Tiberius (AD 14–37), Antipas named his capital Tiberias. The rest of Herod's kingdom, to the east and north of the Sea of Galilee, was entrusted to Philip (4 BC–AD 33/4). He rebuilt the old Greek town of Paneas and named it Caesarea Philippi in honor of the Roman Emperor. This was the site of Peter's confession (Mark 8:27–33 and paral.). The world into which Jesus was born and carried on his public ministry emerged out of the Jewish struggle against Hellenization, the breakup of the religious unity, and the appearance of groups within Judaism, as well as the conquest of Palestine by the Romans.

The Four Gospels

Our knowledge of the particulars of Jesus' ministry is found in the narration of the four Gospels, which are our main source for what Jesus said and did. So much depends on them that it is no wonder that they have been subjected for the past two hundred years to a thorough literary and historical investigation. Written between AD 65 and 95, following the apostolic preaching and teaching, these founding Christian documents invite historical research.

Of the four Gospels, most scholars agree that the Gospel of Mark is the earliest written, John is the latest, and Matthew and Luke used Mark as their major source. What Matthew and Luke have in common that are not found in Mark, some scholars ascribe to a hypothetical source, Q [*Quelle*, German for "source"]; so, Matthew and Luke contain some traditions of their own. The first three canonical Gospels are known as "Synoptic Gospels." Their texts can be seen harmonizing when arranged in parallel columns. While the majority of scholars endorse this two-source theory, some try new approaches to the synoptic premise. They reject the view that the formation of the Gospels was simply a literary problem. The Gospels grew incorporating both oral and written traditions.[7]

---

[7]See Veselin Kesich, *The Gospel Image of Christ* (2d ed.; Crestwood, NY: St Vladimir's Seminary Press, 1991), p. 92.

Even if the early dates of the Gospels are accepted, scholars have been working to determine which sayings attributed to Jesus are genuine and which are of later origin. Most scholars would accept two exegetical methods. On the one hand, some accept a saying as authentic if it is found in several layers of gospel tradition. On the other hand, others would insist that to be authentic, a saying ascribed to Jesus must be dissimilar "to characteristic emphases both of ancient Judaism and of the early church."[8] This latter approach is known as the "criterion of double dissimilarity." If applied without being supplemented by other criteria, this distinction would separate Jesus from his environment and isolate him from the followers who bear witness to him. It "disincarnates" Jesus and offers a limited view of the originality of his teaching. Scholars who rely heavily on the criterion of double dissimilarity accept as authentic very few of Jesus' sayings.

Out of the quest for the historical Jesus came a group of biblical scholars concentrating upon the Synoptic sayings, and applying an extreme form of the criterion of double dissimilarity—the group who started the Jesus Seminar in 1985, publishing the results of their research in *The Five Gospels: The Search for the Authentic Words of Jesus* in 1993. They claimed that out of a great number of sayings attributed to Jesus in the four Gospels (as well as the Gospel of Thomas) only a few actually were spoken by Jesus. In the Gospel of Mark, for instance, out of more than a hundred sayings only one was accepted as authentic: "Render to Caesar the things that are Caesar's, and to God the things that are God's" (Mark 2:17). All other sayings were excluded as too "Jewish" or too "Christian," that is, as the church's creation. They separated Jesus as a historical figure from first-century Judaism as well as from the Christian community, which preserved the memory of his eyewitnesses and followers. Adding a dramatic flourish, they cast their votes with colored beads: red for Jesus' authentic sayings, black for those created by the church, and pink or gray for those sayings in doubt. In their evaluation of the Lord's Prayer, for example, the seminar accepted only the first two words, "Our Father," as spoken by Jesus. They deemed Jesus' proclamation of God's kingdom as applying to the present only. There is no future kingdom in the teaching of Jesus, they concluded. For members of the seminar, eschatology was a product of the early church. Clearly, seminar participants did not simply

[8]Norman Perrin, *Rediscovering the Teaching of Jesus* (New York: HarperCollins, 1967), p. 39.

separate "authentic" sayings of Jesus from "non-authentic," but offered a new image of Jesus, a revisionist Jesus, their version of Christian origins.

To the four canonical Gospels the seminar added the Gospel of Thomas, which in their view originated in a very early period, between AD 30 and 60, antedating the Synoptics and used as an independent source. Many scholars have sharply questioned these claims. This gospel, discovered at Nag Hammadi in 1947 in Egypt in a fourth-century Coptic text translated from Greek, was written probably in the second century. It consists of 114 sayings of Jesus without a historical framework or narrative and without eschatology. Some of those sayings may have been derived from the Synoptic Gospels or their sources, but are clearly edited under the influence of gnostics. As a whole, the Gospel of Thomas has a gnostic orientation.[9] Further, the Synoptics and John testify to the life, death, and resurrection of Jesus, but members of the seminar rejected the Fourth Gospel as a historically valid source of Jesus' sayings.

However, the overriding result of modern critical investigation has firmly established that the Jesus of the Gospels belongs to history, not to mythology, and that "the quest for the historical Jesus gives concrete context to our theological statements and thus does play a useful role in theology."[10] The evangelists, who belonged to the second Christian generation, incorporated into their Gospels traditions that had been circulating from the earliest period of the Christian community. They knew Jesus as the disciples had remembered and witnessed to him. Their main impetus for writing was to compile an account of what Jesus had said and done. Clearly, evidence in support of the four canonical Gospels as the founding documents of history and faith has been accepted by the prevailing number of scholars, despite the publicity of the Jesus Seminar and despite the current popular fascination with gnostic gospels and writings.

Jesus of the Gospels

BIRTH, BAPTISM, AND PUBLIC MINISTRY

Jesus was born into a pious Jewish home, brought up with the Scriptures and prayer books of the Jews. Mary was his mother and Joseph his legal father.

---

[9]See our *Gospel Image of Christ*, p. 125ff, and Robert J. Miller and Ben Witherington, III, "Battling over the Jesus Seminar," *BR* 13.2 (1997): 18–26.

[10]See J.P. Meier's article on "Jesus" in *NJBC* 78:10.

His mother Mary is mentioned by name in the Synoptic Gospels (Matthew, Mark and Luke) as well as in the Book of Acts. Her name appears in Luke about thirteen times, in Mark only once (Mark 6:30). Matthew and Luke tell us that the birth took place in Bethlehem during the reign of Herod (Matt 2:1; Luke 1:5, 2:4–6). Jesus was brought up in Nazareth (Matt 2:23, Luke 2:39).

Around AD 27 Jesus withdrew into the Judean desert and was baptized by John, known as "the Baptist" in Jewish and Christian sources. There were several Jewish groups or sects baptizing along the Jordan River. While their baptisms were repeatable purification acts, John's baptism was a onetime unrepeatable rite. John the Baptist was a prophet who called Israel to repentance, to "bear fruits that befit repentance," for the "tree that does not bear good fruit is cut down and thrown into the fire" (Matt 3:7–10). In God's judgment, the repentant, the renewed people of God, would be spared that fire. The dialogue between Jesus and John that we find in Matt 3:7–10 confirms Jesus' baptism by John. His subordination to John here may have been an embarrassment to some Christians.

The synoptic tradition relates Jesus' baptism to his temptations by the devil (Mark 1:12–13; Matt 4:1–11; Luke 4:1–13). The historicity of the temptations is beyond the reach of historians; Jesus himself was most likely the source of his trials in the wilderness, translated into figurative language. Not only in the wilderness was Jesus tempted, but throughout his public ministry, as people requested signs and miracles from him.

Unlike John the Baptist, Jesus did not stay in the wilderness but returned to Galilee. After John was imprisoned (Mark 1:14; Matt 4:12) or even before (John 3:22–24), Jesus appeared in public preaching "the gospel of God." He transcends John's message of judgment and destruction; the joy of salvation permeates Jesus' announcement that "the kingdom of God is at hand" (Mark 1:15). In the teaching of Jesus, the age of salvation has already begun. God's reign is here, although its end is still to come. There are numerous references in the Gospels to the present as well as the future kingdom. Attempts to express what would be central in Jesus' proclamation and teaching of the kingdom of God are often labeled "realized" and "futurist" eschatology, separating the present from the future. More satisfying are the scholarly efforts to overcome these divisions, relating Jesus' sayings about the kingdom of God both to the present and the future. In "inaugurated eschatology," neither the present nor the future kingdom can be separated from the life and person of Jesus and his future coming. The kingdom of God is "already here" and "not yet." These two aspects of the kingdom are distinct but inseparable.

Jesus proclaimed the message of salvation to the excluded. He had meals with tax collectors and sinners, as well as with his followers. He ate with those working for the Roman authorities as well as with those who did not submit entirely to the Jewish law and its demands. Jesus' opponents criticized his friendship with tax collectors and sinners (Luke 7:34). They would only accept repentant sinners into the company of the righteous. In argument with his adversaries, Jesus defined his mission: "Those who are well have no need of a physician, but those who are sick; I came not to call the righteous, but sinners" (Mark 2:17). As the Father in heaven "makes his sun rise on the evil and on the good, and sends rain on the just and on the unjust" (Matt 5:45), Jesus mirrors God's character by manifesting limitless love and goodness. His parables reveal how God acts, and his mighty works point to the saving power of God in the world and to Jesus himself as the bearer of God's kingdom.

Jesus' treatment of women challenged taboos against them in Jewish society at the time. Women were regarded and treated as inferiors. They could not study the Torah or teach it. In the synagogue they were separated from the men by a curtain. They were not protected in marriage; their husbands could easily divorce them. In courts of law their testimony was not accepted as reliable. They were the property of their husbands, and other men were not expected to have contact with them. In Jesus' Kingdom, salvation is offered to all, to women as well as to tax collectors and sinners. He freely conversed with them, healed them, and pictured them in his parables. To illustrate the irresistible power of the kingdom of God, Jesus takes an example from a woman's work: she hid leaven "in three measures of meal till it is all leavened" (Luke 13:20–21). Woman is also the image of God's search for the lost (Luke 15:8–10). Jesus displayed an unprecedented attitude toward women. He does not warn men against "the wiles of loose women," but admonishes men for their aggressiveness and lust (Matt 5:27–28). A group of women followed him during his public ministry (Luke 8:1–3), and he visited and taught those who stayed home (Luke 10:38–47). Neither John the Baptist nor the Pharisees had female followers. The memory of Jesus' revolutionary approach to women was alive and strong in the earliest Christian community in Jerusalem, to which both men and women belonged. Women who were witnesses of the crucifixion and resurrection have been remembered throughout the centuries.

As Jesus willingly came into contact with women, he also did not avoid encounters with Samaritans (John 4:7ff) and Gentiles. For an observant Jew the very term "Samaritan" denoted an enemy (John 8:48). He praised a Samaritan and a Roman pagan (the centurion) for their faith (Luke 17:19; Matt 8:13). By prophesying the inclusion of the Gentiles in the peoples of God (Matt 8:11–12), Jesus stood in the tradition of the Hebrew prophets. Isaiah had spoken both of the salvation and destruction of the Gentiles. They will be saved and they will be destroyed (Isa 45:22, 54:3, 56:6–8). Micah had a vision of the defeat of the Gentiles (Mic 5), but prophesied of the pilgrimage of many nations to the mountain of the Lord, to the house of the God of Jacob, where all would live in peace and security. Although Jesus did not go beyond the prophetic vision of the pilgrimage of all nations, yet the story of the healing of the centurion's servant contains a new element, for it stresses trust in Jesus' power as the way toward the gathering of the people of Israel and all nations. The early church extended Jesus' mission to the Gentiles, drawing a line of separation between "Jew" and "Gentiles," not on the basis of their race or ethnicity but on their relation to the crucified and resurrected Christ, in whom the dividing line of hostility is broken down (Eph 2:14).

Jesus left a profound impact upon his audience, for he taught "as one who had authority, not as the scribes" (Mark 1:22). The scribes were those who had been trained by renowned teachers and were proud of their knowledge. Without a permanent residence, Jesus taught in synagogues, houses of his disciples, and even of Pharisees (Luke 7:36–50). He taught in the hills as well as in the plains, in the open air as well as in the temple. What he taught he had lived. He criticized those who honor God with their lips while their hearts are far from him. He did not teach about God, but made him known and present in his life and in his works.

WHO WAS JESUS?

By addressing God as *abba*, Father, Jesus expressed his close relationship with the "Father of Israel," the creator and ruler of the universe, author of the law and maker of the covenant. It was customary among Jews at the time of Jesus to call upon God as *abinu* [our Father]. The word *abba* was used within the family by children addressing their father. We do not know how a pious

Galilean Jew who spoke Aramaic addressed God in his daily prayers, but we know that the term *abba* was not used in synagogue worship as it belonged to the circle of the family. J.D.G. Dunn speculates that this "may be the reason for its exclusion in solemn prayer."[11] In Jesus' consistent use of *abba*, in his filial relationship to the heavenly Father, lies the "real root" of the post-Easter title "Son of God."[12] By confessing the resurrected Christ as "Son of God," the early Christians did not ascribe a new identity to Jesus but recognized what was implied in his regular use of *abba*.[13]

Jesus' contemporaries tried to understand who Jesus was by associating him with one of the figures of Jewish prophetic tradition. Some thought that Jesus was a prophet (Mark 6:15, 8:27; Luke 7:16; John 6:14). Some of his acts were prophetic. Like a prophet, he criticized contemporary religious practices: sacrifices of purchased animals and neglect of the poor and sinners. The common people shared the views of his disciples, who saw him as "a prophet mighty in deed and word before God and all the people" (Luke 24:19). For the religious authorities, his opponents, he was a false prophet (Mark 14:65; Luke 22:63–64). And the Romans saw him as a dangerous pretender who might provoke an uprising against the occupying power. When Pilate delivered Jesus to be crucified, the Roman soldiers "clothed him in a purple cloak," mocking him (Mark 15:16ff). With this robe and the crown of thorns, Jesus was accused of the political crime of claiming to be a king. By mocking him, they also accused him as one of those false prophets.[14]

To see Jesus as a prophet was an attempt to identify him, but it was not adequate. Jesus never used the prophetic introductory formula: "Thus saith the Lord," to underline that his prophecy was a message received from God and not a product of his own insight or wisdom. Instead he introduced his revelatory sayings with "Amen, I say to you," as if he made pronouncements on the basis of his own authority, rooted in his intimate union with the Father, in his experience of the certainty of God's presence and the closeness of his relationship with God. It was usual to use the word *amen* to approve or agree with the statements of somebody else. By putting this word at the very

---

[11]James D.G. Dunn, *Christology in the Making* (Philadelphia, PA: SCM Press, Ltd., 1980), p. 26f.

[12]Martin Hengel, *The Son of God: The Origin of Christology and the History of the Jewish-Hellenistic Religion* (Minneapolis, MN: Augsburg Fortress Publishers, 1976), p. 63.

[13]Raymond E. Brown, *Introduction to New Testament Christology* (New York: Paulist Press, 1994), pp. 87f, 109.

[14]Joachim Jeremias, *The Eucharistic Words of Jesus* (New York: Charles Scribner's Sons, 1966), p. 79.

beginning of his sayings, Jesus confirmed the truthfulness of his pronouncements. The Fourth Gospel uses *amen* emphatically, repeating it in about
twenty-five examples: "*Amen, amen* I say to you," as if to indicate the particular significance of his words.[15] His disciples regarded Jesus as higher than
the prophets (Matt 11:9; Luke 7:26). He was "greater than Jonah" and "greater
than Solomon" (Matt 12:38–42, 13:16ff), and more authoritative than Moses
(Matt 5:21–48).

He was addressed as "rabbi." Peter, on the Mount of Transfiguration said
to Jesus: "Rabbi, it is well that we are here" (Mark 9:5). It is worth noting that
in the Gospels according to Matthew and Luke, only Judas called Jesus
"rabbi." The term had one meaning before the destruction of the temple and
acquired another after the Jewish-Roman War (AD 70). In the time of Jesus,
to address someone as "rabbi" was to honor him. The scribes and lawyers
were respectfully addressed as rabbis. They were laymen who had acquired
great learning. After the reorganization of Judaism following the Jewish rebellion of AD 66–70, "rabbi" meant an ordained spiritual leader of a Jewish rabbinic synagogue.

When Jesus, who was called "rabbi" spoke, the people marveled: "How is
it that this man has learning, when he has never studied?" (John 7:15). He
taught "as one who had authority, and not as the scribes" (Mark 1:22). His way
of speaking and working was not that of the scribes, who had studied under
famous teachers, and lawyers. He had no formal training in the Torah and did
not possess their "petty learnedness."[16]

The terms "prophet" and "rabbi" were not sufficient to identify who Jesus
was. His disciples, who were with him, saw him as the Davidic Messiah (Mark
8:29), the anointed one, Christ, the one promised by God (2 Sam 7:12ff). There
is an essential bond between the disciples' estimate of Jesus and the very early
Christian confession of faith: "who was descended from David according to
the flesh, and designated Son of God in power according to the Spirit of holiness by his resurrection from the dead, Jesus Christ our Lord" (Rom 1:3–4).

After the Romans conquered Palestine in 63 BC, a surge of intense popular messianic expectation led to repeated rebellions against the new occupiers
and their subjects. Around the time of Jesus' birth, a sizable force of Jewish

---

[15]See particularly Martin Hengel, *The Charismatic Leader and His Followers* (Eugene, OR: Wipf &
Stock Publishers, 2005), p. 69.

[16]Hengel, *The Charismatic Leader;* see especially the chapter "Jesus Was Not a Rabbi," pp. 42–50.

rebels destroyed the royal palaces at Sepphoris and Jericho. Of all attempts to defeat and expel the Romans from Palestine, two Jewish-Roman wars (AD 66–70 and 132–135) proved particularly bloody and catastrophic for the population of Palestine; Bar Kochba led the last attempt in AD 132 to remove the Romans from this land. Rabbi Akiba, the best known rabbi of the period, proclaimed him "king, messiah." A century earlier, Jesus had repudiated this association of "messiah" with a triumphant political leader. Whereas his contemporaries were looking for a victorious, triumphant messiah, he was predicting his own suffering and death. Like the Suffering Servant of Isaiah 53, he "was wounded for our transgressions" (Matt 8:17). The post-Resurrection Christians saw Jesus' life and ministry as a fulfillment of this prophecy. The suffering Messiah was raised up and exalted to sit at the right hand of God (Acts 2:32ff). The crucifixion and resurrection of Jesus removed from the title "Christ" any political connotation. It enabled the followers of Jesus to confess him as the Christ sent and glorified by God. To share in his glory meant for them readiness to share in his suffering and death.

Central to an understanding of Jesus' vocation is the title "Son of Man," which Jesus used for himself. Found in all strata of the gospel tradition, the title indicates first of all Jesus' humble condition in his daily life (Luke 9:58; Matt 8:20), and refers to his suffering and glorification (Mark 8:31, 9:31, 10:33; John 3:14, 8:28, 12:32). In a vision of Daniel (Dan 7:13–14), in the figure of "one like a son of man" who came before God and to whom "the Ancient of Days" gave "dominion and glory and kingdom," Jesus found the symbol for his own mission.

The author of the book of Daniel lived under the persecution of Antiochus Epiphanes (167–164 BC), and the figure "Son of Man" represents the devout Jews who at a time of severe trials remained faithful and loyal, and whom God vindicated after persecution. Jesus interpreted Daniel's representative figure in reference to his person and his future vindication. The available evidence shows that Dan 7:13 had not been interpreted as a particular individual before Jesus. Only after the fall of Jerusalem (AD 70) was Daniel understood as a messianic vision. An apocalyptic document, 1 Enoch, written before the fall of Jerusalem, prepared the way by using the terms "Son of Man" and "Messiah" almost interchangeably.[17] Jesus was selective in apply-

---

[17]An informative discussion of the Son of Man in 1 Enoch appears in J.H. Charlesworth, *Jesus within Judaism: New Light from Exciting Archeological Discoveries* (New York: Doubleday, 1988), p. 39ff.

ing to himself prophetic or apocalyptic images or visions. He did not share the messianic hope attributed to the Son of Man in 1 Enoch, that he would crush the teeth of sinners.

No single title could fully express the messianic awareness of Jesus.[18] A title such as "Son of Man" conceals as much as it reveals. After the death and resurrection of its founder, the church avoided this title as not conducive to mission, preferring to use the titles "Christ," "Son of God," and "Lord."

TO JERUSALEM FOR PASSOVER

During his public ministry Jesus avoided two large cities in Galilee: Tiberias and Sepphoris. Tiberias and the Sea of Tiberias are mentioned only in John (John 6:1, 21:1, 23). Built on the Sea of Galilee by Herod Antipas around AD 13, it was dedicated, as we have already mentioned, to the Roman emperor Tiberius. Although Jesus proclaimed the coming of the kingdom of God to the people in cities and villages around that sea, he avoided Tiberias. Pious Galilean Jews in the time of Jesus shunned Herod Antipas' place of residence, for they believed that in building the city he had desecrated ancient tombs. Also, Herod Antipas had threatened to arrest him.

The threat of arrest never stopped Jesus from going to Jerusalem, however. John records that he visited Jerusalem more than once (John 2:13, 5:1, 7:10, 12:12). The evangelist Mark concentrates on his last visit to the holy city and emphasizes his determination to reach it in time for the Passover feast. On the road to Jerusalem, Jesus is followed by his chosen twelve disciples, who had left their homes and possessions, as well as their professions, to be with him. By choosing the Twelve (Matt 10; Mark 3; Luke 6; Acts 1), Jesus' aim was to renew Israel (Matt 19:28; Luke 22:30) which would include Gentiles (Isa 2:49; Matt 8:11). The Twelve represented the twelve patriarchs of Israel, the number of which could be neither decreased nor increased (Acts 1:22f, 12:1). With his chosen messianic community, Jesus entered Jerusalem.

Jerusalem at the time of Jesus' final Passover was charged with hope and fear. The population swelled from about 25,000 to 125,000 due to the influx of pilgrims from the surrounding provinces and the Diaspora. Filled with fear of disturbances, the Roman authorities responsible for peace and order were sensitive to any move of the great mass of people gathered in a limited space.

---

[18]See M. Hengel, *Charismatic Leader*, p. 59, and E.P. Sanders, *Jesus and Judaism* (Minneapolis, MN: Augsburg Fortress Publishers, 1987), p. 223.

They were quick to respond to the provocations of Jewish revolutionaries, who saw opposition to cruel Roman rule as their sacred duty. The religious leaders of the Jews, particularly the Sadducees, were afraid of any prophet, as they regarded all prophets as false prophets who would appear in Jerusalem at times when many expected God to intervene on behalf of his people. Jesus was aware of the consequences for himself that his preaching could produce. Although his detailed predictions of his suffering were colored by post-Resurrection events, we cannot dismiss their core as non-historical. Aware that his opponents might unite against him, Jesus regarded his death as an inevitable outcome of his last visit to Jerusalem. His disciples, the new recreated Israel, would share in his destiny (Mark 10:35ff).

Soon after he entered Jerusalem, Jesus visited the temple and overturned the tables of the moneychangers (Matt 21:12–13; Mark 11:15–19; Luke 19:45–48; John 2:13–15). The Synoptics put this at the end of Jesus' ministry, as the event that would lead directly to his death on the cross. John places it at the beginning, suggesting that the shadow of the cross lies over Jesus' proclamation of the kingdom of God from his first appearance. The cleansing of the temple belongs to the final week of Jesus' ministry in Jerusalem. Attempts to posit two cleansings, one at the beginning and the other at the end of his public proclamation of the kingdom, lack scholarly support.

By interweaving the story of the fig tree and its "withering away to its roots" with the cleansing of the temple (Mark 11:12–25), Mark interpreted Jesus' driving out of the merchants and overturning the tables as a prophecy that the temple would be destroyed in the near future. When Jesus predicted that a new temple would arise after the destruction, "he spoke of the temple of his body" (John 2:21; Mark 13:1–2). At his trial he was accused of speaking of the destruction of the Jerusalem temple (Matt 26:60f; Mark 14:57f). Commentators have argued convincingly that if he had wanted to reform or purify this temple, he could have symbolized purification by pouring out water, but instead he "carried out an action symbolic of its destruction," pointing to the present temple as neither adequate nor final.[19] Jesus' symbolic action provoked the temple authorities to seek a way to destroy him (Mark 11:18).

If the temple is not final, then neither is the law, the basis of temple worship. Far from abrogating the law, Jesus fulfilled it. By doing so, he asserted

---

[19] See E.P. Sanders, *Jesus and Judaism*, pp. 70–76, 89f, 251ff.

his own higher authority (Matt 5:21–47). His disciples are asked to follow him, to be totally committed to him. In Matthew's record of the Sermon on the Mount (Matt 5–7), the law is seen in the light of Jesus' proclamation of the kingdom of God. The evangelist does not relate Jesus to the law, but the Law to Jesus. For him "Christ is the center of the faith" and not the law. This would be a source of bitter conflict between Jewish Christians and the leaders of Rabbinic Judaism after the destruction of the temple (AD 70).[20]

FROM THE LAST SUPPER TO THE CRUCIFIXION

All the Synoptic Gospels recount Jesus' Last Supper with his disciples, the group of the twelve (Matt 26:26–29; Mark 14:22–25; Luke 22:14–22), as does Paul (1 Cor 11:23–26). In the Fourth Gospel, the Last Supper is reflected in several chapters (John 13–17), and we may see a reference to the sacramental meal in John 6:35–59. The evangelists agree that the Last Supper took place on Thursday evening, which is already Friday according to Jewish reckoning of the day from sunset to sunset. For the Synoptics it was the first day of Passover, and the meal that Jesus had with his disciples was a Passover meal. However, in the year of Jesus' crucifixion, according to John, this Friday was not the Passover day, Nissan 15 in the Jewish calendar, but Nissan 14, the day of the slaughtering of paschal lambs. Hence the Last Supper and the crucifixion would have taken place on the eve of Passover. When early on Friday the temple authorities brought Jesus to Pilate, they "did not enter the praetorium, so that they might not be defiled, but might eat the Passover" (John 18:28). It was "the Day of Preparation," and the Sabbath that followed "was a high day" (John 19:14, 31). The Passover in the year in which Jesus was crucified, on the basis of these references, fell on a Saturday and not on a Friday. According to the lunar calendar used by the temple authorities, Passover was a moveable feast.

We should note here that not all Jews were celebrating Passover on the same day. The Qumran sect, for example, used a fixed calendar, celebrating each year on the same day of the week. But Jesus was celebrating according to the Jerusalem lunar calendar. We have other evidence that he was following the Jerusalem calendar. John records that he was in Jerusalem for the Feast of the Dedication of the temple, the Feast of Hanukkah (John 10:22). This is

[20]John P. Meier, *Matthew*, New Testament Message, 3 (Wilmington, DE: Michael Glazier, Inc., 1981), p. 46f.

clear evidence that Jesus did not follow the Qumran calendar, for this Feast commemorated a Maccabean victory, whereas the Essenes of Qumran would have hated and rejected this Maccabean celebration. The Gospels do not support those scholars who argue that Jesus followed the Qumran calendar.

Which day did Jesus choose to celebrate the Passover? In view of the gathering of hostile forces and his imminent death, especially after the cleansing of the temple, he apparently decided to celebrate Passover a day earlier than prescribed, giving the meal a paschal coloration and meaning. His words, as they are recorded in all four versions, point to his redemptive death and vindication. Behind the four versions of the institution of the Lord's Supper, two distinct traditions can be detected, Pauline (1 Cor 11:23–26) and Marcan (Mark 14:22–25). Some differences between them are due to liturgical development, centering upon the very meaning of Jesus' actions at the Last Supper. In both traditions there is a link between breaking bread and offering wine and Jesus' coming death. The disciples present at the meal are asked to eat bread that is broken and to drink of one cup. The bread represents his body that is "broken for you" (1 Cor 11:24). The bread Jesus distributes is not a token food furnished for daily needs but an offering of himself for his own. The wine represents his blood "which is poured out for many" (Mark 14:24), meaning for all, not a few. It alludes to Moses, who sealed the covenant by sprinkling the blood of a sacrificial animal (Ex 24:28). Here Jesus seals the covenant with his own blood. "This cup is the new covenant in my blood" (1 Cor 11:25). He sees his coming death as necessary for gathering the people of Israel, for restoring their relations with God, and for their salvation. Death is not strong enough to break the ties that exist between Jesus and the Twelve, for God will vindicate him beyond death (Mark 14:25; 1 Cor 11:26). The disciples therefore are commanded to do what he has done "in remembrance of me." The tradition that Paul delivered has this demand both in reference to the bread and the cup. Luke, who is close to the Pauline tradition, has the same exhortation, but only in connection with the bread (Luke 22:19).

Paul's version of the Last Supper of Jesus, called "the Lord's Supper" or "the Supper of the Lord" (1 Cor 11:20), is the earliest written account of its celebration in the church, developed in liturgical use, and Paul quite likely added his own commentary at the end of the words of institution. In 1 Cor 11:26 he makes explicit what is given in the exhortation "Do this in remembrance of me" (1 Cor 11:24, 25). To remember Jesus is to imitate him. The disciples are asked to mirror his life, to proclaim at their liturgical gathering the supreme act of his sacrifice until Christ returns in glory (1 Cor 11:26). They too are called to sacrifice themselves in the service of others.

Like the Synoptics and Paul, John also links the Last Supper to the death of Jesus. Without recording the words of institution, he offers enough evidence of acquaintance with them. He uses the term "flesh" instead of "body." "Flesh" is a more literal translation of the Hebrew *basar*. The sacrificial phrase "for many" (Mark 14:24) is paralleled with Jesus' discourse on the living bread, which shall be given "for the life of the world" (John 6:51); and "I am the true vine" (John 15:1) stands for "this is my blood." John's highly developed tradition of the Last Supper is anchored to its historical roots.

The Last Supper should also be seen in the context of Jesus' table fellowship meals during his public ministry. It is the last in the series, linked with them and yet distinctly different. At meals, in the most ordinary setting, Jesus had proclaimed the gospel. His opponents criticized him for having meals even with tax collectors and sinners. Here he offered forgiveness and salvation. At the Last Supper Jesus offered himself. Facing death, he anticipates another series of meals in the future, Eucharistic meals. The ancient Eucharistic prayer "Our Lord, come!" [*maranatha*] (1 Cor 16:22) brings together the remembrance of the Last Supper with the joy of his coming. The Lord who was with his disciples at the Last Supper, who after the resurrection appeared to them during meals (Luke 24:13ff; John 21:1–14; Acts 1:4, 10:41) is now present in his body, which is the church.

ARREST AND TRIALS

After the meal was over, Jesus and his companions went to Gethsemane ["the place of the olive press"]. Mark presents Jesus as distraught and troubled, in agony (Mark 14:32–34). His Gospel appears to be the source for Matt 26:36–46 and Luke 22:39–46. Since Caiaphas had pronounced his policy of political accommodation "that one man should die for the people and the whole nation should not perish" (John 11:50), Jesus was under threat, and in Gethsemane was aware that his death was imminent. He was praying "that if it is possible the hour might pass from him" (Mark 14:35). Seeing death as an enemy, he prays for deliverance. Then, as to a mirror of his character and his teaching, he commends himself to his *abba*, Father, and accepts his destiny: "not what I will but what you will" (Mark 14:36). Gethsemane manifests his full humanity, for he was "as we are, yet without sin" (Heb 4:15), and his complete trust and commitment to God, as he had taught: "Blessed are the poor in spirit" (Matt 5:3).

The night of agony was also the night of Jesus' arrest. Judas, one of the Twelve, who had been present at the Last Supper, betrayed Jesus' whereabouts and brought an armed group from Caiaphas to take him captive. While historians accept Judas' betrayal as historical fact, they see as a major concern in two accounts of his death the fulfillment of Scripture (Matt 27:3–10; Acts 1:16–20). Peeling away transmitted popular traditions on which these accounts are based, the interpreters who shun a "forced harmonization" and "frozen contradiction," point to a tradition based on very early memories that Judas' violent death followed his betrayal.[21]

Jesus underwent two trials: before the Sanhedrin, at which he was mocked as a prophet (Mark 14:65), and the Roman trial before Pontius Pilate, prefect of Judea, at which he was mocked as a king (Mark 15:1–5). There have been divisions among historians over whether the "Jewish trial" preceded the Roman trial. While some deny the historicity of the trial before the Sanhedrin altogether, others support the earliest Gospel accounts. According to Mark, followed by Matthew, after his arrest Jesus was led "to the high priest, and all the chief priests and elders and scribes were assembled." That night there was a formal trial of the captive before the Sanhedrin (Mark 14:53ff; Matt 26:57ff). Luke refers to an informal morning hearing (Luke 22:54, 66ff). In John, there is neither a formal trial nor an informal hearing. Jesus was led to Annas, the father-in-law of Caiaphas, who had been high priest for nine years. The next morning Annas sent him to his son-in-law the high priest, and from the house of Caiaphas he was taken to the Praetorium (John 18:12ff, 24ff). Thus, there is neither a formal setting for a trial nor an informal hearing. Yet, John does not differ so radically from the Synoptics. He records the session of the ruling body of the temple after the raising of Lazarus, a few days before Jesus was arrested (John 11:45–53). Out of fear that many would follow Jesus and that the Romans would come to "destroy both our holy place and our nation," Caiaphas expressed the view that one man should die and prevent the destruction of the whole nation. And "from that day on they took counsel how to put him to death" (John 11:53). But the Jewish authori-

---

[21]See "The Death of Judas" in Pierre Benoît, *Jesus and the Gospel* (1st ed.; New York: Herder & Herder, 1973), pp. 189–208.

ties at the time of Jesus, John points out, did not have the right to "put any man to death" (John 18:31). It appears that the Sanhedrin could condemn Jesus but could not carry out capital punishment.[22] The Romans alone had the right to carry out executions.

Historians will continue to analyze, compare, and interpret the Gospel Passion narratives and will express views for or against the historicity of the Sanhedrin trial before that of Pilate. Whatever their views on details, all must agree that the main opponents to Jesus were the Sadducees. In order to preserve their privileged position, the temple authorities collaborated with these Roman rulers. Caiaphas' tenure as high priest for an unusually long period (AD 18–36) can only be explained by his way of dealing with and pleasing the Romans. After Pompey conquered Palestine, the chief priest served as head of the people on behalf of the Romans.[23] He presided at the Sanhedrin, and as high priest exercised considerable influence over the court. He could not act without its support, however. In addition to the chief priests, Sadducees and scribes, mostly Pharisees, sat on the court as well. Caiaphas needed their support too. "In any case," writes E.P. Sanders, "the immediate occasion of Jesus' death was the temple scene, which doubtless persuaded the leaders of Judaism that this Galilean should not be allowed to create further trouble."[24]

RESPONSIBILITY FOR THE CRUCIFIXION

To improve Jewish-Christian relations and to prevent anti-Jewish hostilities, some have suggested a need for rewriting, "improving," or removing the offensive Gospel passages, particularly Matthew 27 and John's polemic against "the Jews." Others warn, however, that manipulating historical documents would not contribute to dialogue. The Passion Gospels must be examined in the context of the larger historical and religious events to which they belong. Without this examination, they may "lead to simplistic accusations about guilt for the death of Jesus," warns Raymond E. Brown, among others.[25]

---

[22]For views of the trial before the Sanhedrin, see our article, "The Historical Jesus: A Challenge from Jerusalem," *SVTQ* 30.1 (1986): 30ff.

[23]Sanders, *Jesus and Judaism*, p. 317.

[24]Ibid., pp. 294–318. Sanders offers a historical reconstruction of the events during the last week of Jesus' life in Jerusalem.

[25]Raymond E. Brown, *A Crucified Christ in Holy Week: Essays on the Four Gospel Passion Narratives* (Collegeville, MN: Liturgical Press, 1986). In a recent study, *Constantine's Sword: The Church and the Jews* (New York: Houghton Mifflin Co., 2001), James Carroll questioned the entire structure of the Gospel Passion narrative. He gives priority to the dialogue between Judaism and Christianity, particularly

The Gospels are unanimous in their testimony that Pontius Pilate condemned Jesus to death on the cross, and that the Romans carried out the sentence. They are also in agreement that Jesus was held captive by the temple authorities before the trial and was presented by them to the Romans as a dangerous rebel. The Jewish historian Josephus wrote that "Pilate at the suggestion of the principal men among us" condemned Jesus (*Ant.* 18.63f). Later, around AD 115, the Roman historian Tacitus wrote that "Christ was executed by sentence of the procurator Pontius Pilate in the reign of Tiberius" (*Ann.* 15.44).

The moment of the death of Jesus is described with slight variations in all four Gospels. Whatever words are used, they conveyed that his death was not a defeat but rather a moment of victory. The death of Jesus in the early Christian tradition was seen to be more than a moral act of love and obedience. They counted it an offering to God, a sacrifice (John 17:19).

All Jesus' "acquaintances and the women who followed him from Galilee" watched his crucifixion and burial, which underlines the reality of his death. The burial of Christ is included in the early Christian creedal statement (1 Cor 15:4). It also belongs to the apostolic sermon on the day of Pentecost attributed to Peter (Acts 2:27–31).[26]

The very moment of Jesus' resurrection was not an observable event and could not be captured in categories of time and space. Therefore, the Gospels do not narrate it. They do present evidence for the resurrection, however. The post-resurrection appearances of the risen Jesus led the disciples to understand why the tomb was found empty and made them witnesses of the resurrection and leaders of the earliest Christian community in Jerusalem. The post-resurrection appearances do not belong to the category of ecstatic experience, such as Paul described in 2 Cor 12:1ff, nor to any recognizable category of spiritual experience. Without them, there would have been no church or New Testament Scripture.

---

to what he regarded as the "distorted importance" given to the cross and the crucifixion. For the sake of better Jewish-Christian relations, he suggested "improving" the Gospels. Eamon Duffy warned in his review that this road would not lead to real understanding and reconciliation: "Interfaith dialogue can only be fruitfully conducted by those engaged with and committed to the central affirmation of their respective tradition, for only such partners can offer real reconciliation or deliver the confidence of their coreligionists" ("A Deadly Misunderstanding," *New York Review of Books*, May 5, 2001, pp. 24–27).

[26]We offer a detailed account of the death and burial of Christ in our study *The First Day of the New Creation* (Crestwood, NY: St Vladimir's Seminary Press, 1982), pp. 60–65.

On the day of Pentecost, Peter, the leader of the Twelve, proclaimed to those who were dwelling in Jerusalem: "Jews, devout men from every nation under heaven," that God raised up Jesus of Nazareth who had been crucified by "lawless men," "and of that we are all witnesses." God "has made him both Lord and Christ" (Acts 2:22ff). Those who received Peter's word were baptized, and, united with the eyewitnesses of Jesus' words and deeds, formed the nucleus of the earliest Christian community. The door to this messianic community was opened to everyone who would be baptized "in the name of Jesus Christ" (Acts 2:38).

CHAPTER TWO

THE BIRTH OF THE CHURCH IN JERUSALEM

N ew Testament historians usually distinguish three periods in the life of the first century church.[1] The first, the subject of our study, covers about five years, from the crucifixion and resurrection of Christ (AD 30) up to the call and conversion of Paul (ca. AD 35). The second ends with the destruction of the temple (AD 70), and the third takes up the events following the First Jewish-Roman War to the end of the century. We must remember that throughout these stages the Christian communities were not separated from Judaism. They preached the message of the risen Christ from within Judaism, where they clashed and competed with other Jewish groups. As long as the temple stood, until AD 68–70, they participated in the life of the Jewish community, although often as harassed members.

Diversity continued within Judaism before and after the destruction of the temple. Although the Jewish-Roman War (AD 66–70) eliminated the Sadducees and the Essenes from historical record, it did not end diversity. When the Pharisees brought their teaching of the oral law to the new religious center at Jamnia—which was accepted by the new leaders—they also brought their love for passionate debates and interpretations. These types of disputation gave birth to further groups. Whether diversity was "external" or "internal," however, it remained within clearly marked boundaries. Jewish Christians could maintain themselves in Jerusalem by attending the temple and practicing circumcision. The authorities did not tolerate attacks on the law and the temple. Jewish Christians who spoke against the temple and the law were persecuted and expelled from Jerusalem because they had broken the limit of diversity. The temple authorities did not expel those Jewish Christians who lived within the limits, however.

---

[1]Material in this and the following chapter appeared as "The Church Before Paul" *SVTQ* 43.1 (1999)–Author.

In this chapter, we shall examine the life of the church in the period when it established the foundations for surprisingly successful Christian missions as well as for theological development and creedal statements. Our primary interest is what happened in the Christian community in Jerusalem before Paul started his missionary activities. What did the new messianic group accomplish under the leadership of the Twelve? How did they respond to the needs of the faithful?

Sources for the Study of the Jerusalem Church

Our sources for the life and activity of the church in Jerusalem are Acts 1–12, a few fragments in the letters of Paul, and some scattered references in other New Testament documents. Contemporary scholars have subjected Acts, the main source, to stringent historical analysis. The dating of Acts is still disputable. Was it written before the destruction of the temple (AD 70), as some have suggested, or after the Jewish-Roman War, as many would argue? In any case, Acts remains the indispensable source for studying the earliest Christian church in Jerusalem. Drawing on oral and written data, as he had in his Gospel, Luke included in Acts his own sources and personal experience, as well as information he had acquired as Paul's traveling companion.

Scholars recognize that Luke used what they have termed the "Antiochian source" (Acts 6–8, 11:19–30, 12:25–15:35). Critics disagree over which passages in these chapters come from this source and which should be excluded. This dispute concerns the reconstruction of the Antiochian source, not the rejection of it. In Luke's accounts of Paul's second and third missionary journeys, the so-called "we source" reads as a "travel diary." From the "we" passages the reader learns that Luke was present at the most important events recorded in Acts 16–28. As Paul's traveling companion (Col 4:14; Phlm 24), Luke came with Paul to visit James in Jerusalem (Acts 20–21). Before they reached the city, they had been guests in Caesarea of "Philip the Evangelist" (Acts 21:8), one of the leaders of the Jewish Christian Hellenists. From him Luke probably received precious information about Christian beginnings, about the substance of the accusations against Stephen and his subsequent trial and persecution. As he compiled the historical record, Luke relied upon the testimony of participants in these early events and may have drawn upon written sources.

Characteristic of Acts are the various speeches and sermons attributed to Peter, Stephen, and Paul. They take up about twenty percent of the entire book. By using speeches, Luke seems to be in the tradition of Hellenistic historical writings. Undoubtedly they are not a verbatim record, nor are they free compositions promoting Luke's ideas. They illustrate how the apostles addressed the Jews and Gentiles (Acts 2, 13, 14, 17). Stephen's sermon (Acts 7) serves as an example of Christian Hellenist preaching. Each speech has its own special features. Luke "gave them their outer form, but this does not prevent us from thinking that he had reliable sources, and that he really gives specimens of the apostolic message," writes Bertil Gartner.[2] Helped by his knowledge of Christian Hellenist missionary preaching, Luke elaborated on available information and sources and gave Stephen's speech its "outer form," as he had done with speeches attributed to Peter and Paul. He preserved the distinct character of Stephen's preaching and the reason for his persecution, however.

The evangelist skillfully presented his sources, weaving and shaping them, and grounding his interpretation on facts. His main purpose was to present the origins of the Christian community, its expansion and Paul's missionary activities. An edifying writer, Luke brings theology and history together. The evidence also suggests that he is reliable as a historical source. Where it is possible to compare the historical data in Acts with works of Jewish and Roman historians, some of the facts in Acts may be confirmed. For example, the record of the death of Agrippa I in Acts 12 when compared with the account in Josephus' *Antiquities of the Jews* 19 indicates that Luke used reliable independent sources. Suetonius likewise confirms the references to the banishment of the Jews from Rome in Acts 18:2 (*Claud.* 25). Luke could not have depended on Josephus, who wrote around the end of the first century, or on Suetonius, writing during the first two decades of the second, but he used trustworthy sources available to him. As one who was intimately involved in the life and development of the Christian church, Luke conveys the atmosphere in which the earliest Christians lived and worked, the problems they encountered, and the harassment and persecution they experienced. He made history more attractive by personalizing it, concentrating upon Peter, Stephen, and Paul.

---

[2]Bertil Gartner, *The Areopagus Speech and Natural Revelation* (Uppsala: C.W.K. Gleerup, 1955), p. 33, cited in C. K. Barrett, *Luke the Historian* (Peterborough, UK: Epworth, 1961), pp. 30–32.

Acts first focuses on Peter. Here presumably, Luke reflects the apostle's role in the earliest years of the church in Jerusalem. He is selective in his material, abbreviating and even telescoping two separate events (the decision about circumcision and dietary laws) into a single occasion (Acts 15). A.N. Sherwin-White, a specialist in Roman history, asserts: "Any attempt to reject the basic historicity [of Acts] now appears absurd. Roman historians have long taken it for granted." He goes on to comment on the remarkable accuracy of Acts "in its record of the legal, administrative, or social background" of the Greco-Roman world.[3]

Trilingual Palestine

The languages of Palestine, Greek, and Aramaic, as well as Latin, were the languages of conquerors. Aramaic entered Palestine with the Assyrian conquest in the eighth century BC and Greek with the military successes of Alexander the Great in the fourth century BC. After the fall of Jerusalem in 586 BC to the Babylonians, Aramaic gradually became the language of the people, whereas Hebrew remained the sacred language, the language of prayer. Aramaic is not a dialect of Hebrew, but a language of its own. The ancient Israelites used Aramaic in their daily contacts. Greek was widely used in the cities, coastal areas, and trading centers, and particularly in Jerusalem, as the religious, political, and commercial center. The Latin language entered with the Roman army and was used within the military after the conquest of Palestine in 63 BC. For three hundred years, Latin was the official language of the Roman Empire in Palestine. In the fourth century, with the establishment of Constantinople, the second Rome, Greek slowly replaced Latin as the language of the Eastern part of the empire. Thus, by the time of Jesus, Palestine, that is Judea, Samaria, and Galilee, was a trilingual region.

Acts 6 speaks of two distinct groups among Jewish Christians: "Hellenists" and "Hebrews." The "Hellenists" [*Hellenistai*] were Jewish Christians who habitually spoke only Greek, and whose knowledge of Hebrew or Aramaic was minimal. There were also Hellenists whose main language was Greek, who lived in Jerusalem, but who did not join the Christian movement and remained Mosaic loyalists (Acts 9:29). When Luke had in mind non-Jews

[3]A.N. Sherwin-White, *Roman Society and Roman Law in the New Testament* (Oxford: Clarendon Press, 1963), p. 189.

whose mother tongue was Greek and who lived according to the Greek fashion, he used the term *Hellenes* (Acts 21:28), not *Hellenistai*. The very context of Acts 6 makes clear that *Hellenistai* are not *Hellenes*.

The upper classes in Jerusalem had been exposed to the influence of Greek education and culture for over three centuries before Jesus. Jewish or Christian Hellenists, however, spoke Greek without undergoing a Greek education. They were predominantly Jews of the diaspora, who had returned to settle in Jerusalem and organized their "diaspora synagogues" in the city. One of the Jerusalem "houses of assembly" is identified as "the synagogue of the Freedmen" [*libertini*] (Acts 6:9). The builders had been Roman slaves who managed to obtain their freedom. While slaves, many had been very enterprising, learning new skills and a new language. Their wealthy masters used them as their agents in various business transactions.[4] When they obtained their freedom, however, they opted to return to the land of their fathers. It is possible that the first-century BC Greek inscription of the "Synagogue of Theodotus" was the Synagogue of the Freedmen mentioned in Acts. "Theodotus, son of Vettenus . . . built this synagogue," runs the Greek inscription. It has been suggested that the father of Theodotus, who later adopted the Latin name Vettenus, had been captured in Pompey's conquest of Jerusalem in 63 BC. He was sent as a slave to Rome and returned to Jerusalem as a freed man. Many other Greek-speaking synagogues existed in Jerusalem before the destruction of the temple. Their members used the Septuagint and followed the guidance of the Pharisees.[5] Jerusalem itself was a center of Jewish diversity.

Ancient Jews gathered the bones of their dead, after the body decayed, into small chests or ossuaries. Discovery of ossuaries (receptacles for bones) dated to New Testament times reveal the extent that Greek was used among all strata of Jewish society, the upper classes and ordinary people in the cities, the educated and uneducated. Some Greek inscriptions on the ossuaries indicate that the subscribers had received a formal Greek education whereas others lacked it.[6]

[4]See W.A. Meeks, *The First Urban Christians: The Social World of the Apostle Paul* (New Haven: Yale University Press, 1983), p. 20f.

[5]See Martin Hengel, *The "Hellenization" of Judaea in the First Century after Christ* (Philadelphia, PA: Trinity Press, 1989), p. 13.

[6]J.T. Milik, *Ten Years of Discovery in the Wilderness of Judaea* (London SCM Press, Ltd., 1959), p. 130f. See also Steven Fine, "Why Bone Boxes?" *BAR* 27.4 (2001): 39–44.

Among "Hebrews," some had some knowledge of Greek and spoke it when circumstances required. Jesus' disciples included enterprising fishermen who had contacts with the Greek-speaking inhabitants of the Decapolis. John tells of several Greeks [*Hellenes*] desiring to see Jesus who approached Philip, and he in turn consulted with Andrew regarding these Gentiles (John 12:20f). Both Andrew and Philip are Greek names, and we presume they were able to speak Greek.

Simon Peter, the leader and spokesman of the inner circle of Jesus' disciples, was an active missionary in Jerusalem and beyond. As one who was with Jesus and witnessed the resurrection, Peter led missionary activities, delivering what he had heard, seen, and experienced. Antioch, Corinth, and Rome claim him as their own apostolic founder, although he was not directly linked with the work of the founding churches of these three cities. Dionysius, Bishop of Corinth around AD 170, claimed that both Paul and Peter "taught together in this Corinth of ours and were our founders." Peter could not have engaged in missionary activities in areas outside his homeland without being able to communicate and preach in Greek.

Did Jesus himself speak Greek? The Gospels indicate that he had contact with the Greek-speaking population and occasionally may have spoken Greek. He had grown up in Nazareth, a village of about four hundred inhabitants. Only an hour's walk away was the rich city of Sepphoris, with a population of around thirty thousand Jews, Greeks, and Romans. The Romans made Sepphoris the capital of Galilee after their conquest of Palestine. Following Herod's death in 4 BC, the city became a center of Jewish rebellion, and as punishment, the Romans destroyed it. Herod's son, Herod Antipas, who ruled Galilee and Perea from 4 BC to AD 39, started extensive reconstruction, requiring skilled workers. He employed many from Nazareth and the surrounding villages to rebuild Sepphoris. The carpenter Joseph, Jesus' legal father, may have worked on this project.[7] There are no indications that Jesus visited this city during his public ministry. He apparently distanced himself from the luxury of cities such as Sepphoris and Tiberias. He visited Jerusalem several times, however, and selected Capernaum, by the Sea of Galilee, a highly populated area where some traders and fishermen used Greek, for the center of his ministry.

---

[7]Richard A. Batey, "Sepphoris–An Urban Portrait of Jesus," in *BAR* 18.3 (1992): 50–63.

Conversations during which Jesus may have spoken Greek were his encounter with the centurion, a Gentile (Matt 8:5–13; Luke 7:9), with the Syro-Phoenician woman (Mark 7:25–30) and at his trial before Pilate. Certainly, Aramaic was the language Jesus naturally used for preaching and teaching. There is strong possibility that he spoke Greek on some occasions, but it is "unlikely" that he taught and preached in Greek.[8]

The spread of Greek in Palestine contributed to the considerable increase in the membership of the earliest Christian community. The mission quickly expanded beyond Jerusalem and the surrounding country. The message of the crucified and risen Christ made an impact upon diaspora Jews, the Jewish Hellenists in Jerusalem, so that many of them were baptized in the first years after the resurrection. The early church proclaimed and transmitted the gospel tradition in two languages, Aramaic and Greek. "The Gospel tradition which may have sounded too Hellenistic to be authentic may be authentic after all."[9] The church in Jerusalem was bilingual from the very beginning. A substantial number of disciples in the earliest community could communicate in both languages. The leader of the Twelve, for instance, could convey Jesus' message in both. Personal testimony as "eyewitnesses and ministers of the Word" (Luke 1:2) must have had a profound impact on their audiences.

Building Community

The fruit of Christ's death and resurrection was *koinonia:* community, communion, fellowship, or the church. In Hebrew the corresponding term for it is *yahad*, used in the Dead Sea scrolls to denote "unity." With one mind [*homothymadon*] the members of the community "devoted themselves to apostolic teaching and fellowship [*koinonia*], to the breaking of bread and prayers" (Acts 2:42). This summary of the prevailing norms of church life, familiar to Luke at the time he was writing Acts, originated in the church in Jerusalem. The categories may not have been delineated so clearly as they would be in a later period. Apostolic teaching [*didache*] was addressed to those outside the church as well as to those inside the church. Fellowship [*koinonia*] included the public and private activities of the community. "The

---

[8]See Joseph A. Fitzmyer, "Did Jesus Speak Greek?" *BAR* 7.5 (1992): 58–63.
[9]Robert H. Gundry, "The Language Milieu of First-Century Palestine: Its Bearing on the Authenticity of the Gospel Tradition," *JBL* (Dec. 1964): 408.

breaking of bread" is the expression that denotes the opening of a festive Jewish meal; for Luke it stands for eucharistic gatherings. The community met at Troas to celebrate the Eucharist "on the first day of the week" (Acts 20:7ff). In this founding period, the Eucharist was not separate from an ordinary meal.[10]

Luke's comprehensive summary also lists prayer as a corporate and private activity. The earliest disciples prayed in the temple (Acts 2:46, 3:1, 5:12, 21) and at home (Acts 5:42). They went to the temple at the regular hours to participate in public prayers without taking part in the elaborate sacrificial services. Luke observes that the disciples preached "Jesus as the Christ," both in the temple and "at home." To the Psalms, which they were most probably familiar with from childhood, they must have added new prayers inspired by Jesus' custom of praying to his Father. During his public ministry, Jesus had taught those around him how to pray (Luke 11:2–4), and these same disciples continued these prayers in the post-resurrection community, which they led and organized.

The norms of church life presuppose baptism; two references in Acts particularly underline the necessity of the rite. Paul was baptized after the risen Christ appeared to him on the road to Damascus (Acts 9:18), and Cornelius and those around him were baptized after they received the Holy Spirit (Acts 10:47–48). Baptism was performed "in the name of Jesus Christ" (Acts 2:38, 10:48) or "in the name of the Lord Jesus" (Acts 8:16, 19:5). This baptismal formula is found only in Acts. The baptized are those who confess the Lord Jesus and are incorporated into the life of the church. Both the confessional and incorporative senses of baptism are pre-Pauline. Paul developed the concept of the incorporation of the baptized into Christ and underlined its significance.[11] Like baptism, healings were performed in the church "in the name of Jesus Christ of Nazareth" (Acts 3:6, 16; 4:10). The "name" represents Jesus and his power. Only those who are his disciples, utterly committed to him, and incorporated into his community could invoke his name.[12]

Baptism and Eucharist served as settings for the transmission of the gospel tradition. At the initiatory rite, those present would remember Jesus' own

---

[10]See Xavier Leon-Dufour, *Sharing the Eucharistic Bread: The Witness of the New Testament* (Mahwah, NJ: Paulist Press, 1987), pp. 22–25.

[11]Joseph A. Fitzmyer, "Pauline Theology," in *NJBC* 82:112–113.

[12]See J.D.G. Dunn, *Jesus and the Spirit* (Philadelphia, PA: Westminster Press, 1975), p. 164.

baptism, and at the eucharistic gathering they would recall his Last Supper before his crucifixion. In this sacramental setting, they would relive the Gospel events culminating in Jesus' death on the cross. The Twelve, the eye-witnesses and disciples of Jesus who became his apostles after his resurrection, would guarantee the authenticity of the tradition.[13]

Jewish Christians attended temple worship and practiced circumcision with other Jews, but they came together for the "breaking of bread" in their homes (Acts 2:46), which served as Christian synagogues or house churches. In this way, they indicated that they did not ascribe ultimate importance to the temple. With the growth of the community, the number of Christian syn-agogues naturally increased. One of these was "the house of Mary, the mother of John whose other name was Mark" (Acts 12:12), to whom the Gospel of Mark was ascribed. The gathering of Jesus' followers on the day of Pentecost was probably in a private house. Jesus had celebrated the Passover and instituted the Eucharist in such a setting (Mark 14:13–16). A distinct Chris-tian worship evolved in private houses in Jerusalem, the city where the tem-ple stood and where several such Christian synagogues appeared, using either Aramaic or Greek.

The earliest Christian mission in Jerusalem was having an effect upon the surrounding towns (Acts 5:16). The boldness of Jesus' followers disturbed the temple authorities. The council was divided on how to deal with them and what measures should be used to silence them. A Pharisee named Gamaliel, a teacher of the Law who came after Hillel, showed more tolerance in dis-putes than his contemporary Shammai. He appealed for tolerance toward the disciples. Gamaliel asked the other members of the Sanhedrin to let them alone. If what they do and preach "is of men, it will fail; but if it is of God, you will not be able to overthrow them" (Acts 5:38–39). Certainly, Gamaliel too rejected what was being taught in the name of Jesus, but he saw no dan-ger in it, for he believed that it would die by itself. Having made an appeal to the council to "take care what you do with these men," he reminded them about groups in the past who had misled the Israelites but in the end "came to nothing," failed, and "perished" (Acts 5:36–37). Gamaliel thought that the Christian *koinonia* would end in such a manner. At this very early period, the enmity of the Sadducees as the chief opponents of Jesus and the church in Jerusalem led to harassment of Jewish Christians but not to open persecution.

---

[13]Bo Ivar Reicke, *The Roots of the Synoptic Gospels* (Philadelphia, PA: Fortress Press, 1986).

Community Disturbances

Although Luke in Acts repeats that the earliest Christian community was of "one accord" or of one mind (Acts 1:14, 2:46, 4:24, 5:12), yet it was not without problems. Some members violated the life of *koinonia*. Ananias and his wife Sapphira tried to serve two masters, God and mammon, and held back some of the proceeds of the land and lied "to the Holy Spirit" (Acts 5:1ff). In other words, they lied to the community permeated and guided by the Spirit. The story of Ananias and Sapphira reveals the Biblical mentality of the earliest Christians. Luke's readers could see it against the background of "the sin of Achan" (Josh 7), who stole some booty and violated the ban against taking for himself what was dedicated to God. For his disobedience, he was stoned. The story of Ananias in Acts intimates that the ideal Christian community was not free of disturbances and that even this community was not beyond temptation (1 Cor 10:13). As his public ministry approached its end, Jesus reproached Simon Peter: "Simon, Simon, behold, Satan demanded to have you . . . but I have prayed for you that your faith may not fail, and when you have turned again strengthen your brethren" (Luke 22:31–32). Acts uses "brethren" [*adelphoi*] to designate the whole Christian community, the church (Acts 1:15, 6:3, and so forth).

Ownership of property did not disrupt the community; rather, the lying of Ananias and Sapphira was punished. Barnabas' act of selling his field (Acts 4:37) expresses the spirit and desire of the disciples of Christ for "economic *koinonia*." He would hardly have been mentioned specifically if every member of the community had done the same.[14] To give one's property to the community was a voluntary act. Paul's later appeals to the Corinthian community to contribute to the needs of others (1 Cor 16:2; 2 Cor 8–9) summon them to a voluntary sharing of goods. In contrast, in the Qumran community, the practice was mandatory. After the novice had spent two years on probation, if accepted as a member, his property belonged to the community.[15]

The practice of concern for the poor in ancient Israel (Lev 25:35ff) formed the early Christian attitude toward the poor and property, as did Jesus' Sermon on the Mount. Jesus criticized those who are rich: "You cannot serve

[14]Richard J. Dillon, "Acts of the Apostles," in *NJBC* 44:36.
[15]"Rule of the Community," *Manual of Discipline*, 6.17–22.

God and mammon" (Matt 6:24; Luke 16:13). The term "mammon" stands for money first, as well as other goods to which one is inordinately attached. Yet, those who possess wealth can serve God by sharing "mammon" with those who are poor and needy. Jesus did not reject property as such. Peter, his leading disciple, had a house in Capernaum (Mark 1:29–31), where Jesus performed a miracle of healing. The church has continued to remember this site; archaeologists located what had traditionally been accepted as Peter's house, and an octagonal Byzantine church has been erected over it. The fourth-century pilgrim Egeria visited a "house church," *domus ecclesia*, which she heard was the house of this apostle. Jewish Christians gathered in this house remembered Peter's works in Capernaum and preserved the sites of Jesus' ministry here.[16]

Pentecost and the Appointment of the Seven

Luke mentions that the followers of Jesus before Pentecost were in all "about a hundred and twenty" (Acts 1:14–15). They included the Twelve as most prominent, Mary, the mother of Jesus, the women who had been with him during his public ministry, and his brothers. After Peter's sermon on the day of Pentecost and his call to repentance and baptism "in the name of Jesus Christ," "about three thousand souls" were added to the disciples of the Risen Christ (Acts 2:41).

Whether or not we take these numbers literally, we cannot doubt the considerable growth of the primitive Christian community after Pentecost. Jerusalem, the place of the crucifixion and the resurrection, was also the place where the event of the Pentecost occurred. The followers of Jesus, who had left Jerusalem after the crucifixion, were returning to the city to celebrate the closing of the Passover cycle. At the beginning of the Christian era, Pentecost marked the annual celebration of the giving of the law on Mount Sinai. In celebrating the renewal of the covenant, to their surprise the disciples experienced the overwhelming power of the divine Spirit. All those who took part in celebrating were called to enter by baptism "in the name of Jesus Christ" (Acts 2:38) into a new covenantal community. The Spirit given to them led to personal interactions with the risen Christ and confirmed their belief that

[16]*Egeria's Travel*, ed. John Wilkinson (London: SPCK, 1971). See V. and L.W. Kesich, *Treasures of the Holy Land*, pp. 21–25.

God raised him up "because it was not possible for him to be held by death" (Acts 2:24).

The evangelist Luke in Acts does not cover up or minimize the "unpleasant disturbances" in the life of the Jerusalem church. With the growth of the community, inevitably other problems confronted the "disciples" of Christ. They had to solve them, for the future of the Christian mission and its expansion depended upon their resolution. Acts identifies the members of the community [koinonia] as disciples [mathetai] of Christ. This word appears in the Gospels as well. A disciple is one who is utterly committed to the person from whom he received a call. He believes in him and recognizes his voice and teaching. In Acts, Luke uses the word "disciple" for any believer in Jesus (Acts 6:1, 9:19). Paul never used the term mathetai for his followers or companions. Only Jesus could have mathetai.

With the rapid growth of the church, some members of the community began to complain of neglect. Acts 6 reports that the Hellenists murmured against the Hebrews because their widows were slighted in the daily distribution, probably meaning in sustenance given to the poor and needy. The Twelve took the complaint of the Hellenists seriously and dealt decisively with the discontent that was endangering the koinonia. They summoned the body of the faithful [plethos] and asked them to select "seven men of good repute, full of the Spirit and wisdom" (Acts 6:3) to serve tables [diakonein trapezais], whom they, the Twelve, would appoint for this duty. In addition, when the plethos put forward seven Hellenists, the Twelve "prayed and laid their hands upon them" (Acts 6:6).

Luke differentiated the role of the Twelve and that of the "multitude" [plethos] in the appointment of the Seven. The Twelve and the community of believers participated in the decision-making process. The Twelve took the initiative, approving and appointing the seven worthy Hellenists whom the community had selected from among themselves. The leadership of the Twelve was undisputed, while the consent of the faithful was indispensable. New leaders, appointed for the group of Hellenists, all had Greek names. They were not native Greeks, Gentiles, but ethnic Jews, except one, "Nicolaus, a proselyte of Antioch" (Acts 6:5). The reason given for their selection was to "serve tables." This expression covers many duties related to economic and financial matters. In addition to caring for the poor and needy, it is clear from Acts 6–8, Stephen and Philip, the two most prominent, participated in preaching, teaching, and baptizing. Stephen "did great wonders and signs among the people" (Acts 6:8) and Philip proclaimed Christ in Samaria and on the road from Jerusalem to Gaza, where he baptized the eunuch (Acts 8:38). They were engaged in service to the community, for in Acts 6, Luke uses the term *diakonia*, "service," but not *diakonos*, "deacon."

Paul uses *diakonos* for a distinct group in the hierarchy of a local church only once in his undisputed epistles. He addresses his letter to the Philippians to "the saints in Christ Jesus . . . with the bishops and deacons [*episkopois kai diakonois*]." Even here, the ministry of *diakonos* is hardly defined. The term has the meaning of minister or attendant. Acts says nothing about the deacon's function in the church at Philippi. In 2 Cor 3:6 Paul identifies himself and those around him as "ministers [*diakonoi*] of a new covenant," and in the same epistle (2 Cor 11:23), attacking his opponents, he writes, "Are they servants of Christ [*diakonoi Christou*]? I am a better one." He is a better *diakonos* than they are. In these two examples the title *diakonos* stands for "the office of preacher and missionary."[17] Later writings of the New Testament as well, such as 1 Timothy, do not specify the functions of deacons. The author only notes that they "must hold the mystery of the faith with clear conscience" (1 Tim 3:9), which does not distinguish them much from other ministries in the church.

Thus, the Seven probably served as local leaders, administrators in the Christian Hellenist community. The Twelve were in charge of the community of Hebrews as well as of Hellenists, and it appears that they "ordained" helpers from both groups. The role and duties of the Seven would correspond to the tasks performed by the elders [*presbyteroi*] (Acts 15:4, 22).[18] The elders dealt with local problems (Acts 11:30), and worked with the apostles to solve the dispute over circumcision that would affect the life of the whole church (Acts 15).

The appointment of the Seven recalls the appointment of the seventy helpers for Moses in Num 11. Not satisfied with manna, the Israelites in the wilderness complained and asked for meat. "Why have you treated your servant so badly?" Moses asked the Lord. He continued, "These people are too heavy for me . . . For they come weeping to me and say 'Give us meat to eat!' "

[17] Helmut Koester, *History and Literature of Early Christianity* (vol. 2 of *Introduction to the New Testament*; 2d edition; Berlin/New York: Walter de Gruyter, 1982), p. 98.

[18] Raymond E. Brown, "Early Church," *NJBC* 80:15.

(Num 11:11–13). The Lord lightened Moses' burden by putting onto seventy elders "some of the Spirit" that was on Moses. Similarly, the complaints of the Hellenists murmuring over food distribution led to the appointment of the Seven.

This similarity has led some to question the historicity of Acts 6. But what leads to a better understanding of the connection between these two events is a well-established use of the Old Testament in the New. Luke recalled the event in the life of Moses to stress the historical importance of what was happening in the church at Jerusalem. He is "interpreting" the appointment of the Seven, not "inventing" it. What he received from his sources he transmitted. In composing the account, he brings out as forcefully as possible the meaning of the appointment of the Seven in the life of the new covenantal community. His creative use of the Old Testament Scripture serves that purpose.[19] Luke also revealed an intimate knowledge of the primitive Christian church and its leader by giving the names of the Seven, who thereupon became a distinct group in the apostolic church. When Paul and his companions came to Caesarea on his last visit to Jerusalem, they stayed with "Philip the Evangelist, who was one of the Seven" (Acts 21:8).

With the appointment of the Seven, the *koinonia* in Jerusalem grew, and church missions spread beyond the city. The number of disciples increased considerably, and "a great many of the priests [*hiereon*] were obedient to the faith" (Acts 6:7). However, Acts reveals nothing specific about the priests. If they had come from the official priesthood, would this imply that the Christian movement had even penetrated the temple?

More likely, these priests had previously belonged to the Essenes. The Essenes lived in a number of towns in Judea as well as in the wilderness. The Christians were acquainted with them, and they had met and observed them in the city of Jerusalem itself. According to Josephus, they were living in Jerusalem as a closed community, where they had probably settled after the 31 BC earthquake, which had disrupted their lives in Qumran. Some archeological findings suggest that Essenes settled on Mount Zion, which also became the center of Jewish Christianity. This shared proximity facilitated contacts between the disciples of Christ and the Essenes.[20]

---

[19]For Luke's perspective of history, see C.K. Barrett, *Luke the Historian.*
[20]See our article, "The Historical Jesus," *SVTQ* 30.1 (1986): 26.

Whether these priests came from the temple or from the Essenes, they did not perform any special "priestly" role in the church. If they had been priests from the temple, they would presumably continue to serve there. In the New Testament, the word *hiereus* [priest] is never used for an office holder. The author of Hebrews applied the term to Christ, who is "high priest [*archierea*] of our confession" (Heb 3:1). The expression "royal priesthood," used in 1 Pet 2:9, does not refer to one who holds an office in the church but to God's people. The text of 1 Pet 2:9, echoing Ex 19:6, is addressed to Christian believers: "You are a chosen race, a royal priesthood, a holy nation, God's own people." In the context of Exodus 19, the author of 1 Peter reminds Christians that they are bound to God by a special covenantal relationship. Here the writer points to the holiness of the people, not to a priestly function. The term *hiereus* was used for an office holder in the church "only in the last quarter of the second century AD," with the final separation of the church from the synagogue, and with "growing recognition of the Eucharist as a sacrifice."[21] The pre-Pauline creedal statement "that Christ died for our sins" (1 Cor 15:3) transcended the entire sacrificial system of the temple, and the Eucharist as a bloodless sacrifice fulfilled it (*Did.* 14).

[21]Daniel Harrington, *The Light of All Nations: Essays on the Church in the New Testament Research.* Good News Studies, 3 (Wilmington, DE: Michael Glazier, Inc. 1982), p. 134.

CHAPTER THREE

THE EXPANSION OF THE CHURCH BEYOND JERUSALEM

T he growth of the Christian community and the boldness of Jesus' disciples provoked the Sadducees and led to the harassment and persecution of the Christian Hellenists. The Sadducees accused Stephen, the leader of the Jewish Christian Hellenists, of blasphemous words against the law and the temple, just as they had charged Jesus. Later, around AD 58, the Sadducees also accused Paul of defiling the temple and breaking the law (Acts 21–27ff). Then in AD 62, Josephus records that James the brother of Jesus was killed by stoning, at the instigation of the high priest Ananos and the council leadership, not at the demand of the people. The accusation against James and the others was that they had transgressed the law.[1]

Stephen's preaching was the first to be met with opposition by other Greek-speaking Jews who had remained loyal to the law. They disputed with Stephen and his followers, who had made inroads into their synagogues. These included the Synagogue of the Freedmen [*libertini*], as well as "of the Cyrenians and of the Alexandrians, and of those from Cilicia and Asia" (Acts 6:9). They could not all have been members of the same synagogue. Diaspora Jews returning to Jerusalem would keep ties with Jews from their own regions and the places in the Hellenistic world that they had left. Each group would try to organize its own house to study the Scripture. Some of these house synagogues were more open to new ideas and criticism of the Jewish institutions than others. The Alexandrian Jews were more receptive to Jewish Christians, for instance, than those from Asia Minor. The Hellenists from "Cilicia and Asia" were probably the main opponents and persecutors of Stephen. Pre-Christian Paul had been a Mosaic loyalist, as were many Hellenists from "Asia." Later, in AD 58, Paul's life was in danger when "the Jews from Asia had

---

[1]Josephus, *Ant.* 2:200. See also E.P. Sanders, *Jesus and Judaism*, p. 285.

seen him in the temple." They laid hands on him, claiming that he was an opponent of the law and the temple (Acts 21:18ff). This same faction, the Asian Jews, had attacked Stephen twenty-five years earlier. Again, their accusations were centered upon the law and the temple.

These accusers, the Mosaic loyalists, fundamentalists, charged Stephen of speaking blasphemously against Moses (Acts 6:11), and of being negative toward Moses and his achievements, although he had not referred to Moses in his speech. To the contrary, Moses was for Stephen a highly esteemed figure who delivered his people from Egyptian slavery. He "was mighty in his words and deeds" and he received living oracles; but the people, "uncircumcised in heart and ears," resisted him and did not keep his commandments (Acts 7:35ff). Stephen spoke as one from within Judaism.

Christian Hellenists looked critically upon the people's use of the law. Their attitude is well illustrated in the account of Philip baptizing the Ethiopian eunuch (Acts 8:26–40). The eunuch was not a proselyte, a convert to Judaism, but a "God fearer." A number of Gentiles in diaspora were attracted to Jewish monotheism and its moral code. Under the influence of the synagogue, they observed some Jewish traditions, particularly the Sabbath day, and undertook pilgrimages to Jerusalem. The eunuch was one of these. In the view of the synagogue authorities, all these "God-fearers" were part of the pagan Gentile population and they could not be buried in Jewish cemeteries. Proselytes, on the other hand, were circumcised, lived under the law, and were buried together with other deceased Jews. By baptizing the eunuch, Philip went beyond the legal requirement. According to the law (Deut 23:2; Lev 21:17–23), eunuchs could not be included in the assembly of God, as they could not be circumcised. Philip brought him into the newly formed community of God's Israel.

The second accusation against Stephen referred to the temple. "False witnesses" heard him say that "Jesus of Nazareth will destroy this place and will change the customs which Moses delivered to us" (Acts 6:14). Stephen saw clearly the meaning of Jesus' teaching, as well as of his death and resurrection (Mark 14:58; John 2:20). The new temple, the temple of his body, would replace the old (John 2:19–22). He spoke critically about the temple and provoked a violent reaction among the loyalists. Stephen described the temple as "made with hands" [*cheiropoietos*], a phrase known to those in the Hellenistic world who opposed idolatry. The Jews in diaspora used the same word to condemn paganism. By applying this expression to the temple, Stephen iden-tified the place as an idol, for "the most High does not dwell in houses made with hands" (Acts 7:48).[2]

Stephen attacked the temple in a very radical manner. For the Jews, the temple was the "house of God," and Jerusalem, where it was located, was the holy city (1 Kings 8:10–13). Some argue that Stephen regarded the "tent" or tabernacle, not the temple, as the true locus of worship. An exegetical analy-sis of the text does not support this view, however. Admittedly, he uses the term "tent" [*skenoma*] (Acts 7:46) and "house" [*oikos*] (Acts 7:47), but in his summary (Acts 7:48), he avoids both terms, removing the alleged opposition between the tent and the temple.[3]

The temple authorities led the forces that drove Stephen out of the city and stoned him to death. Acts specifically mentions that a "young man named Saul" participated and consented to his death (Acts 7:58–8:1). Some scholars have disputed the trustworthiness of Acts on the ground that Paul himself stated that although he had persecuted "the church of God," he was unknown to the Christian community in Judea (Gal 1:13, 22). They doubt that Paul took part in the stoning of Stephen and the subsequent persecution of the church in Jerusalem (Acts 8:3). They suggest that the persecutions Paul referred to in Galatians could have occurred outside the city, most likely even outside Palestine.[4] The reliability of the account in Acts for others rests pre-cisely in the confessional autobiographical passages in Paul's letters. Here he confesses that he was "as to the law a Pharisee, as to zeal a persecutor of the church" (Phil 3:5–6). As a Pharisaic student in Jerusalem, he probably consid-ered the use of violence against the disciples of Jesus justifiable in defense of the law. If Paul was brought up in Jerusalem and educated in the strict tradi-tion of the law (Acts 22:3, 26:4f), then Stephen's "blasphemous words against Moses and God" (Acts 6:11), would have stirred him to violent action. Unknown "by sight to the church of Christ in Judea" (Gal 1:22), Paul was known to the Christian Hellenists in Jerusalem. Christian communities out-side Jerusalem "only heard" about him and his use of violence against the

---

[2]J.D.G. Dunn, *Unity and Diversity in the New Testament* (Philadelphia, PA: Westminster Press, 1977), p. 267ff.

[3]See Craig C. Hill, *Hellenists and Hebrews: Reappraising Division within the Earliest Church* (Min-neapolis, MN: Augsburg Fortress Publishers, 1992), p. 74.

[4]H. Koester, *History and Literature of Early Christianity* (vol. 2 of *Introduction to the New Testament*), pp. 97–99.

disciples (Gal 1:23). These interpreters insist that Acts is trustworthy concerning Paul's eagerness to persecute Greek-speaking Jewish Christians in Jerusalem.[5] It is revealing that on his first visit to Jerusalem after his conversion, the disciples whom Paul attempted to join were afraid of him (Acts 9:26).

Because of Stephen's criticism of the temple, the Hellenists could no longer survive in Jerusalem. Although Judaism allowed diversity within well-defined boundaries before the Jewish-Roman War and the destruction of the temple, this act went beyond what was permitted. Jewish Christians, "Hebrews," maintained themselves in Jerusalem by participating in the temple, practicing circumcision and observing Jewish dietary laws; but to attack ritual law and temple worship, as the Christian Hellenists did, led to the stoning of Stephen and the expulsion of the other Hellenists. They could not remain in Jerusalem and consider themselves Jews, as they had broken the limits of permissible diversity. In consequence, their missionary activities intensified.

The Expansion of the Christian Movement

Paradoxically, the persecution of the Hellenists in the 30s and Hebrews in the 40s brought about an unexpected expansion of the church. As a result of "a great persecution [of] the church in Jerusalem," the Hellenists were scattered throughout the region of Judea and Samaria. Philip proclaimed the Christ to the Samarian people, and then he moved south toward Gaza. In the cities of the coastal plain and particularly in Caesarea, where Greek was the language of communication, Philip could have reached the inhabitants of these cities if he preached in Greek.[6]

The expansion of the Christian movement in a short period, between AD 30 and the call of Paul around AD 35, was by all accounts phenomenal. Acts, our principal source, does not answer many questions regarding this early expansion. Apparently, there were Christians in Damascus even before the expulsion of the Hellenists from Jerusalem. Paul was sent to persecute those

---

[5]For this view, see particularly Martin Hengel, *The Pre-Christian Paul* (Philadelphia, PA: Trinity Press, 1991), and his earlier work, *Acts and the History of Earliest Christianity* (Philadelphia, PA: Trinity Press, 1980).

[6]M. Hengel, *"Hellenization" of Judaea*, p. 14.

who belonged to "the way" [*hodos*, designating Christians].[7] Who had founded the church in Damascus? There were also references to the existence of Christian communities in Galilee (Acts 9:31), but Luke does not identify the missionaries who were active there. Acts gives an outline of the missionary development. The Christian movement started in Jerusalem, then expanded in the city, moving into the surrounding area (Acts 5:16), and then into Samaria and the coastal towns (Acts 8, 9). This may well correspond to what really happened in the earliest years.

Before Paul's conversion, a group of Christian missionaries may have founded the church in Antioch,[8] a major city of the East, third largest in the Roman Empire. Here a great number of Jews enjoyed privileges in practicing their religion. Their synagogues attracted a considerable number of Gentiles, some of whom became proselytes. One of them, "Nicolaus, a proselyte of Antioch," whom we have previously mentioned, was among the Christian Hellenist leaders in Jerusalem (Acts 6:5). So even before the persecuted Hellenists settled in Antioch, a Christian mission had preceded them. The Roman authorities had noted the mixed Christian community of Jews and Gentiles and were probably the first to call them "Christians" (Acts 11:26), to distinguish them from the Jewish community.

The concept of the church as a "third race" may have had its origins in Antioch. For Christians this meant that the church in its eucharistic gathering transcended race or racial divisions. Apparently, the church in Jerusalem did not try to stop the course of events in Antioch, but on the contrary helped and guided the church there. The apostles sent Barnabas, who had very close ties with the church in Jerusalem, to Antioch (Acts 4:36f, 9:27). He was pleased with their active mission and only urged them "to remain faithful to the Lord with steadfast purpose" (Acts 11:23). Antioch did not aspire to be a rival of Jerusalem or to be independent from the mother church, free from its control. The only control that Jerusalem cared about derived from

---

[7]The word *hodos* appears only in Acts (9:2, 19:9, 23, 22:4, 24:14, 22). It was also used in the Qumran documents; that community saw their life in the wilderness, devoted to the study of the law, as preparation for the Lord. The source for both groups most probably is Isa 40:3: "A voice cries: 'In the wilderness prepare the *way* of the Lord.'" John the Baptist announced "the way of the Lord" (Mark 1:3), and Jesus declared that he himself was the way (John 14:6).

[8]H. Koester, *History and Literature of Early Christianity* (vol. 2 of *Introduction to the New Testament*), pp. 93, 96–7.

shared faith. By taking the initiative to get approval for its work, the church in Antioch displayed unity with Jerusalem (Acts 15, Gal 2).

While the persecution of the Hellenists was conducted by the temple authorities, that of the Hebrew Christians was initiated by King Agrippa (AD 41–44), the grandson of Herod. He had James, the brother of John, killed in AD 42. Agrippa's father, Herod Antipas (4 BC–AD 39), had beheaded John the Baptist (Mark 6:14–29). Herod Agrippa emulated his father in cruelty and was well aware that the masses of the Jewish people hated him and those who had preceded him because of their Idumean origin and their collaboration with the Roman occupying power. At the time of the persecution of the Hebrews, Peter departed Jerusalem and "went to another place" (Acts 12:17). He only returned to Jerusalem around AD 50 for an apostolic conference (Acts 15).

The persecution and expulsion of the two Jewish Christian groups from Jerusalem expanded the missionary activities of the early Christians. The earliest Christianity was a missionary religion. Jesus was the "primal missionary." The apostles after Pentecost were sent to "make disciples of all nations." Peter, the leading member of the Jerusalem community, was a missionary both before and after the persecution. He was a missionary among Jews in Palestinian towns, yet he did not exclude Gentiles (Acts 10). In Joppa (now part of Tel Aviv), "he stayed for many days with one Simon, a tanner" (Acts 9:43). Peter, like his Master, did not despise downgraded or outcast people. The tanner was despised because of his ritually "unclean" trade. Peter was not an independent missionary; in his activities, he was responsible to the apostles in Jerusalem who had sent him (Acts 8:14; 11:1–8).

The Brothers of Jesus

As we explore the expansion of the church, we turn to the role of the "brothers" of Jesus. Mark, the earliest written Gospel, names Jesus' brothers as James, Joses, Judas, and Simon. The evangelist also mentioned sisters without naming them (Mark 6:3). The word brother [adelphos] in the New Testament covers various degrees of blood relationship. It can mean stepbrother, neighbor (Matt 5:22–24), or "kinsmen by race" (Rom 9:3). The Gospel passages mentioning the brothers of Jesus when compared (Mark 6:3 with Mark 15:40, and parallels in Matt 13:54–6, Matt 27:55–6) indicate that these brothers are cousins. Paul refers to them as missionaries (1 Cor 9:5), but without elaboration. In the view of some historians, Jewish Christian missionaries centered in Nazareth brought the message to the Decapolis and even reached Damascus before the Hellenist expulsion from Jerusalem. Prominent among these missionaries may have been the brothers of Jesus.[9]

The brothers of Jesus were based in Nazareth. During Jesus' public ministry they "did not believe in him" (John 7:5), but after his resurrection they are among the small group of his followers (Acts 1:14). On the day of Pentecost, with all others present, they experienced the power of the Spirit and with it the inner compulsion to mission. The words of Paul about the necessity laid upon him to preach the gospel (1 Cor 9:16) can be applied to the experience of the brothers of Jesus after the resurrection and Pentecost. As missionaries they left Jerusalem and returned to Nazareth, making it a new church center, not a rival to Jerusalem nor completely dependent upon it. When Paul mentioned the brothers of Jesus as missionaries, he treated it as a well-known fact. There was no need to elaborate; Jesus' relatives were known in Palestinian Christian circles as *desposynoi*, those who belong to the master, the Lord.[10] Jude, whose author identifies himself as "brother of James," has the title *ho despotes* for the risen Christ: "Our only master [*ton monon despoten*] and Lord [*kyrios*] Jesus Christ" (Jude 4). This is the only place in the New Testament documents where *despotes* is used to identify Christ. (It is generally agreed that 2 Pet 2 is dependent on Jude.) The title is used for God, however (Acts 4:14, Luke 2:29, Rev 6:10), and is generally applied to Christ in the later second century. Jesus' relatives seem to have been familiar earlier with this title.[11] Eusebius cites the second century historian Hegesippus, a Palestinian, who wrote, "Those called the 'brothers of Jesus' led the whole church by virtue of being martyrs and relatives of the Lord."[12] As we reconstruct the history of the formative period, we must be aware of their special contribution to the church and their possible role in its expansion in the post-Resurrection period.

---

[9]See Richard Bauckham, *Jude and the Relatives of Jesus in the Early Church* (Edinburgh: T & T Clark, 1990), p. 68.

[10]*H.E.* 1.7.14.

[11]On Jude's Christology, see Bauckham, *Jude and the Relatives of Jesus*, pp. 282–304.

[12]*H.E.* 3.32.5–6.

The Twelve as Members of the Apostolate

The Twelve accompanied Jesus during his public ministry. They were among the first to see the risen Christ, to whom he made himself known. Only with the post-resurrection appearances did the Twelve become his apostles. As such, they had a special place in the church in Jerusalem and exercised unique authority.

Their number could be neither reduced nor increased. Mere death did not create a need for the selection of a new member. No one took the place of James after he was killed. Judas' apostasy, however, created the necessity for his replacement. The requirements for the selection of a new member were clearly spelled out. He must be one who had accompanied Jesus' disciples during his public ministry, from his baptism until his death on the cross. He must also have witnessed his resurrection. Lots were cast, and Matthias took the place of Judas. The number twelve, representing Israel, is thus completed (Acts 1:21–26).

Ancient Israel had used the method of election by lot to determine the divine will. By casting lots, Israel selected Saul, their first king (1 Sam 10:16–26). The same method determined the ranks of the temple personnel. The Essenes determined the admission of new members and their ranks in the community by lots. The proximity of these two groups, the Essenes and Jewish Christians, raised the question of Essene influence upon this practice of the primitive church in Jerusalem. Matthias' selection by lots does not necessarily reflect traces of Essene practices, but rather provides additional evidence of "a Palestinian matrix of the early church."[13]

Numerous modern studies have explored the origin of the dignity of a Christian apostle.[14] Scholars have made attempts to derive the New Testament apostolate from the rabbinical institution of *sheluhim*. After the destruction of the temple, the Palestinian authorities sent "commissioned emissaries," *sheluhim*, to various Jewish communities in the diaspora to act in their name in legal and administrative as well as religious matters. Yet the New

---

[13]See J.A. Fitzmyer, "Jewish Christianity in Acts in Light of the Qumran Scrolls," in *Studies in Luke-Acts*, L.E. Keck and J.L. Martyn, eds. (Philadelphia, PA: Fortress Press, 1980), pp. 233–257.

[14]Hans Dieter Betz, "Apostles," pp. 356–359 in *Encyclopedia of Religion*, ed. Mircea Eliade (New York: Macmillan Publishing Company, 1987) gives an incisive discussion and selected bibliography. Raymond E. Brown, "The Twelve and the Apostolate," in *NJBC* 81:135–157, offers a more extensive treatment of the subject, as does the bibliography.

Testament apostles apparently predated this institution. There is no evidence that the rabbinical institution of *sheluhim* existed "before or during New Testament times."[15] Apparently, the Rabbinical institution of *sheluhim* and the Christian apostolate while sharing a common background in Hebrew Scripture, developed independently from one another.

Scholars have also tried to trace the origin of the Christian apostolate to the influence of the gnostic myth of a heavenly redeemer on Paul, the Apostle to the Gentiles. According to this myth, the gnostic redeemer was sent into the world to spread the message of salvation: the knowledge [gnosis] of the unity and identity of the human soul with a heavenly realm. These scholars suppose that Paul adapted this pattern to contribute to the concept of the Christian apostolate. This is a shaky and highly questionable theory. No pre-Christian gnostic redeemer myth can be documented, as we shall see in a later section. Such a myth is known only in the highly developed Gnosticism of the second century.[16]

The most telling argument against this theory of gnostic influence upon Paul is given in Paul's own writings. He tells us that there were apostles in the earliest Christian community in Jerusalem before him (Gal 1:17). He incorporates in his letter to Corinthians the most elaborate pre-Pauline creedal statement of the early church (1 Cor 15:7ff), which ties the apostolate with post-resurrection appearances. Then Paul aspires to be recognized as an apostle in the rank of other apostles, with whom he had become acquainted after his conversion. In several of his letters, he refers to his experience on the road to Damascus, and he puts his own experience on the same level with the experience of Peter and the others in the post-resurrection period. As far as apostleship is concerned, Paul claimed to be "equal" to the twelve apostles without claiming membership in the Twelve.[17] Paul "had been entrusted with the gospel to the uncircumcised, just as Peter had been entrusted with the gospel to the circumcised" (Gal 2:7).

---

[15]R.E. Brown, "The Twelve and the Apostolate," *NJBC* 81:150–157.

[16]M. Hengel, *The Son of God* , pp. 33–34. In his *"Hellenization" of Judaea* (pp. 94–96 n. 285), Hengel mentions particularly the description of the gnostic myth in Rudolph Bultmann's easily accessible *Theology of the New Testament*, and also in his widely used *Primitive Christianity in Its Contemporary Setting*, written before the discovery of the Nag Hammadi texts, which is "an ahistorical construction of the history-of-religions school."

[17]T.W. Manson, *The Church's Ministry* (Philadelphia, PA: Westminster Press, 1948), pp. 53–54.

The Christian concept of the twelve members of the apostolate belonged to the very early post-resurrection appearances and the call to mission that followed. The risen Jesus widened the circle of apostles by appearing to some of those who were not with him during his public ministry. He even appeared to Paul, who had persecuted his disciples, and sent him "to serve and bear witness to the things which he has seen" (Acts 26:16).

The crucial expression, he "appeared" [ōphthē] or "made himself known" in the creedal statement of 1 Cor 15:3–8, as well as in other passages (Luke 24:34; Acts 9:17, 13:31, 26:16) indicate the external character of the post-resurrection appearances. Ōphthē could also be translated as "he showed himself," that he is the same person whom they knew and followed during his public ministry.[18] We cannot classify these appearances as the subjective, ecstatic, mystical experiences such as are recorded in the life of the church throughout the centuries. "Ecstatic," "mystical" are not adequate definitions of these appearances. A leading historian of world religions, R.C. Zaehner, has stated that we cannot find anything close in the experiences of holy people presented in the scriptures of world religions "to Christ's appearances as they are recorded in the New Testament." Karl Rahner observed that they are "strictly sui generis."[19] They were limited to the formative period, to the rise of the church and the Christian movement.

The act of "sending" itself did not make one an apostle. During his public ministry, Jesus sent the Twelve to preach and heal, instructed them as to what to take, what to wear, and how to behave if the people refuse to hear the message of repentance. Only after the resurrection did the Risen Christ transform them into apostles and send them to proclaim his victory over death. It is generally agreed that Luke in his Gospel interjects the term "apostle" into the public ministry (Luke 6:13, 9:10, and so forth), reflecting the post-resurrection period.

Except for Peter, we know very little about the missionary activities of the Twelve. They were witnesses to Jesus' resurrection in Jerusalem and probably worked within Palestine. Only Peter was presented as a missionary outside Palestine (Acts 12:17, possibly 1 Cor 1:12). As we have noted, Peter was probably able to deliver the message in Greek as well as Aramaic.

---

[18]On "He appeared" (ōphthē), see our First Day of the New Creation, p. 117ff.

[19]See his "Foundations of Christian Faith," p. 277, cited in Gerald O'Collins, Interpreting the Resurrection (New York: Paulist Press, 1988), p. 20.

The Development in Theological Expression

The first attempt to preach the message of Jesus in Greek to the diaspora Jews in Jerusalem inevitably led to the introduction and development of a new theological terminology, which has been used in the church ever since. The term *apostolos* belongs to this very early stage of the Christian community.[20] With the introduction of Greek terminology, theology developed first in answer to the question of who the Jesus is who rose from the dead. Expanding missionary activities necessitated creedal statements, which are the seeds of subsequent development and which underlined the dominance of Christology rooted in the resurrection. The Jesus whom they knew and whom some had followed during his ministry and who was crucified, "God raised up" (Acts 2:23). He made him both Lord and Christ (Acts 2:36), and "exalted him at his right hand as Ruler [Leader] and Savior" (Acts 5:31).

Paul in Romans records a received creedal fragment, which sheds light on a very early development in Christian understanding of Jesus' identity. The gospel of God concerns "his Son, who was descended from David according to the flesh, and designated Son of God in power according to the Spirit of holiness by his resurrection from the dead, Jesus Christ our Lord" (Rom 1:3–4). We find this emphasis on his descent from David only here and in 2 Tim 2:8: "Remember Jesus Christ, risen from the dead, born of David's line. This is the theme of my gospel."

In many and various ways, Jesus indirectly revealed himself during his public ministry.[21] Particularly his choice of the Twelve shed light on his messianic self-understanding. James Charlesworth wonders: "Is there some self-understanding behind Jesus' apparent desire to have twelve special men follow him?" He goes on to warn: "It is unwise, indeed uninformed, to follow the lead of some New Testament scholars who denounce any possibility of recovering Jesus' self-understanding; and it may no longer be wise to reject the possibility that he had some 'messianic' self-understanding."[22] After his resurrection, the disciples identify Jesus as the Messiah of Israel and the Ser-

---

[20]"Terms like *apostolos, euangelion, ekklesia, charis, charismata, ho huios tou anthropou,* and so forth, must have begun very early . . . and not, say, decades later outside Palestine, in Antioch or elsewhere" (M. Hengel, *"Hellenization" of Judaea,* p. 18).

[21]See discussion in our book, *Gospel Image of Christ,* summarized on p. 193.

[22]J.H. Charlesworth, *Jesus within Judaism,* p. 138.

vant of God according to Isaiah (Acts 3:13, 26; 4:27, 30).[23] These fragments belong to primitive Christology. The impact of Jesus' life and suffering had led his disciples to interpret his death in terms of the Suffering Servant of God (Acts 8:32f). Behind Jesus' saying that the Son of Man "came not to be served but to serve and give his life as a ransom for many" (Mark 10:45), they perceived the image of the Servant of Yahweh who "bore the sins of many" (Isa 53:11–12). The title "Son of Man" disappears in Acts, as well as in the christological creedal confessions and the hymns. Instead of "Son of Man," we have the Davidic Christ, the Son of God united with the Lord.

Jesus did not claim for himself that he was the "Son of God," but, as we have seen, he regularly and consistently addressed God as *abba*. Jesus willed what the Father willed, and in his teaching as well as in his life he expressed and revealed the pure will of God. The word *abba*, more than any other prayer, conveyed Jesus' sense of intimacy and oneness with God.[24] The Fourth Gospel, reflecting upon the historical Jesus from a standpoint after the resurrection, makes this explicit (John 6:38; 8:23, 38, 59; 10:36).

Moreover, Jesus alluded to himself as a special son of his Father. The core of the parable of the tenants in the vineyard (Mark 12:1–12) goes back to Jesus. After the tenants mistreated and beat the servants sent by the owner of the vineyard to get some fruits for their master, the owner finally sent "a beloved son," but the tenants killed him. In the parable, he reveals his special relation with the Master. This is also reflected in the saying in Mark 13:32: "But of that day or that hour no one knows, not even the angels in heaven, nor the Son [*ho huios*], but only the Father." Some are reluctant to accept this as an authentic saying of Jesus because "the Son" is used in an absolute sense. This saying of the historical Jesus could hardly have been a creation of the post-resurrection community, for the early church would have been hesitant to claim that Jesus himself had been ignorant of the Day of Judgment.[25]

Jesus pointed to himself as "a beloved Son" and "the Son." The bilingual Christian church identified and confessed him as "Son of God." His identity

---

[23] See B.I. Reicke, "The Risen Lord and His Church," *Interpretation* vol. 13.2 [The Theology of Acts], (1959): 158f.

[24] J.D.G. Dunn, *Christology in the Making*, p. 26f.

[25] See John P. Meier, "Jesus," in *NJBC* 78:7. Among criteria for judging what in the Gospels comes from Jesus himself and what comes from early Christian tradition, J.P. Meier in this article lists as the first "the criterion of embarrassment," which "focuses on actions and sayings of Jesus that would have embarrassed the early church."

rests on his filial relationship to the Father, displayed throughout his public ministry. The earliest Christian reflections of the risen Christ as "Son of God" did not introduce a new term for a new identity. They recognized the reality already implied in the Synoptic Gospels.[26] Since witnessing the resurrection, the church continued to develop in her understanding of the preceding events in Jesus' life. Believers understood and interpreted what God had already revealed in his birth, baptism, and transfiguration: that he was God's beloved Son (Mark 1:11; 9:7). In the earliest written New Testament book, 1 Thessalonians (ca. AD 50), Paul uses the title "Son of God" (1 Thess 1:10). Obviously Paul was not the first Christian missionary to do so; as we have already mentioned, he had cited an earlier confession of faith in Romans (Rom 1:3–4).

The designation "Son of God" itself had its own history. Many in the Judaic and Hellenic worlds had been called "sons of God." Israel itself is God's "first-born son" among the nations (Ex 4:22). Josephus presented Moses as "a son in the likeness of God" (*Ant.* 2.232). Nevertheless, the title applied to Jesus to characterize his filial relationship to God received a special meaning, a unique character, the "note of exclusiveness."[27]

The earliest Christians also identified and confessed Jesus as *kyrios* [Lord]. During his public ministry, Jesus had already been addressed as "Lord." Aramaic *mare* or Greek *kyrios* primarily meant "master" or "owner." Some undoubtedly used the term, like "sir," to convey their respect for Jesus. When the Greek Syro-Phoenician woman, begging Jesus to heal her daughter, exclaimed *"kyrie,"* however, she had already heard of Jesus' unusual power of healing and authority as teacher (Mark 7:28). There is a range of meanings between "lord" as a title of respect and "Lord" as a title for God. Scholars have disputed at length as to whether the emphatic *ho kyrios* was used as a designation for God in Judaism. It appears in the Greek translation of the Old Testament, the Septuagint, but some authorities dismiss the title *kyrios* for God as a substitute for Yahweh, inserted by Christian copyists. There was another group of Greek translations of the Old Testament which were "made for Jews and by Jews" where the sacred tetragram YHWH [Yahweh] is not translated, as it is written in Hebrew characters. This comparison between the two sets

---

[26]See R.E. Brown, *An Introduction to the New Testament Christology*, pp. 87–89, and C.F.D. Moule, *The Origin of Christology* (Cambridge: Cambridge University Press, 1977), p. 11ff.

[27]J.D.G. Dunn, *The Evidence for Jesus* (Philadelphia, PA: Westminster Press, 1985), pp. 49–50.

of Greek manuscripts of the Old Testament does not solve the controversy as to whether the Jews used "the Lord" for God. Now new available evidence indicates that Palestinian Jews, before Jesus and the rise of Christianity, occasionally referred to God as *ho kyrios* if they spoke Greek, or *adon* if they were Hebrew/Aramaic speaking.[28] There is no compelling reason to attribute the use of *ho kyrios* for the risen Christ to Paul due to his alleged involvement in the Hellenistic world or his knowledge of the mystery cults. He received the title, not from the world outside Palestine, but "from the Palestinian Jewish Christian community in Jerusalem, where 'Hebrews' and 'Hellenists' (Acts 6:1–6) had already fashioned the creedal formula 'Jesus is Lord' (1 Cor 12:3; Rom 10:9)."[29] The disciples who followed Jesus from Galilee to Jerusalem were among the first to worship him as Lord and Christ.

The early Christians before Paul attributed the sovereignty of God to the risen Christ. The Christian hymn Paul cites in Phil 2:6–11 to support his exhortation to selflessness may have originated in Jerusalem in Aramaic or Greek in the early 40s. It depicts the crucified Jesus as a pre-existent divine figure that took the form [*morphe*] of a servant, humbled himself, and became obedient even to death on the cross. God exalted him "and bestowed on him the name which is above every name, that at the name of Jesus every knee should bow . . . and every tongue confess that Jesus Christ is Lord" (Phil 2:9–11). The structure of the hymn, his descent [*katabasis*] and ascent [*anabasis*], can be detected in the early creedal statements (1 Cor 15:3–5), the confession of faith preserved in 1 Tim 3:16, the Epistle to the Hebrews (Heb 2:5; 4:14–10:8), and in the Prologue of John's Gospel. Jewish Christians answered the question of who Jesus was in terms of "descent" and "ascent." They also drew on scriptural text, particularly the Wisdom literature, to articulate their christological faith.[30] Personified Wisdom (Prov 8), not yet a distinct person from God, comes from God, and was present when God made the earth (Wis 9:9); and, by Wisdom "the Lord founded the earth" (Prov 3:19). She is the image of God's goodness, power and glory. Her role in salvation is expressed in language usually employed only in reference to Yahweh. Those who find Wisdom find life itself and "obtain favor from the Lord" (Prov 8:35). Like the

---

[28]See Joseph A. Fitzmyer, "Pauline Theology," in *NJBC* 82:52.

[29]Ibid., 82:53.

[30]See Richard N. Longenecker, *The Christology of Early Jewish Christianity,* Studies in Biblical Theology, second series, 17 (Naperville IL: Alec R. Allenson, Inc.), p. 58ff.

Old Testament image of Wisdom, Christ "is the power of God and the Wisdom of God" (1 Cor 1:24).

Christological reflection and formulation belong to the very life and dynamic of the Christian community from its beginning. This is what characterizes the earliest church and makes it easily distinguishable from all other religious groups. The church had started with these christological formulations and continued developing them. The Jewish Christian community in Jerusalem could not have grown without living and proclaiming them.

Acts suggests that the earliest attempt of Jewish Christians to formulate the nature of messianic expectation was *parousia* Christology. The Jewish expectations of peace and prosperity that would be realized with the coming of the Messiah were applied to Jesus. God eventually would send his appointed Christ, "Jesus, whom heaven must receive until the time for establishing all that God spoke of through his holy prophets" (Acts 3:19–21). In other terms, Jesus would become the Messiah when he comes again. This Christology was of short duration. Early Christians found it inadequate, due to their meetings with the risen Jesus. They accepted the Second Coming, but not as the moment when he would become the Messiah. He was already Messiah, Lord, Son of God. He has already inaugurated the messianic age of salvation. With his future coming, the work of the Messiah would be consummated, not begun.[31]

During his earthly ministry, Jesus revealed himself, though indirectly. Those who were his eyewitnesses "beginning from the baptism of John until the day when he was taken up" (Acts 1:22) bore witness to the identity of Jesus, that the one who died and was buried was the same who rose from the dead and appeared on several occasions to his disciples. The christological titles, Christ, the Son of God, and the Lord, testify to the identity of the pre-resurrection and the resurrected Jesus. The death and resurrection of the preexistent Lord was in the origin of Christian beliefs.

In summary, the members of the earliest Christian community in Jerusalem came from various Jewish groups. It was a bilingual church, praying and worshiping in two languages, Aramaic and Greek. This diversity helped the community to articulate its distinct christological beliefs. The church never existed without creedal statements.

---

[31]R.E. Brown, *An Introduction to the New Testament Christology*, p. 143ff.

The openness of the Twelve to the Spirit of Jesus and to the needs of the community was certainly the most decisive factor in achieving so much in such a short period. As leaders, they represented the historical link between the pre-resurrection and the post-resurrection periods, between the historical and the risen Jesus. By introducing a new institution with the appointment of the Seven, the Twelve clearly displayed their insight into the needs of the community, broadmindedness, and readiness to lead.

In the spirit of our modern times, it has been tempting to see the "Hebrews" as a conservative group and the "Hellenists" as a liberal faction in the primitive church. Such terms are meaningless when applied to the earliest Christian community. Exercising their "freedom in Christ," the "Hebrews" and the "Hellenists" laid the foundation for the mission of the church and its theology. There was no sign of christological division during the formative period. Both "Hebrews" and "Hellenists" proclaimed that Jesus was Christ, the Son of God and the Lord. The Apostle Peter and the martyr Stephen are not representatives of two different christologies (Acts 2, 7:35, 37, 52). The difference between them was in their attitudes toward the temple. Paul, with his "freedom from the law," was to move in the direction already indicated by Stephen.

Led by the spirit of the Risen Christ, the earliest community witnessed that the crucified Jesus and the risen Lord are one and the same person. With expansion the community opened itself to the needs of its own people as well as to the world. We now turn to the Roman world, into which the church expanded.

CHAPTER FOUR

THE CHURCH'S ENCOUNTER
WITH SYNCRETISM

Already in the first century, Christian communities were appearing around the eastern Mediterranean Sea, outside the borders of Palestine. The world the early Christian missionaries encountered was that created by Roman conquest and established by Roman order. This was the age of religious syncretism, to which Alexander the Great (356–323 BC) was the major contributor.

By conquest, Alexander brought Greek culture and language from the eastern Mediterranean to the Indus River. With his untimely death at age thirty-three, the empire he had established began to disintegrate, falling into the hands of three of his generals, who began fighting among themselves. Antigonus (382 –301 BC), a Macedonian general, took over parts of Greece and Asia Minor. Palestine fell to Ptolemy, the ruler of Egypt; but by 198 BC, it came into the hands of the Seleucids, Hellenistic kings who ruled in Syria. The founder of the dynasty was Seleucus, Alexander's third general. Divided and weak, what had been Alexander's empire was ripe for conquest by the rising power of Rome.

The Roman republic established control over Italy around 275 BC and started to expand beyond these borders. The three Hellenistic kingdoms no longer presented a serious obstacle to the better-organized and united Roman army. One by one, they came under the control of Rome: Macedonia in 168 BC, Syria (including Palestine) as a province in 63 BC, and Egypt in 30 BC. Civil war raged after the murder of Julius Caesar in 44 BC, and resulted in the victory of Caesar's grandnephew Octavian, now undisputed master of the Greco-Roman world with the title of Caesar Augustus. He ruled from 27 BC to AD 14, establishing *pax romana* and bringing stability and peace to the empire. The evangelist Luke tied the birth of Jesus to the rule of Caesar Augustus (Luke 2:1).

The conquest had a profound impact on the religious life of the hetero-geneous, mobile population of the Hellenistic cities. Wherever the Roman army advanced and settled, they brought their own gods, and then returned home introducing new religions, new cults. Syncretism, the blending or union of different, often opposing, religions and their practices was one of the main characteristics of this period.

Actually, this trend started with Alexander the Great, whose conquests created conditions for the expansion of new religions to the cities he founded. Citizens and foreigners mixed; men, women, and slaves belonged to the same religious cult. To be a member of one cult did not hinder a per-son from attending and participating in the rites of another religious group. The ancient exclusiveness weakened as the walls between the cults broke down. With the extension of the empire to much of the known world, the nature of divinity broadened. Gods of a particular sanctuary were enriched by attributes and virtues of the gods of neighboring shrines. In Egypt, for instance, the Greek Zeus became Zeus-Amon-Re, and in Syria Zeus-Baal. The Egyptian Isis was assimilated to Demeter and made the author of civilization, law, and even mysteries.

Part of the same movement was a monotheistic tendency searching for one supreme deity. Isis, originally Egyptian, was identified with Demeter, and subsequently with Aphrodite, Tyche, and other divinities; and finally, was elevated to *Pantheos*. She became "Queen of every land." This search for one supreme deity, although not unknown in Sumerian and Babylonian reli-gions, became dominant in the Hellenistic period and acquired new propor-tions. Hellenistic philosophy helped to strengthen the tendency toward monotheism.

One of the first to recognize and encourage monotheistic tendencies was Zeno (ca. 336 –264 BC), the founder of the Stoic school. He recognized an "all wise Destiny" which ruled over all men, decreeing what is best for them. The person who desires what Destiny or Zeus or the Universal Law or Nature ordained is a wise man. Destiny [*heimarmenē*] runs through the whole of life and binds it in an inescapable chain of cause and effect. Destiny is conceived as the Logos of the universe, which is the product of design, in contrast to Tyche [Chance, Risk, Fortune, Luck]. Without rejecting any god, the Stoics allegorized all myths in order to save them all. Stoicism became the predom-inant trend among the educated classes in the Hellenistic world for centuries.

In the second century, Plutarch (AD ca. 46–ca. 120), the preeminent Greek scholar and writer of the time, managed to defend polytheism in a way that would have satisfied educated pagans, including the followers of Stoic philosophy. He asserted that there were not different gods among different people,

> but just as the sun, the moon, the sky, the earth, the sea are the common property of all men, yet are given different names by different peoples, so too the one Reason which regulates all these things, and the one Providence which supervises all, and the subordinate powers that are appointed over all things, have different honors and titles assigned to them by custom among the different peoples.[1]

Political considerations also contributed toward strengthening the tendency toward the concept of one god. The emperor cult stemmed from various sources. The Egyptians believed that divinity rested in kingship.

Asians also regarded kings as divine, as sons of god by adoption if not by descent. The Greeks also believed that man could attain the rank of hero or demigod for their services after death. The belief that a divine king may keep and unite all people generated the public, official emperor cult. This led to consequences not always foreseen: those who refused to take part in official ceremonies related to the cult, who resisted honoring the emperor, were persecuted for disloyalty.

Alongside tendencies toward monotheism, the masses of the people clung to their traditional religions and practices. They still made offerings to gods, shut themselves up in temples to receive messages, manifestations, and oracles from the gods, and believed in the underworld after death. They also practiced magic. Beliefs about good and bad spirits [*daimones*] were widespread, as the cause of human afflictions. Eventually, Christian missionaries to the Gentiles encountered many of the varied beliefs and traditions practiced in the pagan Roman Empire. Indeed, some aspects of these pagan beliefs would help the success of their missions, while others hindered them. The movement toward monotheism and even more to a personal relation with a god and the craving for personal salvation eased the way for their mission.[2] This was particularly true of the cult of Asclepius and the mystery religions.

---

[1]Plutarch, "On Isis and Osiris," in Frederick C. Grant, ed., *Hellenistic Religions: The Age of Syncretism* (New York: Macmillan Publishing Company, 1953), p. 94.
[2]See Adolf Harnack, *The Mission and Expansion of Christianity in the First Three Centuries* (New York:

Asclepius and the Ministry of Healing

Asclepius, the great healer, arrived in Epidaurus from Thessaly. Here he was recognized as a god of healing. His cult spread throughout the Greco-Roman world, and the sanctuaries dedicated to Asclepius are numerous. According to some estimates, no fewer than four hundred have been located. They point to the enormous influence and popularity of his cult. His shrines are found in Rome and in Jerusalem as well. One such site was most likely the Pool at Bethesda [the Sheep Pool] (John 5:1–9), where Jesus healed the sick man. Hydrotherapy was a major characteristic of healing in these centers. Archeological excavation at Bethesda has found five porticoes, indicating that five therapeutic centers may have been located in the caves. The one Jesus entered was located outside the walls of Jerusalem.[3]

Asclepius was concerned with the individual, his needs, and his well-being. Among all the deities of ancient Greece, he appears as "the most humane god." The cure he offered required moral purity, however. Some candidates for therapy were rejected if their conduct of life was impure.[4] In contrast, Jesus during his public ministry was surrounded by people, including the impure, all asking for help, healing, and wholeness. He healed "every disease and every infirmity among the people" (Matt 4:23–24). He came not to call those who think of themselves as righteous "but sinners" (Mark 2:17). When he approached the man waiting in the Asclepius center who had been ill for thirty-eight years, Jesus did not ask him about his previous personal behavior, but "Do you want to be healed?" (John 5:6). Do you desire your health restored, to be whole? His disciples continued Jesus' healing ministry (Matt 10:1, 8). This power was given to the church (Acts 3:6), and Paul included healing in his list of charismatic gifts granted to some members of the community by the Spirit (1 Cor 12:9). The church entered the world as a religion of healing, reconciliation, and salvation. The widespread cult of Asclepius was an unmistakable sign of the deep craving for healing and wholeness. The Christian missionaries made use of this tradition when they

Harper Torchbooks, 1961), p. 108. Translated and edited by James Moffatt. Introduction to the Torch-books edition by Jaroslav Pelikan.

[3]For an account of the archeological excavation of the Pool, see Jerzy Klier, "Bethesda and the Universality of the Logos," *SVTQ* 27.3 (1983): 169–189.

[4]H. Koester, *History, Culture, and Religion of the Hellenistic Age* (vol. 1 of *Introduction to the New Testament*), p. 176.

brought their message that "there is but one physician, Jesus Christ our Lord" (Ign. *Eph.* 8).

Throughout the first two centuries the Christians on the roads or at sea would meet pilgrims traveling to such prominent places as Epidaurus, Cos, and Pergamum, all known as magnificent therapeutic centers of Asclepius. Christians would enter into dialogue with these pilgrims, hearing from them about miracles of healing performed by their god. The followers of Christ in turn would acquaint them with Jesus' miracles and exorcisms. In the end, they would continue to dispute whose god was greater: Asclepius or Christ?[5]

Celsus, a pagan philosopher who wrote *True Word* or *True Doctrine* around AD 178, praised Asclepius and attacked Christians. His work has not survived except in extensive quotations in Origen's *Contra Celsum*. Celsus expressed admiration for Asclepius and his miraculous cures. A great multitude, he wrote "both Greeks and barbarians, confess that they have often seen, and still see, not just a phantom, but Asclepius himself healing men and doing good and practicing the future" (*C.C.* 3.24). Celsus attacked Christians for using magic to get power, which "they seem to possess by pronouncing the names of certain daemons and incantations." He accused Christ as well, saying, "It was by magic that he was able to do miracles which he appeared to have done."

Later Origen answered these charges. First, he noted that when Christians "accept the testimony of the disciples, who both saw the wonders of Jesus and show clearly their good conscience," then "we are called by Celsus 'silly people.'" Christians in their healing practice invoke "the supreme God and the name of Jesus," the same Jesus who lived in history and was crucified under Pontius Pilate. They "make no use of spells, but only of the name Jesus with other words . . . taken from the divine Scripture" (*C.C.* 7.6). Such disputes continued throughout the second century and beyond.

Contacts between Christians and devotees of Asclepius were possible on a daily basis in the Hellenistic cities of Pergamum and Corinth. On the acropolis of Pergamum was the altar dedicated to Zeus, and in the valley by the springs was the shrine to Asclepius. By the first century a small Christian community already existed somewhere between the acropolis and the fertile

[5]See Gustav Adolf Deissmann, *Paul: A Study in Social and Religious History* (2d ed.; New York: Doran [Doubleday], 1926), p. 42.

valley. With its temple dedicated to Augustus, Pergamum was one of the old-est centers of emperor worship. One of the seven letters of Revelation was addressed to the Christian community in Pergamum, so highly hellenized. Here Christ speaks to this church: "I know where you dwell, where Satan's throne is; you hold fast my name and you did not deny my faith even in the days of Antipas, my witness, my faithful one, who was killed among you, where Satan dwells" (Rev 2:13). The context links the death of Antipas with "Satan's throne," which some have interpreted as referring to the altar of Zeus, but more probably was the temple dedicated to the Roman emperor. Antipas' execution was very likely due to his refusal to offer sacrifice to the emperor. It is most unlikely that "the throne of Satan" refers to the shrine of Asclepius [Asclepeion]. His shrine in Pergamum served as a medical school, where practitioners learned methods of healing: the use of medicinal herbs, water therapy, mud baths, fasting, and treatment determined by dreams of the patients. Galen, a well-known physician of the second century, studied in the Asclepeion. In AD 161, he moved to Rome and became the personal physi-cian of the Emperor Marcus Aurelius. At the time when Justin, the Christian apologist, suffered martyrdom, Galen praised Christian moral virtues and their readiness to suffer for their faith.[6] Some of those associated with the temple of Asclepius might have praised Antipas for his readiness to suffer even death for his god.

In Corinth, where the Apostle Paul founded a church in ca. AD 50, there had been a temple to Asclepius. Writing to this community, which was threat-ened by divisions from within and dangers from without, he offered his vision of the church as a "body," as an organic unity. Scholars have debated the sources behind this predominant image in 1 Corinthians. Was Paul inspired by the Stoic philosophical writing, or the Hebrew concept of "cor-porate personality," or even by the gnostic concept of "primal" man? Arche-ological excavation of the Asclepius center in Corinth added another possible source to these speculations for Paul's image of the church as the body of Christ. The excavation revealed that patients often left votive offer-ings, clay representations of body parts that had been cured, as expressions of their gratitude to the healer Asclepius. Replicas of hands, feet, arms, legs, eyes, ears, and other body parts have been discovered. Paul spent a consider-

[6]On Galen, see R. L. Wilken, *Christians as the Romans Saw Them*, pp. 68–93.

able time in Corinth in AD 50 and 51, and was familiar with the practices of those newly healed. When Paul articulated his own vision of the church, he also called them to mind (1 Cor 12:14–25). He moves from the individual, the separated dismembered parts of the body, to their mutual dependence and unity. "The eye cannot say to the hand, 'I have no need of you,' nor again the head to the feet . . . Parts of the body which seem to be weaker are indispensable" (1 Cor 12:21f). Paul insists that the eye, like other body parts, is truly an eye only when it belongs to the whole. The Corinthians are truly "alive" when they belong to "the body of Christ and are individually members of it" (1 Cor 12–27).[7] The cult of Asclepius, like the mystery religions, emphasized the individual and his needs. Asclepius provides cure, and the mysteries promise deliverance from the tyranny of destiny [*heimarmenē*] or the capriciousness of the Goddess of Luck [Tyche].

The Mystery Religions and "Christian Mystery"

The mystery religions had their origin in the pre-Hellenistic age. The best known of them, the Eleusinian mysteries, were at first limited to Eleusis, but spread by the fifth century to Athens and then opened to all Greeks. In the Hellenistic age, the mysteries spread throughout the empire and became open to non-Greeks, even slaves. The initiation rites in all mysteries were kept in secrecy. The most popular among the Hellenistic mysteries were the cults of Isis, Cybele, and Attis, and Mithra. By the end of the Republic and the beginning of the empire (31 BC), emphasis shifted from the Eleusinian mysteries to the myths of Isis and Osiris.

The original story of Isis and Osiris is about fertility and death. Originating in Egypt, the cult spread to Greece and beyond. *Metamorphoses*, or "The Golden Ass" by Apuleius, written in Latin around AD 150, is our principal source for the mysteries of Isis. The book tells of the adventures of a young man who, after carelessly playing with magic, was changed into an ass. With the help of Isis, he was restored to human form, and finally initiated into the cult. Apuleius demonstrates an intimate knowledge of the initiation ceremonies, which may well include some of his own experience, and his own

[7]Andrew E. Hill, "The Temple of Asclepius: An Alternative Source for Paul's Body Theology," in *JBL* 99.3 (1980): 437–443, and Jerome Murphy-O'Connor, *Paul: A Critical Life* (Oxford: Oxford University Press, 1996), p. 245f.

religious pilgrimage, and how he came to see the light and achieve his authentic humanity through the power of the goddess Isis. Yet, in his book he leads us to the threshold of the mystery without revealing the very moment of initiation. He gives the following account:

> Perhaps you may ask with some anxiety, zealous reader, what was said next, what done. I would say, if it were permissible to say; you should know, if it were permissible to hear. But ears and tongues would both suffer alike for their rash curiosity. Yet I will not torment you with protracted torture . . . So hear, but believe, what is true. I approached the border of death and after treading the threshold of Proserpine and passing through all the elements, I returned. At midnight I saw the sun gleaming with right light, I publicly approached the gods below and the god above and worshipped them . . . Behold! I have told you what, although you have heard it, you must yet needs fail to understand.[8]

Apuleius was bound by a vow of secrecy not to reveal the mystery of Isis. With Proserpine [Persephone in Greek], he brings us back to the Eleusinian mysteries. Here too the initiate was brought down to the gate of the underworld and returned to the upper world. When he was delivered from the darkness, he saw the light.

The mysteries of Isis were progressively more popular in the Hellenistic Roman world. Octavian tried to revive the ancient Roman gods and to prevent the spread of the rites of Isis in Rome. His successor Tiberius (AD 14–37) destroyed many foreign cults, but Caligula (AD 37–41) who succeeded him, rebuilt the Temple of Isis in Rome. Vespasian (AD 69–79), after his soldiers in Alexandria proclaimed him emperor, entered the Temple of Isis. With the successful end of the Jewish-Roman War in AD 70, he and Titus (AD 79–81) spent the night in prayer in the Temple of Isis.[9]

The cult of the Phrygian Cybele, the Great Mother, and Attis was a rival to the Isis cult. Both cults attracted women. Cybele ensured fertility and

---

[8]Selected texts from *Metamorphoses* are available in Molly Whittaker, *Jews and Christians: Graeco-Roman Views*, Cambridge Commentaries on Writings of the Jewish and Christian World 200 BC to AD 200, vol. 6 (Cambridge: Cambridge University Press, 1984), and in C. K. Barrett, *New Testament Background: Selected Documents* (rev. ed.; New York: HarperCollins, 1989).

[9]See Josephus, *The Jewish War*, 7.123. In the second century, the Emperor Hadrian was also her devotee. (Jack Finegan, *Myth and Mystery: An Introduction to the Pagan Religions of the Biblical World* [Grand Rapids, MI: Baker Academic, 1997], p. 196f.)

cured diseases. Her companion was a young shepherd, Attis, whom the Great Mother Cybele had driven insane after he left her. Attis castrated himself and bled to death under a pine tree. When the cult of Cybele encountered the Roman world, it took its place among the mystery religions. Despite the success of Cybele, many Romans loyal to the traditional religion and its gods were repelled by this cult and its symbols, particularly by its initiation rite, which led to frenzy and self-mutilation.[10]

In the original myth of Cybele and Attis, there is no hint of Attis coming back to life. The idea of his resurrection does not play any part in the original cultic celebrations. Still, a fourth-century calendar of the cult alludes to the resurrection of Attis.[11] The devotees of Cybele now fast for several days in preparation for the spring festivities in March. A pine tree is cut down and carried into the temple. During the procession, the people would whip themselves so hard that drops of blood fall upon the image of Attis. Several "days of blood" end with the announcement by the priest of the temple of the resurrection of Attis, followed by days of rejoicing. The death and resurrection of Attis "has the nature of a fertility ritual."[12] Some see in this later development in the Cybele cult the influence of the Passion Week as practiced in Christian communities.

Many Romans found the mysteries of Cybele too bizarre to attract them. As Frederick Grant has noted, the old Roman religion "was essentially a political or social religion, not personal." It was ritualistic, practical, and conservative.[13] To overcome this resistance, some influential leaders in the ruling body of the empire worked with pagan philosophers to save the mystery religions by interpreting the rites and practices allegorically. They allegorized the cult of Cybele, for example, by emphasizing its ethical aspects. The pine tree, the image of Attis, for instance, came to represent virtue and piety. The fourth-century Neo-platonic philosopher Sallustius excelled in an allegorical, philosophical reinterpretation of the cult. His treatise, *Concerning the Gods and the Universe*, very likely written during the reign of Julian the Apostate, was considered the "official catechism of the Roman Empire." It provided clearly formulated ideas, which the devotees of Cybele could use in their disputes with

---

[10]On the cult of Cybele, see Arnaldo Momigliano, "Cybele," *Encyclopedia of Religion*, IV:185–86.
[11]Ibid.
[12]M. Whittaker, *Jews and Christians: Graeco-Roman Views*, p. 232.
[13]F.C. Grant, *Ancient Roman Religion* (New York: Macmillan Publishing Company, 1957), p. xxxiii.

Christians.[14] The allegorists explain the act of castration performed by Attis as divorce from all earthly ties, a precondition for spiritual devotion to Cybele, the Great Mother of Gods. Christian teaching apparently inspired Sallustius' presentation. What you Christians have, he implied, we have had from the earliest times, in the form of our myths. We have baptism too in our tradition. The Emperor Julian, after renouncing Christianity, joined the cult of Cybele.

While the Eleusinian mysteries and the cults of Isis and Cybele were originally agricultural fertility rites, the cult of Mithra was an exception. Presumably, Mithraism developed in the time of Roman Hellenism out of the warrior initiation rite. Under the influence of astrological beliefs, the cult became a sort of astral mystery, the ascent of the human soul to the realm of the stars. By introducing a great number of new gods, five planets, the sun and moon, and by thrusting a deity into the eighth sphere, astrology paradoxically paved the way for solar monotheism.

Initiation into the mysteries of Mithra and rites of purification took place in a cave–the temple of the deity–called a Mithraeum. They were built partly underground to resemble the cave in which Mithra sacrificed a mythical bull. More than the other mysteries, the cult of Mithra kept the secret of initiation. We have no Apuleius to guide us into the core of Mithraism, so we depend primarily on archeological excavations of the remains of temples and the iconography found there. The difficulty of interpreting these findings is compounded by the lack of literary evidence that is written by those other than Christians. From a papyrus identified as a Mithraic liturgy, the initiation appears to be a mixture of astrology and magic. There are seven stages of ascent, and on reaching the seventh, the initiate will encounter the godlike Mithras, "Lord of the fiery crowns" (an attribute of the sun). The initiate sees the splendor of "the gods gazing intently at you and advancing toward you." After the initiate performs some magic acts "you would see the gods eyeing you kindly and no longer advancing toward you, but going about their own business."[15] After taking an oath to keep secrecy, the "reborn" receives a seal on his forehead. He now belongs to the army of Mithras.

The temples of Mithras have been discovered from England to Palestine and Asia Minor. The oldest Mithraea are from the middle of the second cen-

---

[14]For the text of Sallustius' treatise, see F.C. Grant, *Hellenistic Religions*, pp. 178–196.

[15]From texts collected and annotated in Whittaker, *Jews and Christians: Graeco-Roman Views*, pp. 257–260.

tury, and a great number belong to the third and fourth. Mithras is reputedly of Iranian origin, but no temple of Mithras has been found in Iran. The Mithraeum furthest east was discovered at Dura-Europos on the Euphrates, built in the 60s of the second century by Roman soldiers. In the iconography of the temple in Dura-Europos, Mithras and the Invincible Sun, two deities, are presented together as equal.

Increasingly the cult of Mithras gained adherence throughout the empire. In AD 274 Emperor Aurelian (AD 270–75) declared Deus Sol Invictus the official deity of the Roman Empire. A temple in his honor was built in Rome, and his birthday was celebrated on December 25. Due to the association of Mithras with the Sun, his birthday was also celebrated on December 25, to convey his victory over darkness and night.[16] The feast of the Nativity was officially added to the Christian holy days in the course of the fourth century. By recognizing the birth of Christ on December 25, the empire affirmed the triumph of Christianity over paganism and its solar monotheism, and the victory of Christ, the "Sun of Righteousness," over Mithras. During his short reign, Julian "the Apostate" restored the Mithras cult to the predominant position it had occupied from Aurelian to Diocletian (AD 274–305) as "the protector of the empire." When the church reemerged from persecution, the mysteries faded into obscurity.

Many have noted similarities between the mystery cults and Christianity, stemming from the general culture. The images of blood, washing, the common meal, anointing and healing are not the property of one religion; "they are common to life itself."[17] The church never lived in a vacuum. The disciples of Christ entered the world to exorcize and transform it. In their mission they used recognizable means of communication. Jesus could only reach his listeners and bring them the gospel of salvation by revelatory stories and shared images. A successful Christian missionary would be to some degree familiar with the life and hopes of the people to whom he preached the gospel.

The Apologists Justin Martyr, Tertullian, and Origen noted some similarities between the mysteries and Christianity. They dismissed them, however, as "demonically inspired imitations" of the truth of Christianity. In exasper-

---

[16]F.C. Grant, *Ancient Roman Religion*, p. xxxiv, and J. Finegan, *Myth and Mystery*, pp. 209–212.
[17]Hugo Rahner, *Greek Myth and Christian Mystery* (New York: Harper & Row, 1963), p. 37.

ation, Justin labels the feast following the initiation into the cult of Cybele, when bread and a cup of water are brought out in their sacred rites of initiation, "the wicked demon's imitation of the Eucharist" (*1 Apol.* 66.4). Clement of Alexandria attacked the pagan mysteries and their "godless sanctuaries," their initiations as "profanities" and their solemn rites "as without sanctity" (*Protrep.* 22). In contrast, he presents Christianity as the "sacred mystery."

External similarities of rites do not touch the inner core and differences between the mysteries and Christianity. The basic difference is that the mysteries deal with myth and Christianity with history. As R. Schnackenburg emphasizes in his study of baptism in Paul, the root of the myth is "the ever-repeated" cycle of nature. The root of Christian mystery is "the unrepeatable event of Jesus, who suffered death on the cross and who was raised from the dead by the glory of the Father" (Rom 6:3–4). In the initiation into pagan mysteries, what happened to the initiate takes "central place," and he becomes "the embodiment of divinity." In Christian baptism, Jesus is the "primary event" and what the believers experience is "derivative." Baptism as dying and rising with Christ is "inseparable from the historical experience of Jesus." While in the mysteries the initiate was identified with the cult deity, in Christian initiation Christ does not become one with the baptized. What happened to the baptized happened to him in Christ and with Christ.[18]

Starting in the nineteenth century representatives of the "History-of-Religions School" tended to define Christianity as a mystery religion. Alfred Loisy, in *Christian Mystery* (1911), wrote that "like Adonis, Osiris, and Attis, [Jesus] died a violent death and like them he returned to life." This trend persists into our own time; A.N. Wilson, in *Paul: The Mind of the Apostle* (1997), identifies them as well, replacing the rhetoric of "like Adonis" with "just as."[19] However, there is no evidence in the formative Christian period that participants in the mystery cults expected a mortal to rise from the dead. There is no suggestion in the original Adonis myth of his rising. Only later do we find texts, possibly under the influence of Christianity, that make this claim. Much later, in the third and fourth centuries, Christian writers, Origen among them, report on the annual festivities honoring the dying and rising

---

[18]Rudolf Schnackenburg, *Baptism in the Thought of St. Paul: A Study in Pauline Theology* (New York: Herder and Herder, 1964), p. 139ff.

[19]See our review essay, "Paul: Ambassador of Christ or Founder of Christianity?" *SVTQ* 43.3–4 (1999): 393–97.

god Adonis "on the third day." As for Attis, who bled to death as we have already described, Jonathan Smith has written, "Neither myth nor ritual offers any warrant for classifying Attis as a dying and rising deity."[20]

Osiris was killed by his brother Set, and his body was dismembered and scattered. Then his body was reassembled and he journeyed to the underworld, where he became the lord of the dead and remained there permanently. He does not return to the world of the living and offers no real parallel to the resurrected Christ.

Neither the church before Paul nor the churches founded by Paul were dependent upon the mystery religions. Paul had his opponents in every community, yet he was never criticized or attacked for supposedly yielding to the influence of the mysteries. Since they accepted men and women, masters and slaves, the mysteries facilitated Paul's preaching of the oneness of all baptized in Christ. For his life, missionary activities and his theology we have precious documents, his own letters, which together with other New Testament sources, clearly show that the church in its formative period was firmly rooted in the events of Jesus' life, death, and resurrection.

It is to the mission of Paul to the Roman world that we now turn.

---

[20]See Jonathan Z. Smith, "Dying and Rising Gods," *Encyclopedia of Religion*, IV:521–27. He writes that the category of dying and rising gods is an imaginative reconstruction and "is of more interest to the history of scholarship than to the history of religions."

CHAPTER FIVE

THE APOSTLE PAUL'S UPBRINGING AND CONVERSION

As a Christian missionary, Paul was the most influential leader in the first-century church. His letters are historical and spiritual documents, sources for the church's life, organization, worship, and theological development. Their influence has endured throughout the centuries.

Paul was a contemporary of Jesus. A Jew born in Tarsus around 6 BC, he came from the large and well-established Jewish diaspora. His ancestors–possibly his grandfather–emigrated from Palestine and settled in this well-populated Roman city. At times, Paul recollected his roots and later, as a Christian missionary, he confirmed his Jewish identity in his undisputed letters (Gal 1:13–17; 2 Cor 11:22; Rom 11:1; Phil 3:4–6).

In Tarsus Paul received both a Jewish and a Hellenistic education. Jewish children in diaspora, particularly those of privileged family in university towns such as Tarsus, were exposed to two demanding types of education. They grew up in two worlds, two cultural environments, and profited from the burden as well as the joy of studying and learning.

Education in Tarsus

The first book Paul learned to read was the Greek translation of the Hebrew Scripture (Septuagint). While reading and rereading this text, he committed many passages to memory. Later, while dealing with his Christian communities, he would quote Scripture extensively for exhortations and teaching. Some have identified in his epistles about ninety explicit quotations from Scripture and many more allusions and references to it. He made the Bible his own. As a boy, it entered his blood stream, and inspired and influenced him throughout his life. At the very end of his life, while waiting in prison for execution, he recalled his educational experience and advised his disciple Timothy: "Continue in what you have learned and how from childhood you have been acquainted with the sacred writings, which are able to instruct you for salvation through faith in Christ Jesus."[1]

To function in Hellenistic life and culture, Paul probably read Homer, the basis of Hellenistic education. In his monumental work, *Judaism and Hellenism,* Martin Hengel gives evidence that Homer was read even in Pharisaic circles in Jerusalem. If Homer was read in the center of Judaism, presumably Jewish schoolboys in the diaspora, particularly the sons of Roman citizens, also read him.

In Tarsus Paul learned and spoke the language of his own people, as well as Greek, the language of the world in which he lived. This bilingual "Hebrew of Hebrews" was at home in two languages, in two cultures. And as would be quite usual for a Jew in the diaspora, Paul had two names, one Hebrew and the other Greek, Saul [Saoul] and Paulos, respectively. His claim to be of the tribe of Benjamin (Phil 3:5), which includes Jerusalem within its territory, would imply that he kept a Semitic name, the name of the first king of Israel, to affirm his identity. Most probably, he used the name Paul in contacts and relations with his Gentile neighbors. There is no suggestion in Luke's Acts that Saul became Paul at the time of his conversion. Even after the revelation on the road to Damascus, he uses the name Saul. When Paul came into contact with the Gentile population during his missionary work, Luke switched from Saul to Paul (Acts 13:9). We learn only from Luke, who gives us some information about the life of Paul before his conversion and involvement in the Gentile mission, that the Apostle Paul had the Hebrew name Saul.

It is also from Luke that we learn that Paul was a Roman citizen. To those critics who doubt this, Martin Hengel warned that a radically critical attitude to Acts might produce a wealth of imaginative reconstruction of Paul's life.[2] One may find examples of such reconstruction in A. N. Wilson's *Paul: The Mind of the Apostle* (1997).[3]

---

[1] 2 Tim 3:14–15. For Paul's education in Tarsus, see J. Murphy-O'Connor, *Paul: A Critical Life,* pp. 46–51. He includes II Timothy among the authentic letters of Paul, p. 337ff.

[2] *Between Jesus and Paul: Studies in the Earliest History of Christianity* (Minneapolis, MN: Augsburg Fortress Publishers, 1983), p. 167, n. 12.

[3] For concrete examples of Wilson's radical skepticism, see our review essay "Paul: Ambassador for Christ or Founder of Christianity?" *SVTQ* 43.3–4 (1999): 390–401.

Paul was a Roman citizen from birth (Acts 22:15–19). As such, he enjoyed a special legal protection: not to be humiliated by flogging, and in case of trial, the right to appeal to Caesar. The fact that Paul never mentioned his citizenship in his letters and that he was "beaten with rods three times" by Roman soldiers (2 Cor 11:25) without claiming his legal privileges led those who doubt Luke's reliability to assert that Paul had not been a Roman citizen. Even if Paul had invoked his citizenship on these occasions, argue others, he probably would not have stopped the punishment. Due to lack of rapid communication, the Roman Empire was not a centralized state in the modern sense. Also, Roman laws regarding the rights and privileges of citizenship were not necessarily applied uniformly throughout the empire. Paul may have remained silent for additional reasons. He may have recalled that Jesus kept silent before his persecutors, and wished to imitate him. "Persecuted for the cross of Christ," he was not ashamed to bear on his body "the marks of Jesus" (Gal 6:12, 17). In addition, Paul would have had to produce his citizenship papers, but as an active missionary moving from place to place, constantly in danger of being robbed on the roads or in inns (2 Cor 11:23ff), he would have been reluctant to carry this document on his person. It is likely that he kept it among his scrolls and tools where he lived and worked.[4] The certificate was too precious to carry around in his pocket.

On one occasion, if we follow Luke's account of Paul's last visit to Jerusalem, to avoid the cruel Roman punishment and to reach Rome, Paul asked the centurion: "Is it lawful for you to scourge a man who is a Roman citizen and uncondemned?" (Acts 22:25). Possibly Paul then possessed the certificate to confirm his claim. As he was moving from Asia Minor, Macedonia, and Achaia, where he had already preached Christ, Paul now aimed to visit the Christian community in Rome, a city he had never visited, on his way to Spain (Rom 15:19–26). He stopped in Jerusalem to hand over money he had collected, as he had promised. Before undertaking this arduous journey, Paul may well have taken the document of citizenship with him. As we have seen, it helped him in Jerusalem, and without proof of citizenship, he would never have been able to visit Spain. At least he got to Rome, although not as a free man.

---

[4]See F. Schulz, "Roman Registers of Births and Birth Certificates," *Journal of Roman Studies* 32 (1942): 78–91, and 33 (1943): 55–64.

Paul's Roman citizenship was not in conflict with his Jewish faith. His Hellenistic education did not prevent him from attending the synagogue in Tarsus regularly. Jews who were Roman citizens were free from obligations that might be contrary to the demands of their faith and practice. They were exempt from serving in the military. They could observe the Sabbath and had freedom to assemble for worship. They supported the temple in Jerusalem, and settled their internal disputes before their own judges. Since the time of Julius Caesar (d. 44 BC), these privileges had been in effect.

From Tarsus to Jerusalem

As a young man, Paul left Tarsus for Jerusalem. Here in the center of Judaism he joined a group of Pharisees, coming under the influence of the well-known teacher Gamaliel, and advanced in the study of the law "beyond many among [his] own people" (Gal 1:14). In the Mishnah list of teachers of Judaism, Gamaliel comes after Hillel, who was active around the beginning of the Christian era. Hillel had stressed the importance of study and he reportedly warned his students: "Do not say 'when I have time I will study.' Perhaps you will never have leisure." Those who came after him imitated his zeal and joy in study. Paul in his letters never indicated who his teacher was before his conversion; this we learn from Acts (Acts 22:3). There was no reason worthy of consideration for Luke to invent that Gamaliel was Paul's teacher. Paul emphasized that he was a Pharisee (Phil 3:6). He could have joined this group only in Jerusalem. There is no evidence that Pharisaic settlements existed in Tarsus or in other towns outside Jerusalem.

After moving to Jerusalem and joining the circle of the Pharisees, Paul undoubtedly heard about Jesus of Nazareth, as a breaker of the law, who ate with sinners, neglected the Sabbath, and flouted the rules of ritual purity. He learned of Jesus' works and the claims of his followers that he was the promised Messiah and that God raised him from the dead. For the pre-Christian Paul, Jesus was a heretical teacher, a false messiah who undermined the very basis of Judaism. There is no suggestion in the letters that Paul saw Jesus himself in Jerusalem. As a Pharisee, he regarded Christ "from a human point of view," or "in a fleshly way" (2 Cor 5:16). He judged Christ by hearsay.

Paul's Journey to Damascus and Conversion

Zealous in defense of the Law, Paul embarked on persecution of the Christian community. He tried to destroy it, as he wrote later (Gal 1:13, 23). Around AD 34, following the expulsion of the Jewish Christian Hellenists from Jerusalem, "Saul, still breathing threats," asked the high priest to send him to Damascus to bring those who belonged to "the Way" bound to Jerusalem (Acts 9:2). Modern scholars have widely questioned Luke's testimony here on the grounds that the High Priest did not have "judicial authority" outside Judea. Some among them conclude that Paul decided to go to Damascus on his own.

Before Paul's conversion, there had been a Christian community in Damascus. It is possible that Damascus was evangelized by Jesus' followers from Galilee, perhaps by the "brothers of the Lord." Mark in 16:7 may reflect the very early existence of a Christian community in Galilee, and Damascus was closely linked with the region by heavily traveled roads. According to Josephus (*J.W.* 2.22.2), the city had a large Jewish population, and "the synagogues at Damascus" are mentioned by Luke (Acts 9:2, 20). Paul found himself on the road to Damascus in pursuit of the expelled Christians, to harass them as well as those who try to protect them. Jewish Christians had been attending the synagogues in Damascus. Ananias from Damascus, who baptized Paul after his conversion, had a good reputation among Jews (Acts 22:12).

On the road to Damascus God "was pleased to reveal his son to me," Paul wrote to the churches of Galatia about twenty years afterward (Gal 1:16). The Risen Christ took the initiative and made himself known [*ōphthē*] (1 Cor 15:8). He writes emphatically to the Corinthians that he had "seen Jesus our Lord" (1 Cor 9:1). In both letters Paul relates the moment of conversion and the call to an apostolic ministry, to preach Christ among the Gentiles.

With his conversion, Paul did not reject the God of Israel when he became a follower of Christ. His sudden conversion revealed that the God of his people was the "Father of our Lord Jesus Christ"[5] (Col 1:3; 2 Cor 1:3; Rom 15:6). For Paul, "the Father" becomes God's proper name. His perception of God radically changes. The appearance of the Risen Christ led Paul to recog-

---

[5]See John Courtney Murray, *The Problem of God, Yesterday and Today* (New Haven: Yale University Press, 1965), p. 27.

nize that the crucified Jesus was the Messiah. To Paul as a Pharisee, Jesus' crucifixion had been a "stumbling block," an "offense" (1 Cor 1:23), for "cursed
be everyone who hangs on a tree" (Gal 3:13, quoting Deut 21:23). Now this crucified and risen Christ had "redeemed us from the curse of the law, having
become a curse for us" (Gal 3:13). On behalf of sinful humanity, Jesus
accepted the penalty of sin. God "made him to be sin who knew no sin," so
that others "might become the righteousness of God" (2 Cor 5:21). The role
of Christ is not unlike that of the Suffering Servant of God (Isa 53:4–9). It is
the role that God assigns to Christ, that through him we might be reconciled
with the Father.

Only a real conversion could lead Paul to this divine plan of salvation.
His belief in the law as the ultimate expression of God's will now required a
thorough re-evaluation. As is the case with any real conversion, Paul's life
changed drastically. Whatever he did, wherever he preached, it was now as a
"servant," an "ambassador" for Christ. He suffered beyond human endur-
ance for the sake of the gospel, for he is put "under necessity" to proclaim it
(1 Cor 9:16). As a Christian, Paul experienced persecution by his own people.
Five times, he wrote, he received at the hands of the Jews "the forty lashes less
one" (2 Cor 11:24), the punishment permitted to the Jewish courts. It is note-
worthy that the leaders of synagogues in diaspora treated Paul as a Jew, not
as one outside Judaism, and therefore subject to Jewish discipline. Paul himself never ceased to be a Jew. The Jewish Christian community that he joined
was within Judaism. He could not but proclaim what the God of Israel had
already done in Christ for us. And his preaching led to the conversion of
many.

The conversion of Paul was of such importance for the early church that
Luke recorded it three times (Acts 9, 22, 26). No account can fully convey the
mystery of how God revealed his Son to Paul.

Paul's Meeting with Cephas

Paul began his missionary work from Damascus (Gal 1:17). Around AD 37,
three years after his conversion, he came to Jerusalem to meet Peter (Gal 1:18).
Cephas [rock, stone in Aramaic], translated into Greek as "Petros," was not a
proper name but a title given by Jesus to Simon Bar-Jona (Matt 16:17–19). Paul
came to learn about the historical Jesus from the leading disciple of the

Twelve who had been with him during his public ministry, to whom Jesus had appeared after the crucifixion, the first among the Christian leaders in Jerusalem. By the time Paul came to Jerusalem after his conversion and call, Peter had already spent several years preaching and spreading the gospel. With the birth of the church, Peter began the process of shaping Jesus' words and deeds into a gospel. Apparently over the course of fifteen days, Paul received orally from Peter all the major parts of the gospel.

After Jerusalem, Paul moved to areas beyond Palestine to start preaching to the Gentiles. We deduce both from him and from Luke that he spent several years (AD 37–45/46) in Syria and Cilicia (Gal 1:21, Acts 11:25). As we have no details of his missionary activities at that time, these have been called the "hidden years." They end in AD 47, when Barnabas brings Paul to Antioch, where he spent almost a year strengthening the Christian community in the city.

The Church at Antioch

There was a large community of Jews in Antioch. The Jewish practices and beliefs had attracted a considerable number of Gentiles. It was not unusual that where there was a strong Jewish presence, not only in Antioch but also throughout the Roman Empire, many among the pagan population observed the Sabbath day. They were further attracted to the moral teaching and the "pure" monotheism of the Jewish religion.

By the 30s, a Christian church had appeared in this important and influential city. Paul does not tell us about the very early missionaries who reached Antioch before him and founded and organized the Christian community. Luke in Acts (Acts 11:19–20) reports, "Those who were scattered because of the persecution that arose over Stephen traveled as far as Phoenicia and Cyprus and Antioch, speaking the word to none except Jews. But there were some of them, men of Cyprus and Cyrene, who on coming to Antioch spoke to the Greeks [*Hellenes*] also, preaching the Lord Jesus." It appears that Luke combined two traditions regarding the founding of the church at Antioch. What is not clear, however, is how these two traditions are related. Who were the first Christian missionaries in Antioch, persecuted Christian Hellenists or others from "Cyprus and Cyrene"? It is certain that the church was founded before Paul and that by the end of the first Christian decade there was a mixed Christian community in Antioch. Barnabas brought Paul to the city to strengthen and expand the life and mission of the church, which might have been founded by Christians whom he had persecuted in Jerusalem.

The church at Antioch included both Jewish and Gentile converts. Murphy-O'Connor suggests that there may have been several house churches in Antioch. The Christian Jews and the Gentile converts had separate house churches, and yet enjoyed a certain unity. The members would meet in each other's house churches to eat together. They would have a common meal in addition to the rite of the Eucharist. The Jewish members would observe dietary laws, while the Gentile converts did not. For their Jewish guests, Gentile Christians would prepare kosher food, which the Jewish Christians would accept without questioning. They mutually trusted each other. For the Jewish Christians, social relations with the Gentile Christians presented no problem "as long as one did not eat their meat or drink their wine."[6]

What had already happened at Antioch was not Paul's achievement. He undoubtedly encouraged and worked on deepening the relations between Jews and Gentiles, who "are all one in Christ Jesus" (Gal 3:28). In the decisive early period before Paul, the Christian Jews had succeeded in forming one mission, not two, in Antioch.

The church at Antioch sent Paul and Barnabas to proclaim Christ in Galatia (AD 46–48) and to the cities of Philippi and Thessalonica in Macedonia (AD 48–50). Eight to ten weeks after Paul was forced to leave Thessalonica, he wrote 1 and 2 Thessalonians (AD 50), the earliest among his letters. From Corinth, where he spent a year and a half, he journeyed again to Jerusalem in AD 51 for the apostolic conference recorded by Luke and Paul (Acts 15, Gal 2:1–10).[7]

The Jerusalem Conference

Before Paul visited Jerusalem for the second time after his conversion, he had founded the churches in Galatia, Philippi, Thessalonica, and Corinth. With

---

[6]See J. Murphy-O'Connor, *Paul: A Critical Life*, pp. 149–150.

[7]J. Murphy-O'Connor presents data for the chronology in *Paul: A Critical Life*, taking into account available historical information, geographical features, and what is known of weather conditions in the regions of Paul's ministry. Luke, in Acts, places Paul's journey to Macedonia and Corinth as subsequent to the Jerusalem conference (Acts 16–18) in order to emphasize Jerusalem as the decisive center of the Christian mission and Paul as its agent.

considerable experience from his missionary efforts, he reached the Holy City for the meeting with other missionaries and the leadership of the church at Jerusalem. What we know about this conference, beside the account in Acts, comes from Paul himself, who took an active part in the deliberations and who gave us his account of what had occurred at the gathering in Gal 2:1–10, written about two years afterward. About thirty years later, Luke, the first Christian historian, recorded the proceedings in Acts 15, on the basis of his sources and possibly oral reports of the participants.

The two Jerusalem conferences reported in Acts 6 and 15 led the community to take decisions of far-reaching consequence for the future of the church and its mission in the world. We have already described the first conflict between the Hellenists and Hebrews. At the second meeting in AD 51, the dispute was over circumcision of Gentile converts. Could they become members of the Christian church without undergoing circumcision, without undertaking the obligation of the law and its demands? During the conference there was "discussion and debate" over the issue (Acts 15:12). Some missionaries from Judea insisted that converted Gentiles could not be saved without circumcision. Paul and Barnabas argued against requiring circumcision and related "signs and wonders God had done through them among the Gentiles" (Acts 15:19). In his letter to Galatians, written shortly after the conference, Paul argued that the pillars of the church, James, Cephas, and John, gave Paul and Barnabas "the right hand of fellowship, that we should go to the Gentiles and they to the circumcised" (Gal 2:9). They approved Paul's mission to the Gentiles and asked only that the Gentile missionaries remember the poor in Jerusalem. This demand Paul enthusiastically accepted and faithfully fulfilled.

Following the Jerusalem council, Paul left for Antioch, where soon after Peter joined him. At this time the problem of food arose: should converts be held to the dietary laws found in Leviticus? At first Peter, who had been entrusted with the gospel to the circumcised, participated fully in the life of the mixed community in Antioch. He ate with the Gentile Christians in their houses. But when certain emissaries from James arrived, he drew apart, followed by the rest of the Jewish Christians. "Even Barnabas" left Paul and sided with Peter (Gal 2:11–13). Paul protested that "they were not straightforward about the truth of the gospel," and opposed Peter and the others. He charged Peter with changing his position radically when the representatives of James arrived. Peter had been living "like a Gentile," that is, he ate with them. But when the emissaries came, he changed his mind, requiring the Gentiles to live like Jews (Gal 2:14–15).

James's delegates insisted that Jewish converts obey dietary laws. They opposed their participation in a common meal with Gentile converts who did not abstain from "what has been sacrificed to idols and from blood and what is strangled and from unchastity" (Acts 15:20, 29). The fourth prohibition refers to Lev 18:6–15, which prohibits marriage to close relatives, as practiced among the Gentiles. The demand from Jerusalem for observance of dietary laws by Jewish Christians may have been a response to the need for Jewish identity and unity in the face of Roman occupation. We may infer that the emissaries from James informed Peter and the other Jewish Christians that the conduct of the mixed community in Antioch was exciting great tension in Jerusalem. Peter, who was well known in Jerusalem, may have sided with them out of pastoral concern in view of the danger in which the Jerusalem Christians were living, while Paul took a more dogmatic position.

Paul was the leader of the Jewish Christians, who did not require his Gentile converts to undergo circumcision or observe dietary laws. While Paul himself observed Jewish feasts (Acts 20:6, 16) and worshipped in the temple (Acts 21:26), the Hellenists, more radical than Paul, criticized the temple and its practices of sacrifice. The Epistle to the Hebrews, now regarded by many as written by a second generation Christian Hellenist, was critical of the temple.[8]

Disappointed by the new policies introduced by James and the departure of the other disciples, Paul left Antioch for Galatia, where he nurtured churches he had founded prior to the Jerusalem meeting. He went from there to Ephesus, where he stayed about three years (Acts 19:8–10, 20:31). Here he wrote Galatians (AD 52). Luke mentioned three places where Paul was imprisoned: Philippi (Acts 16:23), Caesarea Maritima (Acts 23:23ff), and Rome (Acts 28:16). Modern New Testament scholars would add Ephesus to this list, supporting their view by references from the Corinthian correspondence (1 Cor 15:32, 2 Cor 11:23). They also find clear references in other epistles. In the

---

[8]For positions taken in the various missions, see Raymond E. Brown and John Meier, *Antioch and Rome: New Cradles of Catholic Christianity* (New York: Paulist Press, 1983), pp. 2–8; R.E. Brown, "The Twelve and the Apostolate," *NJBC* 80:17–18.

prison in Ephesus, he probably wrote the "captivity epistles" (Philippians, Colossians, and Philemon), and after release from prison he wrote Corinthians 1 and 2 (AD 54–56). Just before he embarked for the last visit to Jerusalem in AD 56, he wrote the Epistle to the Romans.

Paul's epistles are our primary source, aside from the Book of Acts, for the mission and expansion of the church from approximately the 40s to the Jewish Roman War (AD 68–70). The syncretism that prevailed throughout the Roman Empire helped to create favorable grounds for Paul's preaching. It also challenged Paul, helping him to develop a clear message of the gospel in the face of the tendency to blend the mixture of religions. The pressure of Hellenistic cults and practices, along with the Roman occupation, alarmed the Jewish community. Paul in turn challenged both Jews and Gentiles with his preaching: "The gospel of the cross, Christ the power of God and the wisdom of God" (1 Cor 1:18ff).

CHAPTER SIX

THE APOSTLE PAUL'S MISSION
TO THE DIASPORA

As we have learned in the previous chapter, Paul was born and raised outside the territory of Palestine in Tarsus, on the southeastern coast of Asia Minor, now Turkey. By the first century, according to estimates, four to five million Jews, about seven percent of the total population of the Roman Empire, were living in diaspora. They were scattered throughout the empire (Acts 2:9–11), but Babylonia, Syria, Asia Minor, and Egypt were the chief centers of Jewish settlement.

The Babylonian *diaspora*, the first among these centers, stemmed from the "Babylonian Captivity." The conquering army destroyed the temple in 587–586 BC, and deported the population to Babylon. With the rise to power of the Persian ruler Cyrus (538–530 BC), the Jews were permitted to return to Jerusalem. Although most returned, a substantial number elected to stay in Babylon. They kept ties with Jerusalem and shared the Aramaic language, and Babylon remained an important center of Jewish life in the Persian period (538–333 BC) and during the Greek era (333–63 BC).

With the Roman conquest, however, the relationship between the Jews of Jerusalem and those of Babylon became strained. Jews in Babylon disagreed with the tenet of the Jerusalem Jews that the law could not be observed outside the geographical region of Palestine. Then, Babylonian Jews refused to support the two wars against Rome: the one that resulted in the destruction of the temple (AD 66–70) and the rebellion led by Bar Kochba (AD 132–135). As an added expression of their displeasure, the Babylonian diaspora stopped extending financial support to the poorer Jewish communities of Palestine after AD 70. Further, Babylon continued producing legal commentaries on Judaism. Hillel, who was active about the beginning of the Christian era, came from Babylon to Palestine. He was a living example to many in Pales-

tine that the law could be observed outside Palestine, either in the Babylonian or any other Jewish *diaspora.*

There were Jewish colonies in Egypt before the conquest of Alexander the
Great. In the Hellenistic period, the Jewish diaspora significantly increased
and strengthened, particularly in the newly founded city of Alexandria. Two
of the five city districts were identified as "Jewish," and Jews were permitted
in other districts as well. Philo (ca. 15 BC–AD 45) tells us that a million people
of Jewish origin lived in Egypt. The entire population of Egypt under Vespasian (AD 69–79) did not exceed eight million.

Syria at the time of Nero (emperor AD 54–68) had more than a million
Jews out of a population of seven million, a proportionately larger group than
Egypt. Josephus noted that the "Jewish race is thickly spread over the world,
but especially in Syria" (*J.W.* 7.3.3). During this same period, fewer than
750,000 Jews lived in Palestine proper. Adolf Harnack finds "particularly strik-
ing" the large number of Jews living in Antioch.[1] Around 200 BC the Seleu-
cid Antiochus III settled close to two thousand Jewish families from
Babylonia to western Asia Minor, strengthening the Jewish presence there.
Synagogues excavated in that area show signs of their presence and their
wealth.

A numerous Jewish community, mentioned in Roman sources, settled in
Rome. In 139 BC they were expelled from Rome and forced to return to their
place of origin, because they "had tried to infect Roman customs" with the
cult of "Sabazius." Apparently, the Roman authorities may have confused
"Sabaoth," the Lord of Hosts, with Sabazius, a Phrygian deity who shared
orgiastic rites with Dionysus.[2] The Jewish population was also increased in the
first centuries BC and AD by military actions: Pompey brought many Jews as
slaves to Rome after conquering Judea in 63 BC, and Vespasian did the same
after destroying the temple in AD 70. In his *Life of Claudius* (AD 41–54), Suetonius writes that "The Jews were constantly making disturbances at the instigation of Chrestus," and for this reason the emperor "expelled them from
Rome" (*Claud.* 25.4). By "Chrestus," he apparently meant "Christ," using a
Latinized form of the Greek "Christos." He implies that there were conflicts
between two groups of Jews in their synagogues, as the Roman Christians were

---

[1]Adolph von Harnack, *The Mission and Expansion of Christianity in the First Three Centuries* (New
York: Harper Torchbooks, 1962), p. 7, n. 1.

[2]M. Whittaker, *Jews and Christians: Graeco-Roman Views,* pp. 85–86.

of Jewish origin. Non-Christian Jews and Jewish Christians were not yet separated, and the Roman authorities could not easily distinguish them. Luke in
Acts mentioned the edict of Claudius and a Jew named Aquila and his wife
Priscilla as among those forced to leave Rome (Acts 18:1–2). Both had been
Christians before they met Paul in Corinth. Luke may have exaggerated when
he claimed that Claudius "had commanded all the Jews to leave Rome." There
were 40,000–50,000 Jews in Rome, and most probably, the edict attacked one
rioting synagogue, a small proportion of the Jewish Roman population.[3]

Throughout the empire, the Jews in *diaspora* settled primarily in cities,
where synagogues were built by the first century. Under Julius Caesar at the
beginning of the empire, special privileges were extended to the Jewish population. An energetic trading people, they enriched the cities where they
dwelt. Although some Roman citizens in the provinces objected to the special rights granted the Jews, the Roman authorities demanded compliance
with all of their privileges.

The Jews were also exempted from participating in the cult of the
emperor. No official document granting dispensation from this requirement
of Roman citizenship has been found (maybe none was issued), but the
exemption was honored in practice. When the Jews failed to worship the
emperor, their absence "was simply ignored."[4]

Some have assumed that the great number of Jews in the Roman world
was due to organized Jewish missionary activities. They point to Jesus' words:
the Pharisees "traverse sea and land to make a single proselyte" (Matt 23:15).
While there might have been individual efforts to convert Gentiles, as the
words of Jesus imply, they would have lacked an organized mission of the
synagogue toward expansion. Judaism was not a missionary religion.[5]

The law-observing Jews of the *diaspora* did not close themselves off from
the outside world, however. In fact, a number of Gentiles were attracted to
Judaism, to its professed monotheism, the strict moral code, and the Sabbath
observance, as we have already discussed. They even adopted some Jewish
practices, without formal conversion. These friendly and interested Gentiles

[3]See J. Murphy-O'Connor, *Paul: A Critical Life*, p. 333.
[4]H. Koester, *History, Culture, and Religion of the Hellenistic Age* (vol. 1 of *Introduction to the New Testament*), p. 226.
[5]See Shaye J.D. Cohen, "Did Ancient Jews Missionize?" *BR* 19.4 (2003): 40–47, with a valuable
recent bibliography.

are identified in Acts as "God-fearing people" or as "worshippers of God." A number of these God-fearers were converted to Christianity, without joining the synagogue. Paul baptized a Gentile woman, Lydia, from the city of Thyatira, "who was a worshiper of God," that is, a God-fearer (Acts 16:13). These "God-fearers" were not as clearly defined as the much smaller group of proselytes, who actually embraced Judaism and undertook the obligation to keep the law. Both groups are mentioned in Acts. Nicolaus, "a proselyte of Antioch," joined the church and was numbered among the seven Christian Hellenists in Jerusalem (Acts 6:5).

Paul was not the first who started missionary activities among the Gentiles. There were Christian missionaries before him, but it was he who transformed the scattered efforts into a well-planned and organized Christian mission. After founding these missions, Paul worked constantly to maintain and nurture them. As a missionary, he envisioned breaking down the wall of separation between Jews and Gentiles by bringing them together in the body of Christ. The church for Paul is the new temple "without walls" (1 Cor 3:16–17).

His missionary work was mainly centered in large cities, capitals of provinces, such as Corinth and Ephesus. He spent about eighteen months in Corinth (Acts 18:11), the capital of Achaia, the Peloponnese, and much of central Greece. Corinth was the place of the Isthmian games, held every two years, which attracted many spectators from all the Roman provinces. Public accommodations were far too scarce for the throngs of visitors, and many found them prohibitively expensive. In response to the demand for shelter, many sought tents. In AD 50–51 Paul was staying in Corinth with Aquila and Priscilla, who supported themselves as tent makers. At that time Paul took on the same trade (Acts 18:1–3). As a Roman citizen and member of a privileged prosperous family, he had never previously engaged in manual labor, as his comments reveal. In his letters he characterized physical labor as "harsh" (1 Cor 4:12; 2 Cor 6:5, 11:23, 27) or slavish (1 Cor 9:19) and demeaning (2 Cor 11:7), reflecting the attitude of a man who had not previously worked with his hands. Paul worked in order to be economically independent, joining other philosophers who promoted the use of manual labor to teach their disciples "self-sufficiency." When Paul's opponents in Corinth tried to undermine his apostleship, they reproached him for being a laborer, which they regarded as a sign of his inferior status. In this, however, Paul imitates Christ. As Christ had humbled himself, so did Paul. He preached God's gospel without charge to the Corinthians (2 Cor 11:7). He learned how to be self-sufficient, to be abased, to face plenty and hunger, abundance and want. Whatever gain he had he "counted as loss for the sake of Christ" (Phil 3:7–8). By supporting himself with tent making, he came into contact with a number of Gentiles, to whom he proclaimed the gospel.[6]

The next big city he visited was Ephesus, where he spent about three years (AD 52–54). Known as "the first and largest city of Asia," Ephesus was regarded as "temple warden" of the Roman emperors. Here was built the temple to the mother goddess Artemis, the largest edifice in the Hellenistic world, constructed entirely of marble. Acts reports that Paul's missionary activities in the city, and his statement that "gods made with hands are not gods," provoked protests from local craftsmen, led by Demetrius, who made silver shrines to Artemis. They said that Paul's attack on Artemis diminished the goddess, robbing "from her magnificence" (Acts 19:27). They feared for their economic loss and threatened Paul and his co-workers with violence.

Priscilla and Aquila had already founded a church in Ephesus, while Paul was away in Jerusalem for the apostolic conference (Acts 18:19). Upon his return in AD 52, their church served as a basis for Christian expansion. In Ephesus, Paul and his co-workers reached some of the worshippers of Artemis who would return to their households with his new message of salvation. In this way, Christian missionaries started reaching people beyond the cities. Less than half a century after the martyrdom of the Apostle Paul, Pliny, a governor of Bithynia, writing to the emperor Trajan (*Ep. Tra.* 10.96), expressed his surprise that a large number of the people had joined the Christian group, which "has spread not only through the cities, but also in the villages and in the open country." Pliny confronted a crisis: Christian expansion, which had begun before the governor reached the province.

Paul's Life as a Missionary

Paul was constantly at risk during his travels to preach the gospel. Three times he was shipwrecked, and in his frequent journeys he was in danger "from

---

[6]For the world of Paul's missions, see Abraham J. Malherbe, *Paul and the Thessalonians: The Philosophic Tradition of Pastoral Care* (Minneapolis, MN: Augsburg Fortress Publishers, 1987), and A.J. Malherbe, *Social Aspects of Early Christianity* (Minneapolis, MN: Augsburg Fortress Publishers, 1983).

robbers, danger from [his] own people, danger from Gentiles, danger in the
city, danger in the wilderness, danger at sea, danger from false brethren; in
toil and hardship, through many a sleepless night, in hunger and thirst, often
without food, in cold and exposure" (2 Cor 11:24–27). Roman soldiers and the
local synagogue authorities beat and imprisoned him. He experienced daily
pressure and anxiety for his churches. The list of his trials and suffering attest
to the outcome of the gospel he preached.

The disruptive behavior of his opponents within the churches he had
founded and nurtured pained him. After the confrontation in Antioch, the
Judaizers, Jewish Christians who belonged to the circumcision party, never
left him alone, but followed him, disrupting his work and creating divisions
in the churches of Galatia, Philippi, and Corinth. To replace Paul's gospel
with their own, they demanded obedience to the law and observance of it.
Some Gentile Christians, convinced that circumcision was necessary for salvation, joined the group.

These "Judaizers" were not the only ones trying to reform the gospel Paul
preached. In addition, he was confronted in Corinth with "spiritual people,"
who discarded the historical Jesus. They were certain that whatever was linked
with the body was of no importance for them. Their slogan was "all things
are lawful for me." In 1 Corinthians, Paul argues against the views of the "spiritual people," reminding them that their body is a temple of the Holy Spirit:
"You are not your own, you were bought with a price. So glorify God in your
body" (1 Cor 6:19–20). There was not a single community founded by Paul
that did not have in its midst some members who opposed him and tried to
transform his gospel of the death and resurrection of Christ according to their
own models. He asked the Christians of Colossae, a church which Paul had
not founded but was well acquainted with, to separate themselves from false
teachers, leave the worship of the angels and return to Christ, for "in him all
the fullness of God was pleased to dwell" (Col 1:19, 2:17f). Paul was struggling
with the syncretists at Colossae.

Paul warned newly converted Gentiles, to Judaism or Christianity, to
expect distress and ill treatment from their former pagan friends, who considered them traitors to their traditional religion. Like the historian Tacitus,
Juvenal, the Roman satirist and poet (ca. AD 60–ca. 140), expressed the view
that the converts to Judaism "are accustomed to despise Roman laws," and
that "they learn to keep and revere whatever Jewish ordinances Moses handed

down in a mysterious volume." Juvenal blames the corrupting influence of the parents: the father is a god-fearer, in that he observes the Sabbath and abstains from pork; the son goes further and *becomes* a full Jew."[7] Philo of Alexandria (ca. 15 BC–AD 45) asked the synagogue to pay special attention to proselytes, in view of the Roman hostility toward them. They should be respected and on the whole regarded with "benevolent concern." We may assume that the increased Christian missionary activity exacerbated the hostility of the surrounding community. Paul noted the suffering of those "who turned to God from idols" and received the gospel of God "in the face of great opposition" (1 Thess 1:9, 2:14). This was a foreshadowing of the suffering Christians would endure with the withdrawal of the protection of the synagogue and privileges of the Jews.

The House Churches

During the first two centuries there were no public meeting places for Christian gatherings. Christians were "in the public mind, not in the public eye," observed A.D. Nock. The places for their liturgical assemblies and the main settings for preaching and teaching were private houses. As Paul's epistles show, Christians met only in private houses of their better-off brethren (1 Cor 16:19; Rom 16:3–5; Phil 22). A house church could not accommodate all members of the community in cities such as Corinth or Rome. According to some accounts there were in Paul's time forty to fifty Christians in Corinth. In Rome several house churches existed (Rom 16:5, 14, 15). For a special meeting, the gathering of "the whole church," the largest house church would be the meeting place for all brethren. In Rome it was the house of Gaius (Rom 16:23), which probably was also the house where Paul's letter to Romans was read to the community for the first time.

The private houses which served as meeting places offered "privacy, intimacy, stability of place," but also they appear to have been a breeding ground for various conflicts and divisions, as is reflected in 1 Cor 1–4.[8] One house church would try to dominate another or would look down upon other groups in the same city. Then Paul also had to deal with tensions, divisions,

[7] *Satires*, 5.14.96, cited in M. Whittaker, *Jews and Christians: Graeco-Roman Views*, pp. 34, 88; and in A.J. Malherbe, *Paul and the Thessalonians*, p. 44.
[8] W.A. Meeks, *First Urban Christians*, p. 75ff.

and even scandalous behavior at the celebration of the Lord's Supper. The wealthy members humiliated the poor (1 Cor 11:17–23). At eucharistic gatherings, Paul exhorted Christian masters and slaves to sing and praise God, and to eat the bread and drink the cup of the Lord together.

The house churches included more than a nuclear family. Servants and business associates would be members of one household. Members of other urban households would visit their neighbors and friends and would be exposed to new ideas. If the head of the household was converted to Christianity this does not necessarily imply that all other members would follow him to be baptized. Philemon was converted, but not his slave Onesimus. Later, during Paul's imprisonment in Ephesus, he converted Onesimus (1 Cor 15:32; 2 Cor 11:23; Phil 10, 16).

The household was the most fertile place for missionary work. In his earliest letter, Paul uses the household code for daily life, a series of injunctions reflecting conventional morality, when he exhorts believers "to aspire to live quietly, to mind their own affairs, and to work with [their] hands" (1 Thess 4:11). Such an orderly life attracts the respect of outsiders from the pagan society among whom they were living. In the Epistle to Colossians, noting their emphasis "on things that are above, not on things that are on earth," Paul urges them to return to the real world, expressed in part in their household code. There was a prevailing tendency in the church at Colossae to practice mystical contemplation and ascetic "self-abasement." The regulations they imposed: "do not handle, do not taste, do not touch" (Col 2:21) in practice implied escape from the world. The household code (Col 3:18–4:1) should be a constant reminder to them to return and be involved in the world. The code also shields "the gospel from a spiritualistic interpretation," such as the one started in the Christian community at Colossae.[9]

The Rites of Baptism and Eucharist

In their liturgical assemblies, particularly in the two rites of incorporation, Baptism and Eucharist, these house churches reveal distinct characteristics that separate them from numerous Roman cults. Baptism was open to all, Jews and Gentiles, men and women, masters and slaves. To be baptized in the

---

[9]Petr Pokorny, *Colossians: A Commentary* (Peabody MA: Hendrickson Publishers, 1991), p. 177f.

name of Jesus is to belong to him. The baptized separate themselves from previous ties and commitments and enter into a new solidarity with Christ. They "were washed, sanctified, justified in the name of the Lord Jesus Christ and the Spirit of our God" (1 Cor 6:11). They were baptized into his death, buried, and raised with him, that they "might walk in the newness of life" (Rom 6:3–6). This union with Christ in baptism is neither a magical act nor simply a mystical experience. It is a decisive act of God, who was raised from the dead, who wiped out our trespasses and brought union with Christ (Col 2:12–14). The very use of the passive voice in Paul's baptismal passages, such as "you were baptized," indicates "God's primacy in everything."[10]

To belong to Christ is to be incorporated into his body, the church, to become a member of God's household, "the household of faith" (Gal 6:10). The baptized, who are many, are one body in the eucharistic celebration, "for they all partake of the same loaf" (1 Cor 10:17). The Eucharist manifests the church as the visible presence of Christ in the life of believers and by their witness to the outside world. There is no Eucharist outside the church. Paul's account of the institution of the Eucharist in 1 Cor 11:23–26 is the earliest written evidence in the New Testament. He claims that he received the eucharistic words "from the Lord" (1 Cor 11:23). Most probably with this statement he asserts that the eucharistic words have their origin in Jesus' words at the Last Supper, and that he is a faithful, trustworthy link in the chain of receiving and delivering them. He received the eucharistic formulations from the Christian community after his conversion, either in Jerusalem or in Antioch, not at the time of the revelation to him on the road to Damascus or in any other "visions and revelations" (2 Cor 12) he experienced. What he received and delivered was already in use in the worship of the early church. The Eucharist was not his creation by borrowing from the mysteries, as some have speculated.

Paul's account of the Eucharist contains his "minor modifications." The Thanksgiving meal of the church has always been understood as the community's rite "in remembrance of Jesus." Paul underlines it by repeating twice the words: "Do this in remembrance of me" (1 Cor 11:24, 25), and adds his own commentary: "For as often as you eat this bread and drink this cup, you proclaim the Lord's death until he comes" (1 Cor 11:26). Thus, he links the Eucharist to the life of the Christian community.

[10]See R. Schnackenburg, *Baptism in the Thought of St. Paul*, p. 62ff.

In Corinth there was a crisis, reflected in disorderly conduct during the liturgical gathering. This showed lack of love and mutual concern in the church. Some commentators, notably J. Murphy-O'Connor,[11] regard Paul's additions to the eucharistic words as reminders to his converts of the supreme act of the Lord's sacrifice for others. To proclaim his death, to remember him, puts demands on them to follow and "imitate" him. Without love and concern for one another, there is no real community. To belong to the body of Christ implies mutual dependence. There are no independent believers or independent churches. Paul sees the church as an organism, a living body called to proclaim Christ's death and resurrection and to manifest God's incarnate love to the world. Every individual member of the body is needed. "The parts of the body which seem to be weaker are indispensable" (1 Cor 12:22).

Paul used the image of the body of Christ in three distinct ways: for Christ's own crucified body (Rom 7:4), then for the eucharistic body ("The bread which we break, is it not a participation in the body of Christ?" [1 Cor 10:16]), and for the church, the body of Christ. In the church, Christ's corporate body, Jews and Gentiles are reconciled and united (Eph 2:14–16). They experience the peace of Christ. They grow in unity by taking part in the eucharistic celebration. Now they can no longer participate in any mystery religions or other cult of the Roman world. A member of the body of Christ cannot drink the cup of the Lord or partake of the table of the Lord and also participate in pagan sacrifices (1 Cor 10:20–21). The Eucharist by its exclusiveness determines the boundaries between the church and the syncretistic cults.[12]

Ministries in the Charismatic Churches

Paul's churches are charismatic communities. The baptized received "the spirit of sonship." As adopted sons of God, they have the courage to address God as "Abba, Father!" (Rom 8:14–15; Gal 4:5–7). The Spirit is given and is active in preaching, witnessing, and making decisions. The Christian community constitutes a temple of the Holy Spirit (1 Cor 3:16). Paul reminds the one

[11] *Becoming Human Together: The Pastoral Anthropology of St. Paul* (Wilmington, DE: Michael Glazier, Inc., 1982), passim.

[12] W.A. Meeks, *First Urban Christians*, p. 159ff.

who is incorporated into the body of Christ that his own body "is a temple of the Holy Spirit within you, which you have from God" (1 Cor 6:19).

In the charismatic church, all members are responsible for ministry, exercising a diversity of ministries and responsibilities. In the early years there is a "ministry of the Word": apostles, prophets, and teachers, in that order of importance, were appointed by God to constitute a ministry by which the church was founded and built up.[13] We notice ranking from the very beginning of the church's life and organization. These apostles are linked with the local community, in this case with the charismatic church at Corinth (1 Cor 12:27). They were the missionaries and the founders of the church (2 Cor 3:5f). They should be distinguished from the apostles who were called and sent into mission by the Risen Christ in his post-resurrection appearances (1 Cor 15:8), as well as from the larger group of apostles who performed the role of "delegates or messengers" sent to represent their churches. In Paul these two aspects of apostleship merged. The Risen Christ took the initiative and made himself known to him [*ōphthē*], and Paul became an apostle who founded and formed Christian communities.

In addition to apostles there were prophets, not appointed but recognized by the charismatic church as such. They are members of the church and subject to its tradition. There were also teachers. While a prophet derives his authority from prophetic inspiration, the teacher derives his from the received tradition. So the teachers in Corinth, like the prophets, stand under the authority of tradition.[14] The prophet speaks and the others "weigh what is said" (1 Cor 14:29). The teacher interprets tradition in the light of the revelation of the Risen Christ. The Christian community is empowered to test everything and to hold fast what is good (1 Thess 5:19–21). The community as a whole seems to be engaged in one or another form of ministry. All are called to shine "as lights in the world, holding fast the word of life" (Phil 2:15–16).

The diversity of ministries expresses the diversity of spiritual gifts [*charismata*]. In addition to the ministries of apostles, prophets, and teachers in Corinth, there was another type of ministry emerging: some members of the community "devoted themselves to service [ministry] of the saints" (1 Cor 16:15). Paul urgently appealed to the Corinthians "to be subject [*hypotassē*, to

---

[13]J. Murphy-O'Connor, "The First Letter to the Corinthians," *NJBC* 49:60.
[14]J.D.G. Dunn, *Jesus and the Spirit*, p. 283.

submit themselves voluntarily in love, not in blind obedience] to such men and to every fellow worker and laborer" (1 Cor 16:17). The spirit that animated the apostles, prophets, and teachers was the same spirit that stirred recognized local leaders such as Stephanos and his household. The church in Corinth did not lack men with spiritual gifts (1 Cor 1:7). In Thessalonica as well, Paul wrote the church there, asking the "faithful" or "saints" to respect those who labor among you, "to esteem them very highly in love because of their work" (1 Thess 5:12f). In addition to Paul's labor [kopiao, the term used for his own missionary work and that of others], there were others in Thessalonica with defined roles and duties.

Both Thessalonica and Corinth had a hierarchical structure as a constituent element of the body of Christ. Writing to the Christians at Philippi, the apostle greeted them with their "bishops and deacons" [episkopois kai diakonois] (Phil 1:1). More than one "bishop" took part in community affairs. These bishops in Philippi did not yet belong to the "monarchical episcopate" known to Ignatius, for they are not much different from elders [presbyteroi], a title which Paul does not use for the leaders in his churches. Polycarp (AD 70–156), Bishop of Smyrna around AD 110, wrote to the Philippians his only known letter, in which he identified the plurality of leaders as "elders" (Pol. Phil. 6:1; 11:1). The term diakonos used by Paul in Phil 1:1, is not used in a general sense of "servant" or "helper," but as an official of the church. The bishops and deacons of Philippi had official community positions. They were the product of the community in which they used their spiritual gifts and whom the "household of faith" assigned to the position of leadership. Among the responsibilities of a bishop was to collect funds and help the needy. With his assistants (deacons), he helped Paul. "No church entered into partnership with me in giving and receiving except you only, for even in Thessalonica you sent help once and again," Paul wrote the Philippians (Phil 4:15–16). That Paul was receiving regular help from Philippi meant that some organized stable leadership existed. The leaders who took care of Paul probably were local church "overseers" (bishops) and their assistants (deacons).[15] The gifts of the spirit were given to these local leaders for the benefit of all. Both the charismatic ministry of the word and the ministry of the organized local church were expressions of charismata, gifts of the spirit.

[15]J. Murphy-O'Connor, Paul: A Critical Life, p. 217.

There was no division between the charismatic and institutional ministries within the local church. What Paul states in 1 Cor 12:28: "And God appointed in the church first apostles, second prophets, third teachers . . ." has been interpreted as a division between different types of ministry. Yet in the same chapter he writes that all activities in the church "are inspired by one and the same spirit" (1 Cor 12:11). In continuing enumeration of various ministries in 1 Cor 12:28 he put "helpers, administrators" before "speakers in various tongues," that is, before glossolalists. At the end of this section, Paul questions "the spiritual relevance of any distinction between natural and supernatural ministries."[16] Offices, which are for the building up of the body of Christ, are also gifts (Eph 4:11–12).

Women in Paul's Churches

Several women, Jesus' disciples, followed the Lord (Luke 8:1–3). By his actions Jesus sought to remove prejudice against women. The earliest Christian community was a new group, a new movement of men and women within Judaism (Acts 1:14). Paul followed Jesus as a liberator of women, who were his helpers and co-workers in the mission and expansion of the church.

The Apostle Paul mentions several women in his letters. The last chapter of Romans (Rom 16) contains a list of greetings addressed to a number of women, members of that church with whom Paul had become acquainted during his missionary activities in Asia Minor and Greece. Emperor Claudius had expelled Jewish Christians belonging to a particular synagogue from Rome. When the emperor died in AD 54, they returned to the city to continue their apostolic work. They were to "contribute to the needs of the saints and to practice hospitality" (Rom 12:13). At the beginning of Rom 16, Paul commends to Roman Christians "our sister Phoebe, a deaconess of the church at Cenchreae" who "has been a helper [*prostatis*] of many and of myself as well" (Rom 16:1–2). He implies that Phoebe was well known in the community, highly esteemed, and a patroness of the church in her house. She opened her house for liturgical gatherings, as did Lydia of Thyatira, who had become a host to the church in Philippi (Acts 16:35–40). Phoebe now travels to Rome bringing, we assume, Paul's letter to the Romans. When the house churches

[16]See Eduard Schweizer, *Church Order in the New Testament*, Studies in Biblical Theology, 32 (London: SCM Press, Ltd., 1961), p. 182.

of Rome gathered together the first Sunday after her arrival, Phoebe could have been the first person to read and interpret the Epistle to the Romans.

The women whom Paul greeted were engaged in teaching as well as apostolic missionary work. Prisca, mentioned after Phoebe (Rom 16:3) instructed Apollos (Acts 18:24–26), and Mary and Persis toiled "in the Lord" (Rom 16:6, 12). The verb used to describe their activities is *kopiao*, the same verb applied to the missionary work of Paul and his fellow workers.

Women formed the nucleus of the church in Philippi. Referring to the dispute between two women, Euodia and Syntyche, Paul entreats them "to agree in the Lord," and he asks his "true yokefellow" [loyal comrade] to help them "for they have labored side by side with me in the gospel together with Clement and the rest of my fellow workers" (Phil 4:2–3). It is quite possible that Euodia and Syntyche discharged duties in the church at Philippi similar to the role Phoebe played at Cenchreae. Paul is concerned that their competition will bring into question the future of the community. To the members of the church in Philippi he appeals: "Do nothing from selfishness or conceit, but in humility count others better than yourselves" (Phil 2:3).

All the references to specific women by name emphasize that Paul worked together with them in building new communities; that he never forgot their participation in apostolic missionary endeavor. He praised their work and, when necessary, offered advice on how to resolve disagreements among them.

"There is neither male nor female, for you are all one in Christ Jesus" (Gal 3:28). Nevertheless, for Paul, not only is there no subordination between the two genders, but there is also no obliteration of distinctions between male and female. Marriage is not abolished (1 Cor 7), as some gnostic groups maintained, but elaborated on in Gal 3:28. Paul did not sanction homosexuality. Chloe's people were disturbed with what they saw in Corinth, where there were homosexuals presumably leading the services (1 Cor 6:9–10). Paul does not approve of homosexual behavior, referring to it as exchanging "natural" relations for "unnatural" (Rom 1:26–27). In 1 Corinthians against the background of homosexual activity in the congregation, he expresses a twofold theme: distinction between the sexes and the equality of women (1 Cor 11:2–16). Paul made use of Gen 1–2: the first man was not a bisexual being, for "male and female he created them" (Gen 1:27). Sexual differentiation, it follows, is not a consequence of the fall but belongs to God's creation. Expressing the mutual dependence of man and woman, Paul reminds his followers:

"woman is not independent of man nor man of woman; for as woman was made from man, so man now is born of woman" (1 Cor 11:11–12). Paul takes a firm stand for the equality of women, and at the same time maintains gender distinction.

Paul deplored lack of order and decency in the church in Corinth. Everybody spoke at the same time, misleading visitors into perceiving the gathering in church as a cult ritual. It is in this context that Paul's well-known reproach was delivered: "The women should keep silence in the churches, for they are not permitted to speak . . . If there is anything they desire to know, let them ask their husbands at home" (1 Cor 14:34–36). His injunction to silence is given in a disorderly liturgical assembly. Paul does not impose silence on women in general but on those in a particular church to secure order and prevent chaos in worship. He imposes silence on some glossolalists (1 Cor 14:28), some prophets (1 Cor 14:30), and some women in this charismatic church. "For God is not a God of confusion but of peace" (1 Cor 14:33).

Paul was a liberator of women. His teachings about the differentiation yet equality of the sexes put him in opposition to gnostic speculations. The Gospel of Thomas, a collection of "the secret sayings of the living Jesus," many of which were developed and interpreted under the obvious influence of gnostic teaching, ends with a conversation between Peter and "the living Jesus" regarding the salvation of women. Peter says to Jesus' disciples: "Let [Mary Magdalene] leave us, for women are not worthy of life." To Peter's request, Jesus replies, "I myself shall lead her in order to make her male, so that she too may become a living spirit resembling you males. For every woman who will make herself male will enter the kingdom of heaven" (*Gos. Thom.* Saying 114). The text suggests that woman as woman will not enter the kingdom, but only some women, those made male, would be found "worthy of life." For gnostics, salvation required the obliteration of sexual differences. There was nothing in common between this gnostic view and Paul's statement: "There is neither male nor female, for you are all one in Christ Jesus" (Gal 3:28).[17] In the same passage Paul brings up the experience of baptism (Gal 3:27), where previous religious allegiances, social and racial barriers are obliterated, but not the distinction between male and female. Paul firmly believed and taught that gender differences belong to God's design for humanity.[18]

[17]See C.K. Barrett, *New Testament Background*, p. 114.
[18]This confrontation of Peter with Mary Magdalene is found in three other gnostic books. Some

Paul's Exercise of Authority

Strife and opposition by some members beset the churches Paul founded. How he responded to these challenges and how he exercised his authority in troubled communities lays the basis for future strength and expansion of the Christian mission. In his epistles, we find that Paul teaches, admonishes the idle, encourages the fainthearted, defends and helps the weak, and is patient with them all (1 Thess 5:14). He pronounces judgment on an immoral man, but at the same time he asks the community's consent (1 Cor 5:1ff); the local church at Corinth, as the responsible body, must pronounce its own judgment on the man who was living with his stepmother. Paul does not dictate, but wants the community to grow spiritually by making the decision what to do about a "rotten apple" in the barrel that was the church community. However, in contrast, when confronted by intruders in Galatia who preached a "different gospel" from his and the danger that their message would make inroads into his communities, Paul vigorously defended his apostleship and pronounced his judgment upon them: "But even if we, or an angel from heaven, should preach you a gospel contrary to that which we preached to you, let him be accursed" (Gal 1:8–10). His strong admonition in this instance resounds like an ecclesiastical excommunication for a doctrinal reason.[19]

modern historians have seen in these texts signs of tensions in second-century Christianity. While there were tensions, the leading second century writers, Clement of Rome, Ignatius of Antioch, Justin Martyr, and Irenaeus did not suggest a conflict between Peter and Mary Magdalene. Gnostics were not and should not be taken as reliable guides for historical development. There is no hint in the New Testament that a conflict existed.

Did Jesus marry Mary Magdalene? This question arises in popular culture, notably in Dan Brown's *Da Vinci Code* (2002). Brown mentions "countless references to Jesus and Magdalene's union" in the ancient records. Birger A. Pearson, one of the leading scholars of the Coptic (i.e., Gnostic) Gospels, points to only two apocryphal gospels Brown used: the Gospel of Philip and the Gospel of Mary. We know them from fourth and fifth century copies. Two passages in the Gospel of Philip pertain to Mary. In these, Mary appears as Jesus' "companion," in Greek *koinonos* [partner, fellow member, sharer], related to the word *koinonia* [community, fellowship]. This same section speaks of Jesus kissing Mary. This is more likely the liturgical "kiss of peace," than a romantic relationship. References to a liturgical "kiss of peace" are also found in the New Testament.

After examining references to Jesus and Mary in the apocryphal Gospel of Mary and Jesus' teaching about the kingdom of God with particular attention to the Sermon on the Mount, Pearson concludes: "Despite what we might read in the popular press, we have no evidence in the New Testament or the apocryphal gospels that Jesus ever married. Further, Jesus' own teachings from his days as a prophet of the kingdom of God rule out the possibility that he could have been married to Mary Magdalene—or any other woman—at that time" ("Did Jesus Marry?" *BR* 21.2 [2005]: 32–43).

[19]D.J. Harrington, *Light of All Nations*, p. 136.

Moreover, in dealing with members of house churches, Paul does not command but appeals. When addressing Philemon, his "beloved fellow worker," though he is "bold enough in Christ to command," Paul prefers to appeal to him (Phlm 8). He entreats forgiveness for the new convert Onesimus, who had been a slave in Philemon's household, but had wronged his master and fled. Paul asked Philemon to accept him back, "no longer as a slave" but "as a beloved brother . . . both in the flesh and in the Lord" (Phlm 16). In his appeal Paul points out what slave and master hold in common: their humanity and their brotherhood in Christ. In his twenty-five-verse letter to Philemon, the apostle frequently uses terms that express the union of Christ and Christians, such as "in Christ," "in the Lord," and "into Christ." Whatever Philemon does will affect the community. Philemon's incorporation into Christ will be manifested in his treatment of the returning slave, whom Paul had converted during his imprisonment in Ephesus. Paul is confident that Philemon, of his own free will, will do "even more" than asked.

Jesus' life and conduct are the example and call for Paul's converts to be imitators of himself—as Paul is of Christ (1 Cor 11:1). Paul reminds the Thessalonians that they too should become imitators of the Lord (1 Thess 1:6). The idea of imitation belongs to the very foundation of Christian ethics.[20] For example, those Christians who are strong ought to bear the burdens of the weak, "and not to please [themselves]" for Christ did not please himself (Rom 15:1–3); rather, he was concerned for "others." Likewise, in his elaborate appeal for funds to be distributed among the poor of Jerusalem, Paul turns to Christ's life. "For you know the grace of our Lord Jesus Christ, that though he was rich, yet for your sake he became poor so that by his poverty you might become rich" (2 Cor 8:9). In their lives, the Corinthians should reflect, even in such activities as the collection of money, the impact of the risen Christ. For Paul, the power of resurrection affects the moral conduct of Christians.[21] In the thought of the apostle, the resurrection of Christ is the present saving reality as well as the future hope, for Christ comes as "the first fruit of those who have fallen asleep" (1 Cor 15–20).

---

[20]See J.D.G. Dunn, *Unity and Diversity*, p. 6; and F.F. Bruce, "On Phil 2:4" in *Philippians* (New York: Harper & Row, 1983).

[21]Oliver O'Donovan, *Resurrection and Moral Order: An Outline for Evangelical Ethics* (Grand Rapids: Wm. B. Eerdmans Publishing Company, 1986). The author argues that Christian ethics depend on Christ's resurrection (pp. 11–27).

In disputes with his numerous opponents, in his teaching, in exhortation or in exercising his authority, Paul pointed to two sources of his gospel: Christ's appearance on the road to Damascus and the living tradition of the apostolic church. Sustained by Christ's revelation and living tradition, he proclaimed the gospel "not to please men, but to please God" (1 Thess 2:4). He preached "the word of the Cross," Christ crucified and resurrected, and his own martyrdom sealed his message.

CHAPTER SEVEN

THE RIFT BETWEEN CHRISTIANS AND JEWS

Radical change came to the young Christian communities in the 60s. James, "the brother of the Lord" and head of the Jerusalem church from AD 42–62, was stoned to death in Jerusalem. Peter, the first among the disciples of Jesus, was crucified around AD 64, and Paul was beheaded in AD 67, both in Rome. In AD 66 a Jewish revolt against Roman occupation broke out. This had a profound impact upon Judaism, as well as on the relations between the church and the synagogue.

The death of James, recounted by Josephus (*Ant.* 20.200), occurred between the death of the Roman governor Festus (AD 62) and the arrival of his successor Albinos. Ananias, the high priest of the temple, called a meeting of the Sanhedrin and brought James, the brother of Jesus, "the so-called anointed one," and some others. The charge against them was that they had transgressed the law; "he handed them over to be stoned."

Peter, the leading disciple during Jesus' public ministry and one of the pillars of the earliest Christian community in Jerusalem, was active outside Jerusalem as well (Gal 2:7–8, Acts 10–11:1–18; 1 Cor 9:5). The churches of Asia Minor mentioned in the opening of 1 Peter may also have been the fruit of his missionary activities. The Gospel of John records that Jesus addressed Peter in a way that suggests his martyrdom: "Truly, truly I say to you, when you were young you girded yourself and walked where you would, but when you are old you will stretch out your hands and another will gird you and carry you where you do not wish to go" (John 21:18). Jesus spoke, the evangelist declared, "to show by what death he [Peter] was to glorify God" (John 21:19). Clement of Rome, whom tradition considers the third successor to Peter, writing around AD 95, pointed to Rome as the place of Peter's martyrdom, very likely in AD 64. This may have been part of the wave of persecutions following the Great Fire of Rome. In Nero's reign, the fire raged for six days, destroying life and property. To counter rumors that the emperor himself had started the fires, he sought scapegoats. Our main source for accounts of the persecution of Christians at this time was Tacitus (ca. AD 56–120). He recorded that "Nero inflicted most extreme punishments on those, hateful by reason of their abominations, who were commonly called Christians." Those professing Christianity were arrested and condemned to death. "They were clothed in animal's skins and torn to pieces by dogs, or they were nailed on crosses to be set on fire, and when darkness came they served as torches" (*Ann.* 15.44). Suetonius (ca. AD 69–ca. 121) confirms Tacitus' account: "The Christians, a kind of men given to a new and mischievous superstition, he [Nero] tortured and put to death" (*Nero* 16). We do not know if Peter's martyrdom was part of this wave of persecution. Clement of Rome suggests that internal rivalry may have played a role. "By reason of rivalry and envy the greatest and most righteous pillars [Gal 2:9] were persecuted and battled to the death. Let us set before our eyes the noble apostles: Peter, who by reason of wicked jealousy, not only once or twice but frequently endured suffering and thus, bearing his witness, went to the glorious place which he merited" (*1 Clem.* 5.1–5). Clement hints at the quarrelling within the Roman church. The "unholy rivalry" for him is the source of evil. He offers many examples from the Old Testament to show the devastating effect of rivalry. "David because of rivalry incurred the envy of foreigners and also of Saul, the king of Israel, who persecuted him" (*1 Clem.* 4.13). The quarrels within the Roman church might have attracted the attention of the Roman authorities, who were looking for a scapegoat.

Paul reached Rome via Jerusalem. Before leaving Corinth in AD 56, he wrote the Letter to the Romans, informing "all God's beloved in Rome" (Rom 1:7) that his apostolic work in the Eastern Mediterranean was completed. The time had come for him to move to another region of the empire. He expressed the hope "to see (them) in passing" on his way to Spain (Rom 15:22ff). But first, he would go to Jerusalem with the collection of money for the poor. Here he anticipated trouble (Rom 15:31), as Luke tells us in detail. Luke goes on to narrate Paul's transfer to Caesarea and his voyage as a prisoner to Rome (Acts 21:15–28:16). For two years Paul lived under the watchful eye of the soldier who guarded him, yet he was allowed to receive visitors (Acts 28:6–30f). In the view of modern scholars, Luke's description of the conditions of Paul's imprisonment corresponds to what is known about conditions of house arrest in the Roman period. Clement of Rome implies that

Paul was released from house arrest in AD 64, and as a free man reached "the limits of the West," where he preached the gospel.[1] According to 2 Timothy, Paul returned to Asia Minor, was rearrested, and brought back to Rome wearing fetters like a criminal (2 Tim 1:8, 16; 2:9). He was executed by beheading in AD 67. Nero's reign of terror ended with the emperor's suicide in AD 68.

By the end of his life, Paul achieved what he had always desired to be: an "imitator" of Christ, who died for others. He aimed to represent him, so that the life of Jesus might be manifested in his mortal flesh (2 Cor 4:11).

The Destruction of the Temple

After the loss of these most prominent leaders, the Jewish-Christian community in Jerusalem was subject to the devastation of war. The Roman procurators Albinos (AD 62–64) and Florus (AD 64–66) plundered the land, took bribes, and created conditions for an uprising. The Romans provoked the Jews, led by the Zealots with widespread support from the population, into open rebellion. Some joined out of conviction and others out of fear of retribution from the Zealots. There were those who saw the confrontation with Rome as the road to catastrophe and refused outright to take part in the rebellion. These included the Christians and some Pharisees. Vespasian, the commander of the Roman army, moved against Jerusalem in AD 69, and after his troops proclaimed him *Imperator*, he left for Rome. His son Titus succeeded him to complete his work in Judea. Titus destroyed the temple and re-conquered Judea. The war ended with devastation of the country. The Romans destroyed the Qumran settlement (AD 68), burned Jerusalem, razed the temple (AD 70), and ended the Jewish resistance at Masada in AD 74. The Jews were severely punished for their struggle for political independence by the victorious Roman army. Many of them were taken out of Judea as slaves.

The Romans destroyed the temple, but they did not outlaw the Jewish religion. Roman policy was never aimed at its destruction. Given the strategic importance of Judea, they badly needed to keep the country under their control to protect the eastern borders against their traditional enemies, the Parthians, who were dominating the Tigris-Euphrates frontiers. The loss of

---

[1] J. Murphy-O'Connor speculates that the mission to Spain was unsuccessful: *Paul: A Critical Life*, p. 362.

Palestine would put Egypt in danger. For this reason the Romans "tried to please Jews," and did not interfere with their religious activities nor interrupt their study of the Law. Johanan Ben Zakkai (d. AD 83), an acknowledged leader of the Pharisees who had not supported the Zealots in their doomed adventure, managed—by feigning illness and even death—to be taken out of the city under siege by his disciples. He came into contact with the Romans, who gave him permission to establish a rabbinical school at Yavneh [Jamnia], a city on the Judean Mediterranean coast. The leader of the Jamnian Academy did not share the anti-Roman policy of the revolutionaries, and those Romans who were more eager for "reconciliation" with the Jews than for their subjugation received him gladly.[2]

The Jamnian scholars, sages, rabbis, and the "Beth Din" or Law Court, which began to define Judaism, were former Pharisees. As the undisputed religious guides to the people of Palestine, they assumed the duties and privileges of the former Sanhedrin. The rabbinic school was built upon the principle that the study of Torah was of the highest value and far more important than the restoration of the temple. The leaders of Beth Din never gave up the hope that the temple would be rebuilt, however. In time the desire for liberation from Roman rule prompted the conquered people to work for the liberation of the land and rebuilding of the temple. This led to the Second Jewish War (AD 132–35), which had more disastrous consequences than the first for Jews and for Jewish-Christian relations.

The Jewish Christians did not take part in the first revolt. Eusebius wrote that when war broke out they fled to Pella (*H.E.* 5.3), some sixty miles northeast of Jerusalem across the River Jordan. After the expulsion of the Hellenists from Jerusalem around AD 35, the gospel had spread outside Palestine. These Hellenists, along with the "Hebrews" who fled in AD 66, brought to the diaspora the story of Jesus, which would be recorded and preserved in the Gospels. Hegesippus, a second-century Christian of Jewish origin, records that Symeon, son of Clopas, led the community to Pella and back again after the first revolt. Symeon was a cousin of Jesus and remained as the head of the Jerusalem church for forty-five years (AD 62–107). The Jerusalem Christian community, no longer the center of the Christian mission, existed up to the time of Hadrian and the second Jewish war (AD 132–135).

---

[2]Louis Finkelstein, *Akiba: Scholar, Saint and Martyr* (New York: Atheneum, 1975), pp. 60–67.

Whereas the Romans grouped the Jerusalem Christians with other Jews, the rabbis of the newly organized Jewish communities started to draw boundaries around Judaism, which in the course of time became the dividing line between the Jewish Christians and the Jews. Jamnia undertook to create worldwide unity in Judaism and to become its intellectual and religious center.

In the period after the destruction of the temple (AD 70), the relations between Jews and Jewish Christians worsened. It is "perhaps in some way connected with the decisions of the Jewish academy of Jamnia and the expulsion of Christians from the synagogue" writes W.H.C. Frend.[3] He observes that "After circa AD 100 there was less of a tendency for Christians to claim to be Israel and more of a tendency to contrast Christianity and Judaism as separate religions."[4] The rabbinic authority took measures to expel from the synagogue those who believed in Jesus (John 9: 22–23). They revised the prayer of the synagogue, known as the "Eighteen Benedictions" [*Shemoneh Esreh*] and added a twelfth benediction, a petition against the apostates and heretics: "As for the renegades, let there be no hope, and may the arrogant kingdom soon be rooted out in our days and the *minim* [heretics] perish in a moment and be blotted out from the book of life and with the righteous be not inscribed."

We do not know when this change in prayer occurred. In R.E. Brown's view, "Sometime between 85 and 130 the rabbinic distaste for sectarians (*minim*) was enshrined by the curse against them." Considered as *minim*, Jewish Christians were expelled from attending synagogue worship.[5] Brown does not link this procedure with some "excommunication edict from Jamnia" but with "spreading practice dependent on how numerous and assertive Jewish Christians were in a given local synagogue."[6] By the practice of expulsion, D. Moody Smith suggests, "Judaism sought to retrench, excluding Christ confessors (i.e., Christians)."[7]

Among the New Testament books written after the destruction of the temple, the Gospels of Matthew and John reflect some vitriolic disputes between two Jewish groups which survived the war: the Pharisees and the disciples of

---

[3] *The Rise of Christianity* (Minneapolis: MN, Augsburg Fortress Publishers, 1986), p. 124.
[4] Ibid.
[5] "Early Church," *NJBC* 24.
[6] Ibid.
[7] D. Moody Smith on "John" in *Harper's Biblical Commentary*, ed. James L. Mays (San Francisco: Harper & Row Publishers, 1988), p. 1061.

Christ. The Zealots, who had started the revolt, were defeated and would finally be subdued in the Second Jewish-Roman War (AD 132–135). In the aftermath of this war, Rabbi Akiba and other leaders of the Academy of Jamnia perished and "the center of gravity in Jewish intellectual life" moved towards Babylon.[8]

Tensions Reflected in the Gospel of Matthew

The Gospel of Matthew, probably written in the 80s, after the destruction of the temple, has been described as a "mature synthesis" of the earliest gospel and collection of Jesus' sayings.[9] Among the suggestions as for which community and locality the gospel was intended, the church of Antioch and its surroundings is considered the most likely choice. Matthew's Gospel is addressed to a church placed outside the rabbinic synagogues, a community that needed encouragement at a time when its members were facing humiliation and hostility. To strengthen their faith the evangelist undertook to faithfully transmit Jesus' public ministry, his relations and conflicts with various groups within Judaism, and in detail his last week in Jerusalem. All of the four Gospels close with the climax of the narrative: the crucifixion and resurrection. While narrating Jesus' words and deeds, the evangelists could not dissociate themselves from the events so crucial to the life of the church at their time. For Matthew this was the intense dispute between the "scribes and Pharisees" and the followers of Christ, who had been expelled from local synagogues. Matthew's Gospel mirrors the attitude of the Christian leaders toward the rabbis of Jamnia, successors of the Pharisees. Only within this historical context can we try to understand Matthew's harsh denunciation of the Pharisees in his Gospel, and the use of language in Chapter 23, which many regard as neither charitable nor "politically correct."

Reacting to the expulsion of Jewish Christians from the synagogue, Matthew attacked the Pharisees, the leaders of Rabbinic Judaism, in vitriolic terms, as hypocritical, legalistic, blind, and murderous. Those expelled from the synagogue could not reconcile themselves to be people without hope.

Christian and non-Christian interpreters have recognized that the language of denunciation we find in Matthew and the manner in which the

---

[8]Frend, *Rise of Christianity*, p. 162.
[9]Benedict T. Viviano, "The Gospel According to Matthew," in *NJBC* 42:2.

author expressed his scathing remarks have roots in the Jewish tradition of disputes. The Pharisees had been accused by their Jewish opponents as "seekers after the smooth thing." They were characterized as "lying interpreters," as hypocrites "who by their false teaching and their lying tongue and deceitful lip" lead many astray. The so-called "woes" (e.g., "Woe to you scribes and Pharisees") of Matt 23:13–16, "are written in a common form of Jewish admonitions."[10] Matthew, in chapter 27 verse 25 of his Gospel, ascribes to the priests, elders, and the temple crowd the harsh words: "His blood be on us and all our children."

During Jesus' public ministry, the temple was a religious and economic center that employed several thousand people. As we might expect, those loyal to Caiaphas shared the Sanhedrin's hostility to Jesus. On the other hand, Luke reports that when Jesus was led to crucifixion, a multitude of people "followed him," and women "bewailed and lamented him" (Luke 23:27ff). Both Jews and Christians need to use dispassionate analysis in order to understand the historical context of Matthew's so-called "anti-Jewish" passages within their historical context.

There is no doubt that many have used Matthew 27:25 as a pretext to provoke pogroms. Some anti-Semites indeed found in these verses justification for their hostility to the Jews. But this gospel reflects a bitter struggle between two groups who share the same heritage. In polemic of a time that is very different from our own, Matthew condemns the Jewish leaders and their interpretation of their common tradition that would exclude Jewish Christians from having a share in it. Having in mind those who interpret the text according to their own premises, a modern scholar has remarked that their interpretation is like "a picnic to which the evangelist brings his text," and they supply meanings.[11] Matthew was not an anti-Semite. As J.D.G. Dunn writes, the charge of anti-Semitism against him "has either to be dismissed or to be so redefined within its historical context as to lose most of its potential as justification for the anti-Semitism of later centuries."[12]

---

[10]This was "a family quarrel," notes Moshe Weinfeld in "The Jewish Roots of Matthew's Vitriol," *BR* 13.5 (1997).

[11]Graham N. Stanton, "The Communities of Matthew," *Interpretation* 46.4 (1992): 380.

[12]J.D.G. Dunn, *The Partings of the Ways: Between Christianity and Judaism and Their Significance for the Character of Christianity* (London: SCM Press, Ltd; Philadelphia, PA: Trinity Press International, 1991), p. 156.

The historical context of Matthew 23 also helps us to define the reason why the community of which Matthew was a member rejected the title "rabbi" and "father." "You are not to be called 'rabbi,' for you have one teacher, and you are all brethren. And call no man your father on earth, for you have one Father, who is in heaven" (Matt 23:8–9). In pre-rabbinic Judaism, that is, prior to AD 70, there was no official rabbinate, no ordination of the learned to whom the title of rabbi was given.[13] At the time of Jesus' public ministry, the title of rabbi denoted simply particular respect, and honor. His disciples addressed Jesus as "rabbi." Paul wrote the Corinthians that he had become their "father in Christ Jesus through the gospel" (1 Cor 4:15). Only after the school was established in Jamnia was the title "rabbi" introduced as a technical term for an approved, ordained Jewish teacher; and only during that period did the title "father" designate a sage. Christian believers who had been expelled from the synagogues and to whom the Gospel of Matthew is addressed were no longer to apply these two titles to the leaders of post–AD 70 Judaism; but they still preserved them for their own leaders in Christ.

The Evangelist John and Anti-Jewish Polemic

Like Matthew, the evangelist John was a Jewish Christian who transmitted traditions he had received before and after the destruction of the temple. As Matthew's attitude toward Judaism is reflected in his Gospel, so the Gospel of John reflects the conflict between the church and the synagogue.

The Fourth Gospel had a long period of growth. It includes the eyewitness of John, a member of the Twelve. The cornerstone of this "historic document" is the Palestinian tradition, linked with the apostolic source, into which liturgical and kerygmatic material was incorporated in the course of the first century. We should not eliminate the evangelist's interpreting and editing of received tradition.[14] The author, whose identity is unknown, was in close contact with Jesus' disciples. Later, in the second century, he was thought to be John, the son of Zebedee, presented in the guise of the Beloved

---

[13]M. Hengel, *Charismatic Leader*, pp. 28, 43–44.

[14]See detailed discussion on the growth of the Fourth Gospel in R. Schnackenburg, *The Gospel According to St. John: Volume One: Introduction and Commentary on Chapters 1–4*, Herders Theological Commentary on the New Testament, eds. J. Massingberd Ford and Kevin Smyth. (New York: Herder and Herder, 1982), pp. 59–74.

ILLUSTRATIONS

1. Veneranda and Saint Petronilla. Location: Catacomb of S. Domitilla, Rome, Italy. *(Photo Credit: Scala/Art Resource, NY)*

2. General view with Corinthian Columns. Location: Asklepion, Kos, Greece. *(Photo Credit: Vanni/Art Resource, NY)*

3. Scale model of Jerusalem and the second temple at the time of King Herod the Great (ca 20 BCE). The picture shows the temple compound. Location: Holy Land Hotel, Jerusalem, Israel. *(Photo Credit: Erich Lessing/Art Resource, NY)*

4. Silver shekel of the Second Jewish Revolt from Rome. Jewish, AD 133–35. From Judaea (modern Israel). CM 1908,0110.776. On the obverse (front) of this coin can be seen a representation of the façade of the Temple at Jerusalem. On the reverse is depicted the ritual "Lulav," a palm-branch tied together with willow and myrtle branches. Location: British Museum, London, Great Britain. *(Photo Credit: © British Museum/Art Resource, NY)*

5. Interdiction for non-Jews to enter the Inner Sanctum of the temple in Jerusalem. Greek inscription from the outer wall of the temple. Saint Paul was falsely accused of having introduced a former pagan into the precinct. Plaster cast. 3rd BCE–IST CE. Location: Museo della Civilta Romana, Rome, Italy. *(Photo Credit: Erich Lessing/Art Resource, NY)*

6. The theatre of Ephesus, built under Lysimachos. View towards the audience. The theatre was reconstructed during 1st BCE and 1st CE. Saint Paul preached here. Location: Ephesus, Turkey. *(Photo Credit : Erich Lessing/Art Resource, NY)*

7. The victorious army of Titus with the spoils from Jerusalem. c. 90 CE. Marble. 204 x 380 cm. Location: Arch of Titus, Rome, Italy. *(Photo Credit: Alinari/Art Resource, NY)*

8. Gerasa (Jerash) in the north of Jordan, was a Hellenistic-Roman town which became rich as a safe trading post for Nabataean, Jewish and Roman merchants. Columns of the propylaeum of the Artemis-Temple on a hill above the cardo (main street). *(Photo Credit: Erich Lessing/Art Resource, NY)*

9. Arrest of Saint Paul. Detail from the "Travellers sarcophagus." Early Christian. Location: St. Victor Basilica, Marseille, France. (*Photo Credit: Erich Lessing/Art Resource, NY*)

Disciple. The Gospel was composed in Ephesus, attaining its final form in the 90s of the first century. Together with John's epistles, it throws light on the life and experience of the Christian communities in Asia Minor at the closing decade of the century.

John's Gospel also reflects a crisis between the Christian group and newly redefined Judaism under the leadership of the Pharisees. The account of the healing of the blind man in John 9 illustrates the dispute. The Pharisees seek to know the identity of the healer, as the miracle occurred on the Sabbath. The parents of the healed man deny knowledge of the healer's identity, "for the Jews had already agreed that if any one should confess him to be Christ, he was to be put out of the synagogue" (John 9:22). We should stress that only in this Gospel the term *aposynagogos* ["put away from the synagogue"] appears, not once but three times (John 9:22, 12:42, 16:2). By the time John's Gospel was written, those who confessed Jesus as Messiah were treated as *minim* [heretics] and, as such, were expelled from the synagogue.

The church with which the evangelist John was associated found itself in great danger. Expulsion from the synagogues exposed them to the threat of the Roman authorities. The Romans, who respected Judaism as an old traditional religion, were suspicious of new cults and considered them troublesome to the Empire. The Christians of Asia Minor regarded themselves as heirs of a very old tradition, which they shared with the Pharisees, and not as members of a new religion. Before the Jewish revolt and the destruction of the temple, the Palestinian Jews who believed and confessed that Jesus of Nazareth was the Messiah were often harassed, and occasionally persecuted, but as a rule were left unpunished. But after the war, they were expelled from the synagogue for confessing Jesus to be Christ.

Readers have noted the resemblance of passages in John's Gospel to Essene writings, especially those passages against the priests in the temple at Jerusalem, who, the Essenes claimed, "belong to the ream of darkness," whereas they, the Essenes, claimed to be "sons of light." Likewise, Essenes identified the temple authorities as being on Satan's side, and for that God hated them and would destroy them. Here, we note parallel imagery, if not direct influence, of the Essenes on the Gospel of John. Can we see these Qumran texts as well as the Fourth Gospel as anti-Semitic? Only if we ignore the original historical context, and the prevailing manners of dispute at that time.

Matthew and John used language that was not unusual in "intra-Jewish" disputes.[15] While condemning the Jewish religious authorities, the early Christian leaders struggled within Judaism and the tradition from which they had emerged and still regarded as their own. Expelled from the synagogues, they denounced the new synagogue authorities as untrustworthy interpreters of their common tradition. C.H. Dodd observed: "Many of the propositions referring to the Logos in the Prologue [of John] are the counterpart of rabbinic statements, referring to the Torah."[16] The evangelists regard Jesus as the self-revelation of God. The rabbis focused upon the Torah without providing for revelation in Christ, as they expected their own messiah. They never renounced their messianic hope and their desire to rebuild the temple.

The Second Jewish-Roman War

Memory of the first temple destroyed by the Babylonians in 587 BC and its restoration fed expectations that something similar would follow the destruction of the second temple by the Romans. The diaspora Jews negotiated with Emperor Trajan, asking for his approval for restoration of the temple of Herodian times. Trajan gave permission for a very modest structure for the purpose of sacrifice, but did not approve the rebuilding of the second temple. The emperor's refusal provoked a Jewish revolt in Egypt. In Cyrenaica, (now modern Libya), rebellion began in AD 115. Cyrene was a trading center with a large Jewish community closely linked with Palestine (Acts 11:30). Simon of Cyrene had carried Jesus' cross (Mark 15:21), and Christians from Cyrene were found very early in Antioch (Acts 11:20). Lucian of Cyrene was remembered as one who belonged to the group of prophets and teachers in the church in Antioch (Acts 13:1). Sporadic unrest among the Jewish diaspora during the reign of Trajan did not spread into Judea, as the emperor made every effort to keep Judea peaceful, particularly when he was planning to move to the east to confront the Parthians.[17]

Judea became the center of rebellion by AD 132, however, when the Second Jewish-Roman war occurred. Hadrian succeeded Trajan and provoked

[15]See Robert Kysar, "John's Anti-Jewish Polemic," *BR* 9.1 (1993): 26–27.
[16]C.H. Dodd, *The Interpretation of the Fourth Gospel* (Cambridge: Cambridge University Press, 1953), p. 84f.
[17]L. Finkelstein, *Akiba*, pp. 216–234.

Jewish unrest by forbidding the rite of circumcision and transforming Jerusalem into Aelia Capitolina, a pagan city. The name "Aelia" honored his family, and "Capitolina" recalled the Roman temple to Jupiter, located on the Capitoline. Jews, who were looking for the restoration of their old temple and independence, rose against Rome under the leadership of Bar Kochba [or Kokhba] in AD 132.

Bar Kochba's first victories over the Romans excited many Jews, who saw in him their promised messiah. Rabbi Akiba [Aqiba], an eminent authority of this period, hailed Bar Kochba as Messiah and urged his people to support him in the uprising. Three years after the successful beginning, the Jewish war effort collapsed, and the nation underwent a far greater disaster than after the first uprising. Roman troops ravaged the country of Judea and resumed building Aelia Capitolina, which remained the official name of Jerusalem until the Arab conquest of the city in the seventh century.[18] Bar Kochba, the military messiah, had brought disaster on his people. Now, after the war, Jews were forbidden to enter Jerusalem and could be punished by death if caught. "The entire race has been forbidden to set foot anywhere in the neighborhood of Jerusalem" writes Eusebius (*H.E.* 4.6.3). Humiliation was complete when Jewish prisoners were sold as slaves in the Near East.

The Christian community also underwent strain and tension as a result of the break with the synagogue. Christians refused to participate in the second Jewish-Roman War on religious grounds. Since Bar Kochba was acclaimed as the Messiah, the war had a messianic character for the Jews. Christians, who had confessed Jesus as the promised Messiah, could not but reject Bar Kochba's claim, and in consequence they were persecuted.[19] According to Justin Martyr (ca. AD 100–165), Bar Kochba ordered only Christians "to be subjected to terrible punishment unless they would deny Jesus the Christ and blaspheme him" (*1 Apol.* 1.31.6).

The relations between Jewish Christians and their "kinsmen by race" deteriorated considerably during and after these two disastrous wars. The Christians refused to participate in the wars, and the Jewish loyalists accused them of being traitors and heretics. After their expulsion from the synagogues, Jewish Christians continued observing Jewish customs and circumcision. At the

---

[18]J. Murphy-O'Connor, "Where was the Capital in Roman Jerusalem?" *BR* 13.6 (1997): 24.

[19]See David Flusser, *Judaism and the Origins of Christianity* (Jerusalem: Magnee Press, Hebrew University, 1988), p. 636.

same time, some Gentile Christians started avoiding contact with those who observed Jewish law. Justin Martyr, a convert to Christianity around AD 130, wrote that Jewish Christians could observe the law, but should not influence Gentile Christians to undergo the rite of circumcision (*Dial. 47*). Justin wrote *Dialogue with Trypho*, a friendly attempt to persuade the rabbi to acknowledge Jesus as Messiah, around AD 160, after the conversation he had had with him at the end of the second uprising (AD 135). Justin's *Dialogue* points to the complexity of relations between Jewish and Gentile Christians around the middle of the second century.

In contrast, the sharpest Christian attack upon Jews for rejecting Jesus as their divine messiah came from Melito of Sardis (d. AD 190), in his *Homily on the Passover*. He preached this sermon at the Easter celebration following the reading of Exodus 12 (Israel's departure from Egypt). Here the events of Passover are interpreted typologically: the Old Testament points to the New. Jesus is the true Passover lamb, who delivered humanity from bondage. In the second part of the *Homily* Melito accused the Jews of killing Jesus. Compared with the second-century polemics, "the New Testament polemic against the Jews appears mild," and must be seen "in a broader perspective of conflicts within the Jewish tradition."[20]

From the end of the second century, harsh polemics between Christians and Jews intensified. The attacks of the rabbis were not directed against Jewish Christians as heretics, notes David Flusser,[21] but against the faith of the Christian church, particularly the doctrine of incarnation.

The Letter to the Hebrews and Roman Christians

After the first Jewish-Roman War (AD 66–70), there were signs of unrest in the Christian community in Rome. Jewish Christians of Palestinian origin, in a display of solidarity with their suffering countrymen, were moving back to Judaism. They embraced its cults and practices. A number of New Testament

---

[20]Dieter Georgi, "The Early Church: Internal Jewish Migration or New Religion?" *HTR* (1995): 46.

[21]D. Flusser, *Judaism*, p. 636. On p. 644, he interprets the Christian anti-Jewish attitude as the result of their failure to convert the Jews. But the element of failure could hardly have been sufficient reason to produce Jewish-Christian disputes in the first and second centuries. Rather, the aftermath of the first and second Jewish-Roman Wars contributed to the partition of Christians and Jews by the end of the second century.

scholars have argued that the Letter to Hebrews was sent to them and their Gentile allies who also were yearning for the temple sacrificial system. The letter warns them that they are drifting away from the message of the gospel, and the author of the letter urged them to "hold fast our confession" (Heb 4:14).[22]

To overcome the temptation to go back to a revival of the old sacrificial system and their hope that a new temple would soon appear in Jerusalem, the author of Hebrews presents Jesus in terms of sacrifice. Jesus is "high priest of our confession" (Heb 3:1). The temple priests were many in number and they "were prevented by death from remaining in office." But Jesus as the high priest continues forever; his death was essential for his priesthood (Heb 7:23–24). The high priests of the temple would offer sacrifice first for their own sins and then for the people. Jesus, once for all, offered up himself (Heb 7:27). The very fact of repetition in performing sacrifices reveals the distance that always remains between God and the high priest. This distance is removed with Jesus as the high priest, "one who is seated at the right hand of the throne of majesty in heaven" (Heb 8:1).

The Jewish Christians who were drifting away did not forsake Jesus, but saw him as no higher than an angel or Moses. Therefore, the author reminds them with *testimonia*, proof texts from Scripture, that the Son is greater than the angels (Heb 1:5–14), and by way of contrast, he underscores the superiority of Jesus over Moses. "Now Moses was faithful in all God's house as a servant, to testify to the things that were to be spoken later, but Christ was faithful over God's house as a son" (Heb 3:5). In the opening of the epistle, its author confidently proclaims the faith of the church that the final age is inaugurated; God has spoken to us "these last days by a Son . . . through whom he created the world" (Heb 1:1–4). He is "the very stamp of [God's] nature," meaning that he "is the image [*eikon*] of the invisible God" (Col 1:15), who could not be identified with any created being.

To articulate their experience, not their speculation, of Christ as a personal transcendent being,[23] the early Christians turned to the Wisdom literature. As the mediator of creation, the Son is likened to the personified Wisdom (Prov 8:1–9:6; Wis 7:9). Before any act of creation, Wisdom was

---

[22]For a clear and informative discussion regarding the locations of the epistle, see R.E. Brown and J.P. Meier, *Antioch and Rome*, pp. 142–49.

[23]See C.F.D. Moule, *Origin of Christology* (1977), p. 95.

beside the Lord (Prov 8:22). God made all things by his word and wisdom (Wis 9:1–2). Wisdom is the image of his goodness (Wis 7:26). To Christians who are moving back toward Judaism, the author of Hebrews reiterates the fundamental Christian belief that Christ is God's self-revelation. The law is "but a shadow of good things to come" (Heb 10:1). The new covenant has been inaugurated, and the first is "becoming obsolete and growing old, ready to vanish away" (Heb 8:13).

We do not know who wrote this letter. Origen (ca. AD 185–ca. 254), the Christian apologist and biblical scholar, remarked, "only God knows who its author was." Modern scholars speculate that its author was a Jewish-Christian Hellenist of the second Christian generation (Heb 2:3), who in his "anti-Judaic" attitude goes beyond the "intra-Jewish" disputes of which we find examples in Paul's letters before the destruction of the temple, as well as the Gospels of Matthew and John, written after that. The author of Hebrews appears to be more radical in repudiating the temple than either one of them, even than Stephen, the earliest leader of the group of Hellenists in Jerusalem (Acts 7–8).

The Jewish-Christian Sects

In the second century, several Jewish-Christian sects appear that do not differ essentially from the group whom the Letter to the Hebrews warned of apostasy. Hegesippus (ca. AD 100–ca. 180), a Christian historian of Jewish origin, traveled from east to west to collect material related to the early church. Around the mid-second century, he reached Rome, where he stayed for two decades. Upon his return to the East, he wrote his *Memoirs,* mainly known to us from fragments preserved by Eusebius. In his traveling, Hegesippus came in contact with Jewish Christians, among which he distinguished two main groups, one "orthodox," and the other "heretical."[24] What they believed about Jesus distinguished one group from another. To make their views known, the "heretical" sects produced their own gospels, epistles, and apocalypses, opposing some beliefs of the "orthodox" groups.

The Ebionites (i.e., "poor persons," as the original group of Jerusalem Christians were known as "the poor") represent these sectarian groups. Ire-

---

[24]Hans Conzelmann, *History of Primitive Christianity* (Nashville, TN: Abingdon Press, 1973), p. 134f.

naeus observed that they drew on the Gospel of Matthew, but with significant omissions (*A.H.* 1.26). They rejected the virgin birth and Christ's divinity. They regarded Jesus as a prophet, like Moses (Deut 18:15). They omitted all passages that clearly presented Jesus as more than a prophet, that is, as a prophet with divine authority.[25] In principle, they rejected any development or growth in understanding the person of Jesus, beyond their own.

The Ebionites denounced Paul as an apostate, and made him responsible for failure to convert the Jews, because he preached against the Jewish law instead of urging Christians to continue keeping it. As an expression of their animosity, they rejected his letters and even went so far as to reject his Jewish heritage. The second-century Judeo-Christian apocryphal work, *Ascension of James*, asserts that Paul of Tarsus was not a Jew but "a Greek, the son of a Greek mother and a Greek father." He came to Jerusalem with a plan "to marry a daughter of a high priest." Toward this end, he underwent circumcision. Rebuffed, he "became furious and began to write against circumcision, the Sabbath and the law."[26] As we have seen, Paul stressed his Jewish roots and his life in Judaism in his letters (Gal 1:13–17; 2 Cor 11:22, Rom 11:1). He identified himself as an "Israelite" and a "Hebrew," who was emotionally attached to his people (Rom 9:1–5, 10:1ff, 11:17–24).

Those who rejected Paul as their enemy considered James, the brother of the Lord, as their friend and portrayed Peter as one of their own. An Ebionite document, the *Letter of Peter to James*, which serves as the preface to the "homilies" of Pseudo-Clementines, reveals a high estimate of James and Peter.[27] Here Peter considers James "my brother," and addresses him as "Lord and Bishop of the holy church." Peter, as keeper of the law, does not conceal his disappointment that some among the Gentiles have rejected his "lawful preaching and have preferred a lawless and absurd doctrine of the man who

[25]J.D.G. Dunn, *Unity and Diversity*, pp. 246–49.

[26]For the text and comments on this bizarre story, see J. Murphy-O'Connor, *Paul: A Critical Life*, p 63. Even more surprising is the number of people in our time who doubt that Paul was a Jew. The best known of them is Hyman Maccoby, *The Mythmaker: Paul and the Invention of Christianity* (New York: Harper & Row, 1986).

[27]F.L. Cross, *The Early Christian Fathers*, Studies in Theology (London: G. Duckworth, 1960), p. 98. "Pseudo-Clementines" is a collection of apocryphal stories and homilies ascribed to Clement of Rome. The text of "The Letter of Peter to James" is given in Edward Hennecke, *New Testament Apocrypha: Volume Two: Writings Related to the Apostles, Apocalypses and Related Subjects.* Wilhelm Schneemelcher, ed. (2d ed.; Philadelphia, PA: Westminster Press, 1991). Also in Bart D. Ehrman, *After the New Testament: A Reader in Early Christianity* (Oxford: Oxford University Press, 1999), pp. 136–9.

is my enemy." It is assumed that here Peter had Paul in mind and the confrontation between Paul and Peter in Antioch (Gal 2:11–14). In the homilies, Peter claims that both Jesus and Moses can bring salvation. "One and the same teaching becomes known through both. God accepts those who believe in one of them" (*Ps.-Clem.* 8.5, 6). In all circumstances, good works are needed.

James, Peter and Paul, who suffered martyrdom in the 60s of the first century, were very much alive in the memory of the second-century Christians. While James was lauded in Judaizing circles, Paul was vilified. Paul was at the center of the storm in his own time, as well as in the second century. Whatever he said or did continued to generate controversies. The image of Peter as a friend of the Ebionites, taking the side of James against their archenemy Paul, distorts the image of both Peter and James known to us from first-century sources, the Gospels and Epistles. The historic Peter "stood somewhere between Paul and James."[28] At a decisive moment, church authorities agreed that circumcision was not necessary for salvation. James, Peter, and Paul were of one mind not to put the yoke of the law on Gentile converts, not to trouble those who turn to God (Acts 15).

With the expansion of Christianity and the appearance of new Christian centers replacing Jerusalem, the Ebionites did not disappear. In the second part of the fourth century there was a resurgence of Jewish Christian sects, encouraged by the Roman Emperor Julian the Apostate,[29] who repudiated Christianity and attempted to revive the pagan mysteries. As part of his program to restore the pre-Christian past, he encouraged the Jews to rebuild the Jewish temple in Jerusalem. However, his death in AD 363 brought his religious designs to an end.

---

[28]R.E. Brown, Carolyn Osiek, Pheme Perkins, "Early Church," *NJBC* 80:26: The cited section of the article is written by Brown.

[29]See Robert L. Wilken, "Ebionites," in *Encyclopedia of Religion,* IV:577.

CHAPTER EIGHT

THE NEW CHRISTIAN CENTERS: ROME, ANTIOCH, AND ALEXANDRIA

After the First Jewish-Roman War (AD 66–70), Jerusalem gradually lost its preeminence and control over Christian communities outside Palestine. Eusebius, depending on Hegesippus, writes that after the martyrdom of James the Righteous (AD 62), Symeon, the son of Clopas and relative of Jesus (John. 19:25; Luke 24:18), "was a fit person to occupy the throne of the Jerusalem see" (*H.E.* 3.22; 4.22). Not much is known about the life of the church in Jerusalem during his long period of leadership (AD 62–107). The Christian community was considerably weakened by the flight of its members to Pella, but survived in places linked with the life of Jesus, particularly in Nazareth. Hegesippus asserts that Symeon, Bishop of Jerusalem, suffered martyrdom under the reign of Emperor Trajan in AD 107. From his martyrdom to the Second Jewish-Roman War (AD 132–135), there were rapid changes in the leadership of the church, a sign of difficulties and decline. The influence of Jerusalem had drastically diminished. By the turn of the century, the new Christian centers, Rome, Antioch, and Alexandria, were replacing Jerusalem in directing Christian mission and expansion. None of these new centers, however, could take the place of Jerusalem as the mother church of Christianity.

The new centers produced new Christian spiritual leaders. Although of diverse origin, they have been grouped together and known as the "Apostolic Fathers" since the seventeenth century. Clement of Rome, Hermas, Ignatius of Antioch, Polycarp of Smyrna, and Barnabas, possibly of Alexandria, flourished from approximately the last decade of the first century to the first half of the second century (AD 90–140). Their writings are precious sources for understanding the life and struggle of the Christian communities immediately after the New Testament period. Given the enormous problems involved in trying to reconstruct the history of the Christian Church in the second century, in this chapter we shall focus on the writings of these Apostolic Fathers and the picture that emerges from their works.[1]

Rome, the Center of the Empire

I CLEMENT

Jewish Christian missionaries from Jerusalem most probably founded the church in Rome. There had been Jews present in Rome from the second century BC, and regular contacts existed between Jerusalem and the Jewish diaspora in Rome. Pompey added many to their number, bringing in Jews as slaves after his conquest of Judea (63 BC). Many traveled from Rome to Jerusalem as well. Luke in his account of the Pentecost mentioned "visitors from Rome, both Jews and proselytes" (Acts 2:10). No specific conversion is recorded, but after Peter's address, and call to repentance and baptism, the Evangelist Luke writes, "about three thousand souls were baptized" (Acts 2:41). The number of the newly converted is possibly exaggerated, but not the fact of conversion of many, among whom were probably also visitors from Rome. The church in Rome was a Jewish Christian church, open to the Gentile world. By the turn of the century the majority of Roman Christians were probably of Gentile background.[2] When Paul was writing the Letter to the Romans around AD 56, he addressed both groups within the church: Jewish Christians and Gentile Christians. He warned the Gentile Christians that they had no basis to feel superior to the Jewish Christians (Rom 11:13ff). He praised them for their faith (Rom 1:8). He had met and worked with Roman Christians during his missions in Asia Minor and Greece. Many of them had been expelled by Claudius around AD 49, and had returned to Rome after the emperor's death (AD 54). By the end of the century, the church there had emerged from persecution as an important center of Christianity. While in the 50s it was the responsibility of Jerusalem to inform Christians in Antioch,

---

[1]Fundamental for an understanding of the early history of the Roman Church is Peter Lampe, *Die stadtrömischen Christen in den ersten beiden Jahrhunderten* (2d revised edition; Tübingen: J.C.B. Mohr [Paul Siebeck], 1989); translated as: *From Paul to Valentinus: Christians at Rome in the First Two Centuries* (London: T & T Clark [Continuum], 2003). Its lessons are probably applicable to other major urban centers, such as Antioch and Alexandria.

[2]R.E. Brown, "Early Church" *NJBC* 80:22.

Syria, or Cilicia about decisions of the Jerusalem conference (Acts 15:23), by the 90s Rome took the initiative to intervene in the rebellion that was spreading in the church in Corinth.

When a group of younger men deposed the legitimate ruling elders in Corinth, the occurrence was described in antiquity as rebellion and "unholy schism." Upon hearing what was happening in Corinth, Clement, the leader in Rome acclaimed by tradition as the third successor to Peter, sent the Corinthian Christians a letter. This correspondence, known as *1 Clement*, was not sent in the name of an individual but by "the church of God, living in exile in Rome," to "the church of God, living in exile in Corinth." Its main purpose was to expose "the dishonored" who had risen up against the elders, thus destroying the established order and undermining the very existence of the community. The Roman Christians regarded this as "exceedingly disgraceful" (*1 Clem.* 47.6). They demanded that the leaders of the rebellion give up their unlawfully acquired authority and surrender to the legitimate leadership of the church. To bring them to repentance, Clement turned to the essential part of his argument: the divine origin of church order (*1 Clem.* 40–44). We find in the letter one of the earliest expressions of "apostolic succession." The leaders of the Christian churches were appointed by the apostles' successors, the apostles were called and chosen by Christ, and Christ was sent from God. Fully convinced that Christ had risen from the dead, the apostles "went out in the confidence of the Holy Spirit to preach the good news that God's kingdom was about to come." The apostles appointed their first converts "to be bishops and deacons of the future believers" (*1 Clem.* 42.1–4). "Apostolic succession" is the succession of truth. The apostles received the gospel of truth from Christ, who is the Truth. In 1 Clement, the leaders are called "bishops" (*1 Clem.* 44.1–4), but are identified as "elders" (*1 Clem.* 47.5; 57.1). Clement was a presbyter-bishop, one among the elders, not the sole bishop of Rome. Bishops and deacons are mentioned together (*1 Clem.* 42.4) implying that they had different ranks and duties in the same body. The author, however, does not spell out their functions and responsibilities. We may note that Ignatius' concept of a single ruling bishop (in modern terms, "monoepiscopacy") did not yet exist in the church in Rome, just as it did not in the church in Ephesus (1 Tim).

At the end of the first century, the church in Corinth had appointed leaders, like the church in Rome. They were challenged by young men claiming to possess charismatic gifts of the Spirit, "with their pretensions to fine speech" (*1 Clem.* 21.5) and of mystical knowledge, who removed them from their positions of authority. It is possible that the crisis in Corinth was provoked by some teachers of gnostic tendency, whom we shall describe later. They created a schism that led many astray, into despair and doubt (*1 Clem.* 46.9). Clement's letter particularly stressed their lack of Christian love and concern for the community. "Love knows nothing of schism or revolt. Love does everything in harmony" (*1 Clem.* 49.5). The church of Rome appeals to the ringleaders "to reflect upon the common nature of our hope" (*1 Clem.* 51.1), to submit to the presbyters, and to curb their "arrogant tongues" (*1 Clem.* 57.2).

Clement wrote his letter to the Corinthians out of Christian concern, to help another church in crisis. It is not an assertion of the authority of the Roman church over the church in Corinth. The Christian communities located in various geographic areas were neither isolated nor independent. They shared common beliefs and practices and were linked with one another. Clement apologizes that due "to the sudden and successive misfortunes and accidents" the church in Rome had not been able to turn its attention to the quarrels in Corinth earlier (*1 Clem.* 1.1). He is probably referring to the persecutions by Domitian around AD 95.

2 CLEMENT

By his intervention, Clement appears to have been successful in dealing with the rebellion in Corinth. Some have argued, based on the so-called "second letter of Clement," that the deposed presbyters were reinstated. This second letter is a homily presumably delivered by the legitimate elders and preserved with a copy of *1 Clement*. It might explain why the homily has been designated as *2 Clement*. Although attributed to Clement, we have no compelling reason to exclude Corinth as the place of its writing, a city that was no stranger to platonic and gnostic views–views that also had influenced the rebellious leaders. The second letter of Clement emphasizes throughout the divinity of Christ: "We ought to think of Jesus Christ as we do of God" (*2 Clem.* 1.1). Likewise, Paul's high estimate of "the flesh" in 1 Corinthians 3 is restated in the homily: "We should guard the flesh as God's temple." Christ "who saved us was made flesh," and the homilist warns, "let none of you say that this flesh will not be judged or rise again" (*2 Clem.* 9.1–5). All of these points–the body as a temple of the Holy Spirit, the Incarnation, "the Word became flesh and dwelled among us," and the bodily resurrection–are fundamental Christian teachings and experiences that separated Christianity from platonic or gnostic views.

The homily, when it presents two aspects of the church–the spiritual and the living church–appears to be close to a gnostic idea of the Aeons.[3] The homilist's inspiration, however, is Christian. The two-fold vision of the church corresponds to the two-fold nature of Christ. The church is from above, as Christ was also. The spiritual church, a pre-existent church, "was made manifest in the flesh of Christ," which is his living church.

THE *SHEPHERD OF HERMAS*

From Rome also comes Hermas, who composed *The Shepherd of Hermas*. This book written around AD 120 consists of *Visions, Mandates* [commandments, or *mandata*], and *Similitudes* [parables, or *similitudines*]. In form, it is an apocalypse, and its title comes from the mediator of the story, who appeared to Hermas as a shepherd.

Hermas was a contemporary of Clement, who is also mentioned in the text (*Herm. Vis.* 2.4.3). It seems that both Hermas and Clement were former slaves: Clement probably in the household of Titus Flavius Clemens and Flavia Domitilla. As a freedman, he took his name from this household. Archeological evidence raises the possibility that the house church to which Clement belonged was located on land owned by the Flavians, a family documented by a few ancient historians.[4] By the second century, the cemetery of Domitilla had become a Christian burial place [catacomb]. The Roman historian Suetonius (ca. AD 69–121) writes that the emperor Domitian "suddenly put his own cousin Flavius Clemens to death . . . on the slightest suspicion" around AD 95 or 96.[5] Dio Cassius, another Roman historian, (ca. AD 150–235), recounts that Flavius Clemens and Flavia Domitilla "were accused of atheism, a charge under which many were condemned who had drifted into Jewish practices." Dio Cassius does not mention Christians in the surviving parts of his *History of Rome*, as if they did not exist, but we surmise that the victims had indeed been Christians.

---

[3]See Aloys Grillmeier, *Christ in Christian Tradition: From the Apostolic Age to Chalcedon, 451* (New York: Sheed & Ward, 1965), p. 69.

[4]See James S. Jeffers, *Conflict at Rome: Social Order and Hierarchy in Early Christianity* (Philadelphia, PA: Fortress Press, 1991), p. 28ff.

[5]*Life of Domitian*, 15.

However, Clement and Hermas appear to have been members of two different house churches. Clement held an official position as presbyter-bishop for "inter-church affairs." But Hermas, a prophetic voice without an official position, criticized and expressed dissatisfaction with those in the leadership. From his parable of two cities, it appears that Hermas' community was composed of both rich and poor (*Herm. Sim.* 1.1–11). Some of its members accumulated a considerable amount of riches, and their main concern was how to increase and profit from their business. His message to them is simple and clear: turn your efforts from purchasing fields and dwelling places to those who are in distress and show your care for "widows and orphans." The Master of us all made you rich "so that you might fulfill these ministries for him" (*Herm. Sim.* 1.8–9). Hermas is interested in those who were "despised by all men" (*Herm. Mand.* 7.2), but the solution he offers is not radical. As one of the "poor" in his house church, he urged cooperation between the social divisions. The rich man has wealth that comes from the Lord, and the poor is rich in prayers on behalf of the rich. "So they both become partners in righteous work" (*Herm. Sim.* 2.8–10).

Clement and Hermas differ in their attitudes toward the state and its governing authorities. Hermas is more radical regarding the Roman government. He follows the tradition of the Christian *apokalypsis* (Rev 17), reproaching the authorities for their cruelty to those who are faithful to Christ. He could not call them "our rulers," nor could he ask obedience to them, for he believed that the emperor was not merely subject to a higher authority, but as a governor, stood under God's judgment, manifested in Jesus Christ.

For Clement, the rulers of the empire are still "our governors," despite the persecutions of Christians under Nero and Domitian. In a prayer close to the end of *1 Clement*, its author asks the Master to "grant that we may be obedient to your almighty and glorious name, and to our rulers and governors on earth . . . Grant them, Lord, health, peace, harmony and stability, so that they may give no offense in administering the government you have given them" (*1 Clem.* 60.4–61.1). This petition is not essentially different from Rom 13:1ff and 1 Pet 2:13–17. The rulers are not outside God's concern. Christians pray that all may live on the earth in harmony and peace. But if the earthly rulers do not administer in accordance with God's will and persecute God's people, then obedience may be replaced by disobedience to the governing authorities. Both Clement and Hermas reject violence as Christian responses to unjust treatment or punishment. In suffering for being Christians, they share in Christ's suffering. Suffering without violence "is the very principle of the incarnation."[6] The radical exclusive claims which Christians make for Jesus Christ contains a revolutionary feature: the possibility of resistance is implied, yet without resorting to violence.

The church in Rome was both a "charismatic" and an "institutional" church. Both aspects were necessary for its life and future development. Both were gifts of the Spirit. Hermas looks at the church "as a heavenly body that was created before the world and for whose sake the world originated" (*Herm. Vis.* 2.4.1).[7] The vision of the church as a high tower takes the church back in time and history. Hermas tells us that the stones that go into the building are the leaders of the church. "The stones that are square and white and fit their joints are the apostles and bishops and teachers and deacons, who have walked according to the holiness of life" (*Herm. Vis.* 3.5.1). The stones rejected represent unrepentant Christians. Yet in this "charismatic" work the ethical drive is obviously predominant: to speak the truth, to give alms, to avoid immorality, and above all to repent. Hermas is known as a preacher of repentance for forgiveness of post-baptismal sin. Some believed that "it is impossible to restore again to repentance those who have once been enlightened" and fallen away (Heb 6:4–6). In contrast, Hermas insists that repentance can lead to forgiveness.

The authority of the writings of Clement and Hermas was quickly recognized in the church. By AD 170, the Christians of Corinth regarded *1 Clement* as Scripture. Irenaeus wrote around AD 185 (*A.H.* 3.3.3) that Clement had faithfully transmitted the apostolic teaching to that church when it was in turmoil. By Origen's time (ca. AD 185–ca. 254), *1 Clement* and the *Shepherd of Hermas*, as well as the *Letter of Barnabas*, were considered Scripture.

Antioch, the Center of Early Mission

As we have noted, in the first century, missionaries were already reaching Antioch from Jerusalem, and Antioch was becoming a missionary center. There also was vigorous trade between Jerusalem and Antioch. Acts 13:10

---

[6]See C.F.D. Moule, *The Birth of the New Testament* (London: Adam & Charles Black, 1962), p. 139.
[7]E. Schweizer, *Church Order in the New Testament*, p. 156.

records that here the disciples were first called Christians, supposedly by the Roman authorities, distinguishing them from other Jews.

THE *DIDACHE*

Around the beginning of the second century from this area came the *Didache* [*The Teaching of the Twelve Apostles*], the oldest extant church manual. It was written around AD 100, after the Gospel of Matthew and before Ignatius' letters. The manuscript was discovered in 1873. A number of scholars presume that the *Didache* was intended for Christian communities surrounding Antioch.

The *Didache* opens with the assertion that "There are two ways, one of life and one of death, and between the two ways there is a great difference." The teaching of "two ways" had been used in diaspora synagogues to instruct proselytes. This basic Jewish moral instruction, augmented by Jesus' teaching to his disciples as recorded in the Gospel of Matthew, was used to prepare candidates for baptism. The Sermon on the Mount (Matt 5–7) is extensively cited in the first part of the *Didache* and concludes: if one "can bear the Lord's full yoke," he "will be perfect. But if he cannot, then let him do what he can" (*Did.* 6.2). Then follow pre-baptismal instructions (*Did.* 7–9). Baptism is performed "in the name of the Father, Son and Holy Spirit" (*Did.* 7.3) or "in the Lord's name" (*Did.* 9.15). Those who are baptized "should fast on Wednesdays and Fridays" (*Did.* 8.1) and should pray the Lord's Prayer, "Our Father," three times a day (*Did.* 8.3), presumably at the third, sixth and ninth hours, the hours of the Lord's suffering. The *Didache* uses the Evangelist Matthew's text of the prayer (Matt 6:9–13) with an added doxology "for yours is the power and glory forever." The Lord's Prayer is appropriate for use by only those who are baptized.

There are two accounts of the eucharistic celebration. The first (*Did.* 9–10) gives us the oldest recorded prayers for the eucharistic meal with the newly baptized. The setting is apparently the annual celebration of baptism and Eucharist at Easter.[8] The second account refers to regular eucharistic gatherings on Sundays. "On every Lord's Day–his special day–come together and break bread and give thanks, first confessing your sins so that your sacrifice may be pure" (*Did.* 14.1f). Justin Martyr, writing in the middle of the second

---

[8]Robert A. Kraft, *The Didache and Barnabas;* vol. 3 of *The Apostolic Fathers: A New Translation and Commentary,* ed. Robert M. Grant (New York: Thomas Nelson & Sons, 1964–1968), p. 168.

century, describes early Christian worship in more detail (*1 Apl.* 65–67). According to both accounts, the *Didache* and *1 Apology*, no one except the baptized is allowed to participate in the Eucharist.

Moreover, in the church of the *Didache* there are two distinct ministries: local and itinerant. Bishops and deacons are elected local residential leaders (*Did.* 15.1), as they were in Paul's church at Philippi (Phil 1:1). As in Paul's writings (Rom 16:7; 1 Cor 12:18), apostles belong with prophets and teachers to the itinerant ministry. To characterize the local ministry as "non-charismatic" and the itinerants as "charismatic" is an "artificial" distinction without basis in reality.[9] However, the *Didache* does distinguish between acceptable and non-acceptable conduct for itinerant ministers: some help and some exploit (*Did.* 11.3–6). The community elects bishops and deacons, who offer instruction on how to judge who is a true prophet and who is false. True prophets have a charismatic role. At the same time, they are responsible for the tradition that they received, as well as for its development under their leadership.

The *Didache* describes the church as local and universal at the same time. The author conveys the unity of the church by using the metaphor of sowing and gathering. "As this piece [of bread] was scattered over the hills and then brought together and made one, so let your church be brought together from the ends of the earth into one kingdom" (*Did.* 9.4). By "breaking bread," Christians celebrate God's way of bringing people together.

THE LETTERS OF ST IGNATIUS

Antioch's greatest Father of this period was Ignatius (martyred ca. AD 110). Ignatius was arrested and taken to Rome to be thrown to wild beasts. As he traveled on this fateful journey, he composed seven letters, sending four from Smyrna: to Ephesians, Magnesians, Trallians, and Romans. He then sent three from Troas: to Philadelphians and to Smyrnaeans, as well as his letter to Polycarp. Ignatius reveals himself in these letters more vividly than any other second-century Christian author. He writes that Polycarp, the Bishop of Smyrna, who had been a personal acquaintance of John the "Disciple of the Lord," came to greet him. In his letter to the Romans, Ignatius appeals to Christians not to try to stop his execution but to allow him to imitate the suffering of the Lord.

---

[9] See W.H.C. Frend, *Rise of Christianity*, p. 139.

As the leading pastor, Ignatius struggled to defend the church from those who tried from the inside to distort its doctrinal teaching. He warns Christians "against wild beasts in human shapes." "Avoid them," he stresses, "just pray for them that they may somehow repent, hard as that is." But Christ, our life and hope, he notes, "has the power to bring it about" (Ign. *Smyr.* 4.2). To believe that Christ was "actually crucified for us in the flesh" and that he was really raised up has practical implications for the faithful. The doctrinal teachings appear to be constantly calling them to a new level of living and hoping. "We are part of this fruit which grew out of his most blessed passion," wrote Ignatius (Ign. *Smyr.* 1.2). The followers of Christ have shown themselves as "branches of the Cross" (Ign. *Trall.* 11.2).

Ignatius is our earliest witness to the church under the rule of a sole bishop, surrounded by a group of presbyters and deacons. In all his letters, except *To the Romans*, Christians are asked to be obedient to the bishop. In *To the Romans*, however, there is only one mention of himself as "Bishop of Syria" (Ign. *Rom.* 2.2). Rome did not yet have a single ruling bishop. He therefore urged the Christians in Rome to be obedient to their presbyters. Christians in the communities of the western part of Asia Minor were also instructed to obey their bishops, along with the presbyters who are "as closely tied to the bishop as the strings to a harp." Only united as one body may they all sing praises "to the Father through Jesus Christ" (Ign. *Eph.* 4.1–2).

Ignatius clearly states the bishop "presides in God's place, and the presbyters take the place of the apostolic council, and let the deacons be entrusted with the ministry of Jesus Christ" (Ign. *Mag.* 3.1; 6.1). These analogies are a clear sign of a special, considerable development in the hierarchical structure of the church. Ignatius presents it not as an innovation but as something already established before his time. Robert Grant has written that these analogies of Ignatius are inspired by the Gospel of John: the Evangelist John provides us with the model of Jesus and the Father as the pattern for relations between Christians and their bishop (John 13:30; 17:18, 23ff).[10]

Nothing in the church, Ignatius insists, is to be done without his approval (Ign. *Trall.* 3.2). Either the bishop or someone he authorizes is to celebrate the Eucharist. Without his supervision, no baptism or love feast [*agape*] is permitted. "Where the bishop is present, there let the congregation gather, just

---

[10]"Scripture and Tradition in Ignatius of Antioch" in Robert M. Grant, *After the New Testament* (Philadelphia, PA: Fortress Press, 1967), p. 46ff.

as where Jesus Christ is, there is the Catholic Church" (Ign. *Smyr.* 8.1–2). This is the first known appearance of the adjective *katholikos* in Christian literature, meaning "whole" or "entire." Justin Martyr uses the term for general resurrection (*Dial.* 81.4).[11]

Ignatius's exhortation in his letter to the Smyrnaeans indicates some people in the community presented a serious danger to the eucharistic unity of the church. Presumably, they had separate gatherings without the bishop's presence or his authorization. The churches in Smyrna or Tralles were in danger of deceitful teachers, of "those people who mingle Jesus Christ with their teachings," just to gain the confidence of other members "under false pretenses" (Ign. *Trall.* 6.1–2). They abstain from Eucharist "because they refuse to admit that the Eucharist is the flesh of our Savior Jesus Christ, who suffered for our sins" and who was raised from the dead (Ign. *Smyr.* 7.1). The Smyrnaeans and Trallians were in danger from docetic teachers, who professed that the Word of God did not really become a human being, but only appeared or seemed to be human. They denied Christ's humanity. To fight docetism, denial of the physical incarnation of Christ, Ignatius emphatically affirmed the historical reality of Jesus: he really "was born, really was crucified and died. He was really raised from the dead" (Ign. *Trall.* 9.1–2). This is the creedal statement or proclamation of the apostolic faith preached in Antioch. The docetic teachers regarded Jesus' suffering as "sham," but to Ignatius it is "really they who are a sham." In denying the Lord's suffering, the heretical teachers are not "branches of the cross," for through the cross "he summons you who are his members" (Ign. *Trall.* 11.2). In combating docetic tendencies in the several churches he addressed on his way to his martyrdom, Ignatius emphasized the unity of the divine and human in Christ: he was "born yet unbegotten, God incarnate, genuine life in the midst of death, sprung from Mary as well as God, first subject to suffering, then beyond it—Jesus Christ our Lord" (Ign. *Eph.* 7.2). The churches in Asia Minor were in danger from docetics, who in their midst were proclaiming a new Christology and threatening the unity of the church.

In two particular communities (Ign. *Magn.* 8–10; Ign. *Phld.* 5–9), another threat to the unity of the church presented themselves—the "Judaizers." At the time of Ignatius, the Judaizers insisted on following Judaism and its rites.

---

[11]For other usages in the second century, see R.M. Grant, *Ignatius of Antioch;* vol. 4 of *Apostolic Fathers,* p. 121.

They probably were Gentiles converted to Jewish Christianity, similar to the group that had presented difficulties for Paul's mission in Galatia (Gal 6:13). Of them, Ignatius warns: If anyone tries to convince you to follow Judaism, "pay no attention to him. For it is better to hear about Christianity from one of the circumcised [Jewish Christians] than Judaism from a Gentile. They say that they are Jews and are not" (Ign. *Phld.* 6.1). They disrupted the life of Christian Asia Minor (Rev 3:9), and continued propagating their version of Christianity. Their claim to be Christians, while at the same time leading the people astray, forced Ignatius to use the word "Christian" often. It had been used very rarely in the New Testament (Acts 11:26, 26:28; 2 Pet 4:16), but became more common in the second century. The word "Christianity" [*Christianismos*] appears for the first time in Ignatius' letters (Ign. *Rom.* 3.3; Ign. *Phld.* 6.1). Condemning false teachers, Ignatius defined the Christian as one who believes in Jesus Christ, "who came forth from one Father, while still remaining one with him, and returning to him." To go on "observing Judaism" is to admit that you "never received grace" (Ign. *Magn.* 8.1–2). The divine prophets, he writes, "lived Christ Jesus' way." They "anticipated the gospel in their preaching," were saved by believing in him, and announced his coming (Ign. *Phld.* 5.2; 9.2). Ignatius maintained that the prophets spoke of Christ; they lived according to Christ and were inspired by his grace. What the apostles saw and proclaimed, the prophets foresaw. Here Ignatius uses typological interpretation, which establishes an inner correspondence between events or persons belonging to two different periods of history. The ancient Christian interpreters considered the Scriptures as the prefiguration or preparation of the gospel. As a prefiguration, it implies that the reality is already present, and as a preparation, it points to a promise that is to be fulfilled. For those who are Christians, Ignatius concludes, to practice Judaism is absurd. "Christianity did not believe in Judaism, but Judaism in Christianity" (Ign. *Magn.* 10.3). In dealing with schismatic heretical teachers, he turns their attention to the events recorded in the Gospels but does not search for texts to refute them.

By their preaching and practices, the Judaizers were introducing schism into the churches. It appears that they held separate Eucharist meals, not on regular Sundays, but on the preceding day, Saturday. Ignatius insists on the celebration of a "single Eucharist. For there is one flesh of our Lord, Jesus Christ, and one cup of his blood that makes us one, and one altar, just as there is one bishop along with the presbytery and deacons" (Ign. *Phld.* 4.1). "Meet together, all of you, with a single heart," Ignatius urges. "Pay heed to the bishop, the presbyters, and the deacons" [and] avoid schism, for "where there is schism and bad feeling God has no place" (Ign. *Phld.* 6.2; 7.2; 8.1). As Christ in the flesh was visible, so the unity of the church is to be visible to all. The unity of the church is manifest in Christians praying together, professing the same faith, and in the eucharistic celebration, together with the bishop, who is the celebrant, the leader, and the teacher. He is the local point of unity, the guardian and the charismatic teacher of apostolic tradition. And he who fails to join in common worship displays "his arrogance by the very fact of becoming a schismatic" (Ign. *Eph.* 5.2–3).

The transition in the church of Antioch from the leadership of "prophets and teachers" (Acts 13:1) to a single bishop occurred probably after the Gospel of Matthew was written and before Ignatius became Bishop of Antioch. Apparently, this three-part hierarchical organization strengthened the church to confront false teachers from within, without transforming the charismatic church into one that was solely institutional. For, the bishop is not above the church; he is a member of the community known for his faith, love, and deeds. Conversely, false teachers lack faith and love for the community and are easily recognized by their deeds. In the person of Ignatius, the "charismatic" and the "hierarchical" merged.[12]

A further development by Ignatius, also common among some other of the first Christian fathers, is the explication of a "two-nature" Christology: Jesus Christ is both God and man, spirit and flesh. To be a Christian, he insists, means participation in the passion, death, and resurrection of Christ. Ignatius could join the Apostle Paul in saying: "I have been crucified with Christ. It is no longer I who live, but Christ who lives in me" (Gal 2:20). In that belief, he calls himself *theophoros*, "God-bearer." With his life and martyrdom, he conveyed the spirit of the early church, its faith and doctrine, to a new generation.

Alexandria, the Second City of the Empire

By the first century, this Egyptian city of about a million inhabitants had a diverse population. It was the capital of Egypt, and a major trading and intel-

---

[12]R.E. Brown and J.P. Meier, *Antioch and Rome*, p. 74f.

lectual center. Here the Hebrew Scriptures were translated into Greek, in a text now known as the Septuagint. Almost half the population was Jewish, comprising the largest Jewish diaspora in the Roman Empire.

Alexandria was rich in philosophers and famous teachers with speculative gifts. Philo (ca. 25 BC–ca. AD 15), a well-known Jewish philosopher, lived and worked in Alexandria. Basilides and Valentinus, the leading gnostic teachers, flourished there around AD 130. Origen, the most prominent Christian apologist, theologian, and biblical scholar of the pre-Nicene period, was born about AD 185, probably in Alexandria. Under his influence, the city became the center of the most prominent Christian Catechetical School.

In view of the large number of people traveling from Palestine or Syria to Alexandria,[13] we can hardly doubt that Christian missionaries were among them. We lack written documents attesting to the origins of Christianity in Alexandria, but must assume its establishment there by the end of the first century.

Eusebius tells us that "Mark is said to have been the first man to set out for Egypt and preach there the gospel which he had himself written down and the first to establish churches in Alexandria itself" (H.E. 2.16). Modern scholars question the reliability of this tradition. Eusebius seems to be eager to attribute the mission to Mark as parallel to the role of Peter in Rome. What the story of Mark tells us is that Egyptian Christianity had Palestinian origins. More likely is the tradition that Barnabas, a missionary of the Jerusalem community (Acts 11:19ff), may have been among the first to reach Alexandria. Also, Jews, with Christian missionaries among them, traveled from Jerusalem to Alexandria in great numbers. There were three groups in the church at Alexandria: in addition to "orthodox" and gnostics, there was also a distinct Jewish Christian group.[14]

The first attested Christian in Alexandria some time in the late 40s was "a Jew named Apollos, a native of Alexandria, [who] came to Ephesus. He was well versed in Scriptures" (Acts 18:24). From Ephesus he moved to Corinth after Paul left the city for Jerusalem (AD 51). When Paul wrote 1 Corinthians, Apollos was with him in Ephesus. Acts 18:24 indicates that Apollos had

---

[13]See H. Koester, *History, Culture and Religion of the Hellenistic Age* (vol. 1 of *Introduction in the New Testament*), pp. 219–228.

[14]For a recent discussion, see Birger A. Pearson, *Gnosticism, Judaism and Egyptian Christianity: Studies in Antiquity and Christianity* (Philadelphia, PA: Fortress Press, 1990), pp. 194–213.

become a Christian in Alexandria. There "he had been instructed in the way of the Lord," and "he spoke and taught accurately the things concerning Jesus" (Acts 18:25), although it is true that he was acquainted only with the baptism by John and needed further instruction by Priscilla and Aquila. Here we see the integration of this independent Christian teacher into the apostolic mission and fellowship.[15] As a teacher who was "well versed in scriptures," Apollos made a great impression in the synagogues and house churches in Corinth. Interestingly, Martin Luther ascribed the Letter to the Hebrews to him.

The second Alexandrian Christian recognized by name is Basilides. Of Jewish origin, he came to Alexandria from Antioch, and in the latter part of Hadrian's reign (AD 117–138) distinguished himself as a Christian teacher. Together with orthodox teachings, however, Basilides proclaimed some basic gnostic tenets: he presented an unknown God beyond the God of the Hebrew Scriptures, and viewed Jesus as a man who was enlightened at his baptism and served as an example for "spiritual" human beings. In contrast to Valentinus, an Alexandrian who went to Rome and was excommunicated there, Basilides remained a member of the church in Alexandria until his death.[16] Those Christians who remained faithful to the apostolic preaching resisted gnostic influences and speculations. The *Letter of Barnabas* is regarded as the first important "non-gnostic" document written when the most influential gnostic teachers were active in the Egyptian capital. The letter is attributed to the Barnabas of Scripture (Acts 4:36); but based on a reference to the destruction of the Temple (AD 70) as an event in the past and the letter's "anti-Judaic" attitude, it could not have been written by a contemporary of Paul. *Barnabas* probably was written in the 40s of the second century, before the final separation between Judaism and Christianity, but at the time when the breach between them was widening and hostile rhetoric was intensifying.

Barnabas stressed the historical character of the incarnation, suffering, and death of Christ. The Son of God came in the flesh "that he might destroy death and demonstrate the reality of the resurrection of the dead" (*Barn.* 5.6, also chapters 5–7). "For if he had not come in flesh, how could men be saved by looking at him? They cannot even gaze directly into the rays of the sun, even though it is a work of his hands and is destined to cease existing" (*Barn.*

[15]Richard J. Dillon, "Acts of the Apostles" *NJBC* 44:98.
[16]Gilles Quispel, "Gnosticism from its Origins to the Middle Ages," *Encyclopedia of Religion*, V:571.

5.10). Salvation is to be achieved not by withdrawing from the world in one-self, but rather by participating in the life of the community and seeking "together the common good" (*Barn.* 4.10). The author of *Barnabas* exhorts Christians to "love as the apple of your eye all who proclaim the Lord's word to you" (*Barn.* 19.9).

Although the writer of this letter uses the term "gnosis," knowledge, there is in the letter neither a reference to an evil god of creation nor to matter that is evil—characteristics of gnostic literature. Rather, faith is presented as the saving knowledge, revelation of the real nature of the self and of God. In *Barnabas* the term gnosis is used for knowledge of what God requires from man (*Barn.* 18.1; 19.1; 21.5). The one who is obedient to God's voice has this knowledge (*Barn.* 8.7–9.4). Gnosis refers to the understanding of the Lord's ways and requirements, preceded by "exegetical gnosis," that is, discovering the meaning of the scriptural text (*Barn.* 6.9; 9.8; 13.7). Ultimately, gnosis is not an end in itself, but the beginning of Christian life.[17] *Barnabas* in partic-ular bears witness to the battle of the Christians in Alexandria to preserve the apostolic traditions from gnostics and Jewish sects. The moral instructions we find in *Barnabas* (chapters 18–21) closely resemble those found in the section titled "Two Ways" in the *Didache* (chapters 1–6).

We may speculate that the battling movements we find in Alexandria led to a restructuring of the church. By the end of the second century, the church at Alexandria had a "monarchical" bishop. The rule of a single bishop appeared in Rome before Alexandria. The first known monarchical bishop of Alexandria seems to have been Bishop Demetrius (AD 189–232). This develop-ment suggests that the orthodox group felt strong enough with the help of Rome to establish a hierarchical structure similar to that church.[18] Irenaeus, writing around AD 185, included the church in Egypt as among those churches that received and preserved the faith of the apostles and their disciples with "one soul and one heart."[19]

---

[17]See R.A. Kraft, *The Didache and Barnabas;* vol. 3 of *The Apostolic Fathers*, pp. 22–24.

[18]The exact time of the establishment of the monoepiscopacy in Rome is disputed. Whether with Bishop Anicetus (mid-second century) or with Bishop Victor (the first Latin-speaking pope, AD 189–199), by the end of the second century it was firmly established.

[19]See B. Pearson, *Gnosticism*, p. 209f. For a contrasting view, see Walter Bauer, who argues in *Ortho-doxy and Heresy in Earliest Christianity* (1935) [Philadelphia, PA: Fortress Press, 1971] that the original form of Christianity in Alexandria was "gnostic," not "orthodox." Only later, under the influence of Rome, did the orthodox form prevail over the gnostic.

The Scriptural Interpretation by the Apostolic Fathers

For the Fathers, the Bible was the Septuagint, the Greek translation of the Hebrew Bible. The process of canonization of New Testament writings had started (2 Pet 3:16), but was not yet completed. The Apostolic Fathers adopted the Septuagint as their own, interpreting it in the light of Christ. Their methods of interpretation, typological and allegorical, had been known both to Jews and Greeks. There are examples of typology and allegory in the writings of the New Testament, the Gospels, and Paul's Epistles. After his resurrection, Jesus appeared to his disciples, and beginning "with Moses and all the Prophets, he interpreted to them in all the Scriptures the things concerning himself" (Luke 24:25–28). For Ignatius, the prophets spoke of Christ, and he exhorted Christians to love the prophets "because they anticipated the gospel in their preaching, hoped for and awaited Him, and were saved by believing in him. Thus they were in unity with Jesus Christ. They were saints, and we should love them and admire them, seeing that Jesus Christ vouched for them and they form a real part of the gospel of our common hope" (Ign. *Phld.* 5.2). The prophets "announced his coming, but the gospel is the crowning achievement forever" (Ign. *Phld.* 9.2).

The author of the *Letter of Barnabas* used allegorical, "radical interpretation" for apologetic purposes. He rejected literal acceptance of the law and the covenant, insisting on the spiritual meaning of the biblical text and the superiority of Christianity over Judaism. Claiming that the Scriptures belong to Christians alone, he argues that Jews who adhere to the literal meaning misunderstand and destroy their Bible. The covenant is "ours, not theirs." The Scriptures must be interpreted allegorically. Christians are now God's new people (*Barn.* 4.6–51).[20] "Let us become a perfect temple of God, the place where God dwells" (*Barn.* 4.11). The author of this letter had a debate with Jews (*Barn.* 1.4) and admitted that he was one of them, "loving you all above my own life" (*Barn.* 4.6). There was a "love-hate relationship between the members of the two 'Israels.'"[21] At the time of writing the *Letter of Barnabas,* the conflict between Christians and Jews was deepening and moving to final separation.

---

[20]R.E. Brown, "Early Church" *NJBC* 80:25.
[21]W.H.C. Frend, *Rise of Christianity,* p. 185.

The *Letter of Barnabas* demonstrates the influence of the Jewish philosopher Philo, who also used allegory for apologetic purposes to defend and
strengthen Judaism. He finds it necessary to show that the truth revealed in
the Scriptures does not differ from the truth of the Greek philosophers.
Philo's interest lay in discovering moral or religious ideas in Scripture. Adam,
Eve, Cain, Abel, and others are symbolic characters. These figures "tell something else" to us than the literal biblical stories.

Paul was the first to use allegory in Christian interpretation. He reminds
the Galatians, who desire to be under the law, that Abraham had two sons,
one by a slave and one by a free woman (Gal 4:24). The former was born
according to the flesh, and the latter through the promise. Now this is an allegory, Paul continues: these two women are two covenants; Hagar represents
Mount Sinai, the present Jerusalem and the covenant of law, and Sarah stands
for the new Jerusalem and the new covenant. The spiritual meaning of Hagar
and Sarah is linked with history. Paul does not deny their existence historically, but he uses allegory in the sense of type. Philo also used allegory to dis-
till the meaning of the Hagar-Sarah story. In his interpretation, Hagar stands
for profane philosophy, while Sarah represents sacred theology. This is quite
different from Paul's interpretation, in Henry Chadwick's view.[22] For Paul,
allegory has a "typological" character. This is also true of the use of allegory
in the *Letter of Barnabas,* but with an important difference: the author of the
Letter of Barnabas is primarily concerned to present ancient Jewish Scripture
as a Christian book. He minimized the historical context of past events, but
stressed the historical character of God's final revelation.

Whether the Apostolic Fathers used the typological or the allegorical
method of interpretation, they saw the Bible as the unity of prophecy and
fulfillment. They searched for an "inner correspondence" between the events
or persons belonging to different periods of sacred history, directed and
guided by the Creator and the Redeemer of the universe. They sought to
establish a relationship between the Hebrew Scripture and the Christian
Gospels. When Ignatius heard some people saying: "If I do not find it in the
original documents, I don't believe it in the Gospel," he reminded them that
the Old Testament was not the original, primary document for Christians, the

[22]See his "St Paul and Philo of Alexandria," *Bulletin of John Rylands Library* 48 (1966): 286–307, here
p. 299 (reprinted in *History and Thought of the Early Christian Church* [London, 1982, item V]).

final authority which verifies the Gospel. Ignatius argued: "It is written there that it is Jesus Christ who is the original document. The inviolable archives are his cross and death and his resurrection and the faith that came by Him" (Ign. *Phld.* 8.2). The final determining authority for Ignatius is the living tradition of the four Gospels.[23]

Early Christians bore witness to Christ with their lives and their writings. They bore witness by the testimony of blood, martyrdom, and "the testimony of writings," that is, by the apologists.[24] Both testimonies arose out of the struggle of the church with the Roman authorities.

[23]For the relationship between Christ, the gospel, and Scripture in Ignatius, see John Behr, "Scripture, the Gospel and Orthodoxy," *SVTQ* 43 (1999): 223–48. He writes that the archives "are Jesus Christ, in the sense that He is embodiment of Scripture–the word made flesh" (p. 240).

[24]A. Grillmeier, *Christ in Christian Tradition*, p. 101f.

CHAPTER NINE

PERSECUTION AND MARTYRDOM: THE TESTIMONY OF BLOOD

With the painful partition between Judaism and Christianity, starting during the Jewish-Roman Wars (completed in AD 135), Christians began attracting punitive attention from local Roman authorities. As they were expelled from the synagogues, they were perceived as a new and dangerous religion. With the separation from Judaism, they lost privileges, such as freedom of worship and exemption from participating in the cult of the emperor, extended to Jews under Roman rule. Emperor worship had come from the East and was gradually accepted in Rome. Octavian had acquired the title "Augustus" from the Roman senate in 27 BC, thereby being elevated above all other citizens. Now the office had acquired a "numinous quality," but he was not yet regarded as personally divine. Only after his death did he become *Theos Sebastos*, the god Augustus.[1] However, his successors began demanding the divine title while still alive. The Emperor Domitian (AD 81–96) requested to be addressed as "Lord and God." For the Romans, the emperor cult was necessary for peace, order and prosperity. It was the religion of all good people. For those baptized into Christ, however, it was sheer idolatry.

"Under the Roman Empire there was no single imperial cult" but "a variety of cults of the emperors, which took three main forms: the official state cult of Rome, municipal cults of cities in the empire, and private cults." Founding these shrines and maintaining worship, "the imperial cult was one of the most vital features of Greco-Roman paganism in the first two centuries of the Christian era."[2] Building and organizing shrines in honor of successive emperors ended in the fourth century when Christianity became the official religion.

[1] H. Koester, *History, Culture, and Religion of the Hellenistic Age* (vol. 1 of *Introduction to the New Testament*), pp. 366–71.

[2] J. Rufus Fears, "Emperor's Cult," *The Encyclopedia of Religion*, V:101–102.

Throughout the vast empire, there were a number of local cults where sacrifices were offered to "the gods." Romans were devoted to their ancient cults and tolerated foreign religions as long as their members participated in activities of their local cults. Worship of the emperor and worship of the gods sometimes merged.

The new cults, which were suspected of illegal activities, were under constant supervision of the police. They were perceived as threats to peace and security in the empire. Christians refused to take part in the cult's rituals, and were persecuted, not for holding new ideas but for belonging to a competing community. The church claimed to be a distinct fellowship, to which obedience to God and to his commandments must be above allegiance to the religion of the empire. The conflict between worship of "the gods" and worship of Christ was inevitable. The position of the Jews was different; they were exempted from the requirement to sacrifice to the gods.

The Persecution of Christians in Asia Minor

By the beginning of the second century, persecutions started in Bithynia-Pontus in Asia Minor. Roman and Christian documents (official correspondence, court proceedings, and reports of eyewitnesses) indicate the reasons for these persecutions. Pliny the Younger, who was governor of Bithynia from ca. AD 110–ca. 112), wrote to the Emperor Trajan (AD 98–117) and asked what the proper course was in persecuting Christians. "It is my custom, Your Majesty, to refer everything about which I have doubts to you," he starts. Christians were already being put on trial, but he did not know what the object of his investigation was or the degree of punishment required. He asked "whether the name itself [being Christian], if free from crime or abominations attached to the name, should be punished." He described his method: "I asked them whether they were Christians. If they confessed it, I asked a second and a third time and threatened punishment; if they persisted I ordered their execution." To justify it, the governor adds: "Their pertinacity and inflexible obstinacy ought certainly to be punished." Those who were Roman citizens he sent to Rome. He then referred to a pamphlet, sent by an informer, which contained many names. If those named denied that they had been Christians, the governor tested them, asking them to pray to the gods "and with offerings of wine and incense pray to your statue, which for this reason I had ordered to be brought along with the images of the gods." And if they cursed Christ, he said, "I thought that they should be let go."

From former Christians, who were on an informer's list but who had left the Christian community some even twenty years before, possibly during the persecution under Domitian, the governor learned that Christians used to meet "on a fixed day" early in the morning "to sing a hymn by turns to Christ as God."

To discover more about Christians meeting and coming together for a meal, Pliny ordered the torture of two slave girls, called "ministrants." The Latin *ministra* expresses the meaning of the Greek *diakonos*, "server." We do not know the function of the two Christian slaves; most likely, they performed distinct duties in the worship of the community. After torture they were questioned, but the governor could discover only "a degrading and extravagant superstition." Now Pliny asked the emperor what to do, as Christianity was spreading throughout the cities of Bithynia-Pontus in Asia Minor. How could the governor check the Christian expansion, which undermined the religion of the empire and the economic base of paganism?

In his reply, Emperor Trajan wrote, "No general rule can be laid down in fixed terms. They [Christians] must not be sought out." Those who are convicted must be punished, but those who say that they are not Christians and who worship "our gods" may be pardoned. Anonymous accusations, the emperor concludes, "should not be entertained on any charge. For they both set a very bad precedent and are alien to the spirit of our age."[3] The Emperor Hadrian, who succeeded Trajan around AD 124–25, continued advising the proconsul of Asia that Christians should not be harassed by informers. Specific accusations against them must be made in court.

Despite these warnings, in fact Christians were punished for "the name" itself. They were tortured to reveal the secrets of their group meetings. Records tell that to gather information that would help the provincial governing authorities to acquire knowledge of activities of this new movement, two women were severely beaten. Rumors that Christians at regular meetings ate human flesh and drank blood proved to be wrong when Pliny discovered that they were eating "ordinary, harmless food." Yet the persecutions contin-

[3]For the text of these letters, 10.96 and 10.97, see M. Whittaker, *Jews and Christians: Graeco-Roman Views*, pp. 150–53. Trajan's edict regarding informers appears to be a contrast to practice in totalitarian states in the twentieth century–Author's note.

ued. Christians refused to worship idols, as the emperor cult spread, gaining acceptance among the educated population. Pliny the Younger, a highly educated man, a man of letters and friend of Tacitus, insisted that the living Emperor Trajan must be worshipped for the sake of the peace and prosperity of the empire.

THE MARTYRDOM OF POLYCARP

Sporadic outbreaks of violence against Christians occurred in various cities and provinces. Reports of eyewitnesses and official court proceedings give us moving accounts of the martyrdom of Christian leaders, teachers, bishops, and philosophers. Christian documents and letters reveal the attitude and convictions of the persecuted people.

We first hear of Polycarp, Bishop of Smyrna, from Ignatius, who wrote to Polycarp on his way to his own martyrdom in Rome. This same Polycarp, forty-five years later, was arrested, tried, and executed for being a Christian (AD 155). Eyewitness reports of his trial and death, sent as a letter from the church at Smyrna to the church at Philomelium, also in Asia Minor, comprise the document known as the *Martyrdom of Polycarp*. This letter apparently describes a persecution in Smyrna where several Christians had been martyred, among them the "blessed Polycarp." The letter ends with praise to Polycarp, "not only as a distinguished teacher but also an outstanding martyr, whose martyrdom all desire to imitate, since it was in accord with the pattern of the gospel of Christ" (*Mart. Pol.* 19). He waited to be betrayed, just as the Lord did. In the most moving part of the letter, we have an eyewitness account of Polycarp's arrest, his refusal to say "Caesar is Lord," and his confrontation with the proconsul, who tried to persuade him to "swear by the genius [divine aura] of Caesar." During this confrontation, the proconsul commanded him to change his mind and say "Away with the atheists!" Polycarp looked at the crowd in the stadium and without hesitation said, "Away with the atheists!" (Christians were often charged as "atheists," as they denied the existence of the traditional gods.) The proconsul insisted: "Take the oath and I will release you. Curse Christ." Polycarp replied: "For eighty-six years I have been his servant, and he has done me no wrong. How can I blaspheme my King, who saved me?" He refused "to swear by the genius of Caesar," saying, "I am a Christian." While preparations were being made to burn him, Polycarp prayed, using words similar in many ways to eucharistic prayers: "I bless you because you have considered me worthy of this day and hour, that I might receive a place among the number of martyrs in the cup of your Christ, to the resurrection to eternal life, both of soul and of body, in the incorruptibility of the Holy Spirit" (*Mart. Pol.* 14). This is part of the prayer he must have recited many times before at liturgical eucharistic celebrations in the church in Smyrna. Central to his spiritual life, this prayer he again recited just before he was burnt, around AD 155. The letter further describes what happened after the martyrdom: his followers sifted his bones from the ashes, "which are more valuable than precious stones and finer than refined gold," then deposited them in a suitable place. The annual liturgical celebration, "the birthday of his martyrdom," started the next year[4] (*Mart. Pol.* 18). This is one of the earliest accounts of the veneration of martyrs in the church.

The letter also records that there was a large and powerful Jewish population in Smyrna. As previously noted, after AD 135 relations between Christians and Jews worsened, and were worst of all in the cities of Asia Minor, where the number of Christians had been increasing. The persecutions leading to the martyrdom of Polycarp and his associates exacerbated the antagonism between the two groups. The letter notes that Jewish Smyrneans shouted with the mob, demanding the execution of Polycarp, that "the father of Christians" should be burnt alive.

THE MARTYRDOM OF JUSTIN

Justin, the best known and most influential Christian apologist of the second century, was brought with six followers to trial before the prefect Rusticus in Rome. This occurred around AD 165, ten years after the persecution of Christians in Smyrna and the martyrdom of their bishop Polycarp. What we know of the proceedings comes from official Roman court records.

The trial started when Rusticus attempted to compel Justin and his followers to accept the beliefs and cults of the Romans. "First, believe in the gods and obey the emperors," the prefect said to Justin. These first exchanges ended with what we may characterize as Justin's confession of faith: "We worship the God of Christians, whom we think to be One, from the beginning maker and creator of the whole creation, visible and invisible, and the Lord

---

[4]*Mart. Pol.* 18. The names of martyrs, the victims of persecutions, in the liturgies "rapidly gave rise to special cults that went far beyond mere commemoration of the dead," writes Patrick J. Geary, "Cult of the Saints," *Encyclopedia of Religion*, IV:172f.

Jesus Christ, the Son of God, who was predicted by the prophets as going to come to the human race, herald of salvation and teacher of good precepts."

Then Rusticus wanted to discover the meeting places of Christians in Rome, so he asked Justin, "Where do you meet?" to which Justin answered, "Where each one chooses and is able . . . for the God of Christians is not limited by place." Not satisfied with such an answer, the prefect insisted: "Tell me, where do you meet, or in what place do you gather your disciples?" Including all necessary details Justin responded: "I live above the bath of a certain Martin, the son of Timothinus, and during all this time I have not known any other assembly but the one there. And whoever wanted to come to me, to him I communicated the words of truth."

The court records reveal Justin to have been a well-known teacher among Christians and to have had his own school. Those who desired to learn or hear about Christian religion would come to him, at his home "above the bath of a certain Martin." He said that he did not know any other place of Christian meetings in Rome. As in Jerusalem, Christians used to meet in the houses of their members even before they were expelled from the synagogue. After their expulsion, they lost the civil privileges granted to Jews: reprieve from universally required emperor worship and the right to found house churches. Now a permit was required for meeting in a private house.[5] Rusticus really wanted to know about unauthorized house meetings.

To seal his case against Justin, Rusticus questioned him again: "Well, finally, you are a Christian?" Without hesitation Justin replied, "Yes, I am a Christian."[6] He then addressed the same question to each member of the group, and each in turn answered affirmatively. One added that he was a Christian "by God's gift." When Rusticus asked another "Did Justin make you a Christian?" he received the answer: "I have been a Christian a long time, and I will always be one." To the question: "Who taught you?" they usually responded that they had been taught by their parents. One of them mentioned Justin: "I gladly heard Justin's discourses, but I too received my Christian training from my parents."

They refused to offer sacrifices to the gods, to fall from "religion into irreligion." Threatened with "torture without mercy," they still insisted that as

[5]See J.S. Jeffers, *Conflict at Rome* (1991), p. 39ff.

[6]"Martyrdom of Justin," in *Second Century Christianity: A Collection of Fragments*, ed. Robert Grant. Translations of Christian Literature. Series VI: Select Passages (SPCK: London, 1957), pp. 109–112.

Christians they could not sacrifice to idols. Rusticus ordered them "to suffer capital punishment in obedience to the laws," and they were beheaded.

The Persecution of Christians in Gaul

Another account of persecutions far from Rome comes from an eyewitness account by the Gallican Christians to their brothers in Asia Minor. The *Letter of the Churches in Vienne and Lyons*[7] starts with the conviction that the servants of Christ in Vienne and Lyons share the same faith and hope of redemption as their brothers in Asia and Phrygia. Lyons, the center of the province of Gaul, had established commercial links with Asia Minor. Connections between the churches in the East with those in the West were maintained through the constant traveling of merchants and their entourage. These ties were strengthened with the arrival of Irenaeus (ca. AD 130–200) from Asia Minor. He had been in Rome on a mission during the persecutions of AD 177, and afterward became Bishop of Lyons.

The Gallic Christians informed the Asian churches about the severity of their trials and the untold sufferings of their martyrs. "No pen could do them justice." They endured abuse, stoning, the plundering of the mob, and then interrogation by the city authorities. Those who confessed Christ were locked up in jail to await the governor's arrival. The arrests went on, and those "who had done most to build up our church life" were added to the number of martyrs. They were hunted out and accused of "Thyestian banquets[8] and Oedipean incest,[9] things we ought never to speak of, think about, or even believe that such things ever happened among human beings."

One who experienced the full fury of the crowd, the governor, and the soldiers was Sanctus, a deacon from Vienne. He stood up to their onslaughts and with determination refused to tell interrogators his own name, race, birthplace, and whether he was slave or free. "To every question he replied in Latin: 'I am a Christian.'" The letter goes on to give a detailed description of the instruments of torture used by the authorities, recounting how some

[7]Preserved in Eusebius, *H.E.* 5.1.3–5.2.2.

[8]Cannibalistic feasts: according to the Greek myth, Thyestes had been served his own sons at a banquet.

[9]According to myth, Oedipus had married his mother: the secrecy of Christian meetings, their calling one another brother and sister, and the exchange of the kiss of peace may have given rise to the suspicion of incest.

victims strengthened others; and of the death of the tortured in dark and filthy prisons. Those who survived the torture were punished according to law: those who possessed Roman citizenship were beheaded, the rest were thrown to wild beasts. Finally, the bodies of the martyrs "were finally burnt to ashes and swept by these wicked men into the Rhone, which flows nearby."

The Proceedings against Christians in North Africa

Shortly after the persecution of the Gallic Christians, seven men and five women were martyred at Scillium in Africa in AD 180.[10] Our knowledge is based on the Latin account of the trial, serving as evidence of a significant Christian presence in North Africa. The account shows the desire of the proconsul Saturninus to reach some compromise with the arrested Christians: "If you return to your senses, you can obtain the pardon of our Lord the Emperor." The prisoner Speratus answered that they had never done anything wrong and that they honored the emperor. The proconsul tried to persuade the prisoners to swear by the "genius" [divine aura] of the emperor. Speratus resolutely replied: "I do not recognize the empire of this world. Rather, I serve that God whom no one has seen, nor can see, with these eyes." He confirmed that he was a Christian and all the other prisoners followed him. The proconsul made a last attempt and offered them time for consideration. Speratus answered that there was no need for that. The last question the proconsul asked Speratus was: "What do you have in your case?" Speratus responded, "Books and letters of a just man named Paul." This lets us know that Paul's letters were already known in North Africa and his influence was widespread by the end of the second century. When the proconsul clearly saw that the Christians "persevered in their obstinacy," he condemned them to be executed by the sword, and they were beheaded.

The persecutions in Rome (AD 165), Gaul (AD 177) and in North Africa (AD 180) took place in the reign of the Emperor Marcus Aurelius (AD 161–180). In his *Meditations* (AD 167), he made a comment about the followers of Christ. As a Stoic philosopher, he defended the act of suicide of one who would attain the state of *apatheia,* impassibility, the mode of existence beyond passion. Such a man, for the emperor, was the model of a "wise man." To the

---

[10]English translation in *The Acts of the Christian Martyrs,* Herbert Musurillo, trans. (Oxford: Oxford University Press, 1972). Reprinted in B.D. Ehrman, *After The New Testament,* pp. 41–42.

Christians who were ready to suffer for their faith, the emperor imputed "theatricality and exhibitionism" (*Med.* 11.3).

Ignatius, Bishop of Antioch, conveys in his letter to the Romans the spirit and the meaning of martyrdom. As a "prisoner in Christ Jesus," he has only one desire: to imitate Christ in his suffering and to "reach God." His zeal and readiness for martyrdom are the outcome of his life in Christ. "If anyone has [Christ] in him, let him appreciate what I am longing for, and sympathize with me, realizing what I am going through" (Ign. *Rom.* 6.3). The Christian martyrs did not rely on their own strength and achievement. They suffered with Christ. His love inspired and strengthened them on the road to martyrdom. The martyrs did not draw attention to themselves, but to the one who died and rose for them. Ignatius had been arrested in Antioch and sent to Rome for trial, as he was a Roman citizen. We have no official account of court proceedings or reports by eyewitnesses of his martyrdom. The edifying stories inspired by his martyrdom appeared much later.

Although the persecutions of Christians were scattered and sporadic, the possibility of being martyred was always present. The churches that did not directly experience attacks, trials, and tortures were in constant danger of investigation by local authorities. Christians were harassed, excluded from the market places, banned from public baths, and attacked by mobs. In some provinces, they would be mercilessly tortured. Throughout the empire in the second century, Christians lived in a hostile environment.

THE MARTYRDOM OF PERPETUA AND FELICITAS

At the turn of the century (AD 202), two young women suffered martyrdom with four other Christians. Perpetua, a twenty-two-year-old Roman aristocrat, and her slave Felicitas were persecuted under Emperor Septimius Severus (AD 193–211) in Carthage, a major center of the empire. Perpetua, the mother of an infant son, was determined to undergo baptism. This brought her into conflict with her family, particularly with her father. Perpetua's experience as a convert separated from her family by membership in the Christian community reflected that of many converts in the first two centuries. The account of her life after her arrest is based on a diary that she kept while in prison.[11] She vividly described her place of detention. She was terrified as never before

---

[11]H. Musurillo, *Acts,* reprinted in B.D. Ehrman, *After the New Testament,*, pp. 42–50.

when she entered "such a dark hole." It was difficult for her to live in a crowded place. "There were the extortions of the soldiers, and to crown all, I was tortured with worry for my baby son." After a long period of anxiety, she was permitted to have her baby with her in prison. Relieved of worry over him, whom she now nursed, Perpetua's health improved, and her prison, as she recorded in her diary, "had suddenly become a palace, so that I wanted to be there rather than anywhere else." Then the time for her hearing and trial came, and all changed.

Felicitas, her servant, who had been pregnant when arrested, was very distressed that her trial would be postponed because of her pregnancy, "for it was against the law for women with child to be executed." Felicitas gave birth to a baby girl before her trial, and the child was "taken by one of the sisters" [Christian women], who "brought her up as her own daughter."

When Perpetua was brought to court, her father confronted her, pleading: "Perform the sacrifice—have pity on your baby!" The governor Hilarion tried as well, saying: "Have pity on your father's gray hair; have pity on your infant son. Offer sacrifice for the welfare of the emperors." Perpetua retorted: "I will not." Hilarion asked once more: "Are you a Christian?" and she answered, "Yes, I am." Thus, they all were condemned to be devoured by beasts.

We recall that at the beginning of the second century two slave girls, called "ministrants," whose names we do not know, were similarly martyred. These events show how slaves and masters were brought together as Christians in the act of martyrdom.

In the third century, under Severus, persecution passed from sporadic outbreaks to systematic attacks against Christians throughout the empire. The Emperor Decius (AD 249–251) undertook a general execution of the leaders of the church. To disorient the faithful and to prevent any organized resistance, the Roman authorities arrested, tried, and executed many of the bishops of Rome, Antioch, and Jerusalem. During that particular persecution, Origen, the Christian apologist, also was arrested and tortured. Some of these bishops succeeded in escaping, but the Bishop of Smyrna, the city of Polycarp, recanted. Some who had shown signs of weakness at the beginning of these persecutions returned to the church later.

By carrying on these persecutions, Decius was trying to eliminate the danger to the peace and order of the empire, coming, as he saw it, from the expanding and increasing membership of the Christian community. The Roman authorities questioned their loyalty, for they refused to sacrifice to the Roman gods and the divine aura of the emperor. The most eloquent of the opponents to the Christians included Marcus Cornelius Fronto (AD 100–166), tutor and friend of the Emperor Marcus Aurelius, who spread popular slanders against the Christians: that they conspire in darkness and hate the light of day. At their common meal, he accused them of drinking blood and then participating in orgies. Some accused Christians of atheism, others of cannibalism, and still others of immorality.[12] The most serious of these attacks came from the public philosopher Celsus, which we shall explore further on. The purpose of this persecution was to unite all, masters and slaves, in their devotion to Rome and the empire. Those who refused to offer sacrifices were executed, and those who participated in the emperor cult received a certificate; they had passed the test of loyalty. Under these severe conditions, many left the church, but some remained faithful.[13]

The Christians saw their conflict with the imperial authorities, not in political but in eschatological terms.[14] For them it was a struggle between Christ and the devil with his powers. The devil used many devices to force arrested Christians to renounce Christ and worship the emperor instead. These public acts of torture also activated the bystanders: some took part in torturing the victims, and others watching egged the torturers on; still others laughed and jeered. On the other hand, some of their pagan neighbors became curious about the Christians and their faith and way of life. Some who had been attracted out of curiosity ended up converting to the faith.

The conflict between the Roman imperial authorities and Christians "remains unique."[15] In contrast to other "criminals," Christians were utterly committed to the founder of their religion and "did not yield or retreat" during the court proceedings. Yet, despite being persecuted they avoided becom-

---

[12]For an account of the slanders leading to persecution, see Stephen Benko, *Pagan Rome and the Early Christians* (Bloomington, IN: Indiana University Press, 1986), p. 54ff., and M. Whittaker, *Jews and Christians: Graeco-Roman Views,* p. 173ff.

[13]On the persecution under Decius, see W.H.C. Frend, *Martyrdom and Persecution in the Early Church: A Study of Conflict from the Maccabees to Donatus* (New York: New York University Press, 1967), pp. 301–304.

[14]Ibid., p. 15.

[15]Arnaldo Momigliano, "Roman Religion: The Imperial Period," in *Encyclopedia of Religion,* XII:469–70.

ing "enemies" of the Roman state. As "apologists" for Christianity, they maintained that the Church was part of the empire.

Justin is an eloquent example of the defense offered. He attacked aggressive paganism with its idolatry, but he did not reject the pagan Greek philosophers, whose truthful expressions, he argued, were inspired by the Divine Logos. He maintained that Greek philosophy is properly interpreted as a preparation for Christianity.

As we look back on the century of martyrdom, we recall that the persecutions were intermittent and widely scattered. The martyrs were a new phenomenon in Roman experience. Many were educated and full participants in Roman life. They argued with their accusers as equals. In contrast, other persecutions of Christianity through history may have been more thorough and vicious (particularly the totalitarian ideologies, Nazism and Communism, of the twentieth century). Still, the martyrs of the second and third century remained the models for all later witnesses to Christianity.

CHAPTER TEN

CHRISTIAN APOLOGISTS:
THE TESTIMONY OF THE WRITINGS

T he position of the Jews, recognized by Julius Caesar and observed by subsequent rulers, exempted them from the requirement to sacrifice to the gods and obey certain other universal demands, in recognition of their longstanding services to the empire. As long as the Christians were regarded as belonging to the "Jewish" community, they were privileged as well. However, as we have seen, they lost that affiliation at the end of the first century, and were grouped together with other "new" religions and required to observe the practices of the empire, including emperor worship.

The age of syncretism fostered toleration of pagan religions and of many gods, but not of Christianity. The imperial authorities and the populace disliked Christians for separating themselves from the society in which they lived. The population as a whole shared the official opinion that the Christians were an obstinate people who did not respect the gods of the empire and, above all, who rejected the cult of the emperor. By not participating in official social and religious events, Christians, in the view of the Romans, represented a disruptive, anti-social force in Roman society, and, when accused of crimes, Christians had to defend themselves. The author of 1 Peter wrote to recent converts from paganism: "Always be prepared to make a defense [*apologia*] to anyone who calls you to account for the hope that is in you, yet do it with gentleness and reverence" (1 Pet 3:15).

Starting around the middle of the second century, the apologists left their mark on Christian development. In their writings, they defended the faith of the church and its practices. Justin Martyr is the best known and the most influential among writers of the second century. Origen of Alexandria, who in many ways carries the concerns of the second century into the third, represents the highest point in the Apologetic movement.

Second-Century Apologists

JUSTIN MARTYR, THE FOREMOST APOLOGIST

The first major Christian apologist, Justin Martyr (ca. AD 100–165), was born in Samaria, in Neapolis (modern Nablus), founded by Romans as a colony after AD 70. Following his conversion around AD 130, he taught in Ephesus and then moved to Rome, where he organized a Christian school. He was martyred in Rome, as we recounted in the preceding chapter.

His work *Dialogue with Trypho*, written around AD 160, is based on a debate with a leading spokesperson of Judaism. Here, it is Justin's intent to present Christianity as the fulfillment of God's plan of salvation. He argues that the Jewish Scripture, when properly understood and interpreted, points to Christ, whose divinity was predicted by the Hebrew prophets. Trypho, conversing with Justin, had stated his difficulties with the Christian gospel: Christians break the law and place their hope in a crucified man. What surprised Trypho most was that Christians "still expect to receive favors from God when they disregard his commandments. Have you not read that a male who is not circumcised on the eighth day shall be cut off from the people?" (*Dial.* 10; Gen 17:4). In replying to Trypho's statement of the major differences between Christians and Jews, Justin starts by affirming monotheism: "There cannot be, nor has there ever been from eternity, any other god except him who created and formed the universe." The God of the Christians does not differ from the God of the Jews. "But our hope is not through Moses or through the law," Justin asserts. The law for Christians is already obsolete, for Christ himself is an everlasting and final law. After quoting Isa 51:4-5 and Jer 31:31-2, Justin adds that through the name of the crucified Jesus Christ many have turned to God and kept the faith even unto death. The crucified Christ "is indeed the new law, the new covenant," and Christians are "the true spiritual Israel and the descendents of Abraham" (*Dial.* 10-11). In the course of their conversation, Trypho tries to explore more fully the Christian attitude regarding the law and asks Justin whether a person who accepts Jesus to be Christ, believes in him and obeys him, yet at the same time observes the Mosaic law, would be saved? Justin replies that in his "opinion" such a person would be saved unless he attempts to influence Gentile Christians to observe the Mosaic law for the sake of their salvation. Here Justin displays a more tolerant attitude than some converts, who refused to have anything to do with Jewish converts to Christianity. In Justin's opinion, Gentile Christians "should receive them and associate with them in every way as kinfolk and brethren" (*Dial.* 47).

In addition to the *Dialogue with Trypho,* we have two other "apologies" by Justin. The first, written around AD 155, was addressed to the Emperor Antonius Pius (reigned AD 137–161), and the second, more in the nature of an appendix to the first, appeared early in the reign of Marcus Aurelius (AD 161–180). In each, Justin addresses the emperor directly because only if the emperor were convinced that accusations against Christians were baseless could the constant harassment and sporadic persecution of them be ended. Justin rejects certain charges against Christians such as atheism, cannibalism, and incest. It is his belief and hope that rational argument might convince the Roman authorities and the people that Christians are loyal to the empire and live according to high moral principles; that they are in fact their best "helpers and allies" for preserving and securing internal peace (*1 Apol.* 12).

In his *First Apology,* Justin asks that charges against Christians should be specific. If a crime is charged to a Christian, he requests, let it be investigated and punished. But no one should be punished just for the name alone, for being Christian. He criticizes this Roman attitude, protesting that the name alone should be neither good nor bad in itself. "So we ask that the actions of those who are denounced to you be investigated, in order that whoever is convicted may be punished as a criminal, but not as a Christian, and that whoever is shown to be innocent may be freed, committing no crime by being a Christian," Justin concludes (*1 Apol.* 4, 7).

Justin's Use of Greek Philosophy

Before his conversion to Christianity, Justin pursued philosophy in search of Truth. After his conversion, he did not give up Greek philosophy but regarded it as the best aspiration of the pagan mind and preparation for the gospel. Yet, for him Hebrew Scripture and Greek philosophy were not of equal importance in the rise of Christianity. Greek philosophy by itself could not have brought him to Christ, as the Hebrew prophets had. In his search for the Truth, Justin had to go beyond the "platonic theory of ideas," which, he acknowledged, "added wings to my mind," and "my folly was so great that I fully expected immediately to gaze upon God, for this is the goal of Plato's philosophy" (*Dial.* 2). After his conversion, Justin expressed his high appreciation of Socrates, who sought to bring people to the Truth. Like Socrates, Christians also were falsely accused as atheists (*2 Apol.* 10). Then he stated that Socrates, Heraclitus, and Abraham among others were Christians before Christ, for they were inspired by the divine Logos [the Word or Reason] (*1 Apol.* 46). The Stoic doctrine of *logos spermatikos*, which pictured the universe as wholly permeated by a cosmic logos, the seminal Word, helped Justin create a bridge between Christianity and philosophy. A seed of the Logos, "implanted in every race of men and women" (*2 Apol.* 8), directs us to the Truth and "dictates that those who are truly pious and philosophers should honor and love only the truth" (*1 Apol.* 2). Human reason has access to the Truth, although frequently deceived and in error.

While granting that the Logos had been sown in every person, Justin presented "the best of pagan thought" as "preparation for the gospel."[1] Justin then moved to develop and interpret the ideas of his Christian tradition against the background of his experience and insight into Greek philosophy. Here he seems to draw as well on the prologue to John's Gospel, but avoided referring more directly to this source, probably because of its popularity in gnostic circles. Some have suggested that the parable of the Sower (Matt 13:3–9), as well as frequent use of the images of sowing and planting in Hellenistic Judaism (Philo), contributed to Justin's usage. His use of the concept of *logos spermatikos*, which stands for "universal activity," or "the logos in a special activity," transcends the meaning ascribed to the logos by the philosophers.[2]

Justin identified the logos with Christ and designated the Logos-Christ as Teacher who is "both Son and Apostle of God the Father and Master of all, that is Jesus Christ, from whom also we received the name Christians" (*1 Apol.* 12). The Logos became incarnate, became man, by the will of God. The purpose of incarnation is "for the conversion and restoration of the human race" (*1 Apol.* 23). The fullness of the Truth was incarnate in Christ (*2 Apol.* 10). The lawgivers and philosophers uttered what is right or true according to their share of the Logos. Possessing a partial knowledge of Truth, they often contradicted themselves and each other because they did not know Truth com-

---

[1] Arthur H. Armstrong and Robert A. Markus, *Christian Faith and Greek Philosophy* (New York: Sheed & Ward, 1960), p. 144.

[2] See our review essay on L.N. Barnard, *St. Justin Martyr: First and Second Apologies* (1997) in *SVTQ* 42 (1998): 85–97.

pletely. The teachings of Plato and Christ "are not in every respect equal, as neither are those of the others, Stoics, poets, and historians." They spoke well because the Divine Logos, the Sower, was present in them. "But they who contradict themselves on the more important points appear not to have possessed the hidden understanding and the irrefutable knowledge. Therefore, whatever things were rightly said among all people are the property of the Christians" (*2 Apol.* 13). Justin confesses that while he strives with all his strength to be found a Christian, he does not claim to possess all revealed truth.

By confessing that the whole Logos, Truth, was revealed in the Word of God become flesh, Justin expresses a fundamental difference between the Christian faith and other religious movements in the age of syncretism. He maintains that what makes Christianity so radically different from other religions is that "we give to a crucified man second place after the unchangeable and eternal God" (*1 Apol.* 13). In his formulation of the doctrine of the Trinity, Justin came under the influence of the predominant philosophy of his time, known as Middle Platonism. Albinus, the best known Platonist of the second century, set forth a theory of a "First God," who transcends the universe, and being unmoved operates through the "Second God" and other lower intermediaries. Justin uses this hierarchical structure, employing the term "First God" (*1 Apol.* 60) and granting second place to the Logos and third place to the Spirit. He thus subordinates the persons of the Trinity. Therefore, some of his formulations would be regarded as inadequate when judged by the standard of the First Ecumenical Council at Nicaea (AD 325). In his apologies, Justin was using ambiguous language, which was in the process of evolving.

Justin's Account of Church Life

Through their writings, the second century apologists furnished many details about life in the church, and Justin gives the fullest account. The gospel is proclaimed and spread among "the powerless" as well as among the powerful: "Not only philosophers and scholars believed, but also artisans and people entirely uneducated" (*2 Apol.* 10). The church is the church of every race, both of "barbarians and Greeks." Those who once practiced immorality now embrace "chastity alone"; those who formerly made use of magic now dedicate themselves to "the good and unbegotten God"; and those who craved wealth and material possessions "now bring what we have in a common stock, and share with everyone in need." The people who belong to different groups with different customs now with the coming of Christ live in harmony with one another and "pray for our enemies" (*1 Apol.* 14). Then Justin cites the Sermon on the Mount to underline the moral power and grandeur of Christianity (*1 Apol.* 15). People who live the life of Christians could not be Rome's enemies, but the empire's "best helpers and allies in securing internal peace" (*1 Apol.* 12). They should be tolerated and protected, and not persecuted. The emperor should punish only those who do not live in accordance with Christ's teaching (*1 Apol.* 16). Justin would have subscribed to the words of Origen, the towering third-century apologist: "The more pious a man is, the more effective he is in helping the emperors" (*C.C.* 8.73).

Justin's account of the Sunday liturgy, reflecting the practice of the Roman church in his time, is among the richest sections of his apology. We may ask why he should write such a detailed description of sacraments, baptism, and Eucharist in a work addressed to the emperor. Apparently, since Christians were being accused of hideous crimes at their secret gatherings, Justin is determined to refute the charges step by step, so that the emperor may know the truth and consider the just demands of Christians that persecution be brought to an end.

Justin begins with an explanation of how citizens are integrated into the body of Christ, the entrance of catechumens into the Christian community. He explains that only those "who are persuaded and believe that the things we teach and say are true" are instructed to pray, fast, and ask God "for the remission of their past sins." Other Christians pray and fast along with the candidate for baptism. When the period of preparation is ended, they are brought to a place where there is water and baptized. They are washed "in the name of God the Father and Master of all and of our Savior, Jesus Christ, and of the Holy Spirit." They are made new through Christ. Thus, Christians have a first birth and a second birth, Justin explains. "At our birth we were born of necessity without our knowledge." At the second birth we become sons "of free choice and knowledge, and obtain remission of sins we have already committed." Justin was probably the first to call the baptismal washing "illumination" [*photismos*] (*1 Apol.* 61).

It is notable that in his description of this rite, Justin does not explicitly refer to the renunciation of the devil, which would, presumably, precede baptism itself. In the early church exorcisms were practiced, and Justin refers to this practice: "Many of our Christian people exorcizing in the name of Jesus

Christ, who was crucified under Pontius Pilate" (*2 Apol.* 6). He often warns about demonic powers that play significant roles in leading people astray, inspiring the persecution of Christians. Demonic powers "get hold of all who do not struggle to their utmost for their own salvation—as we do who, after being persuaded by the Word, renounce them and now follow the only unbegotten God through his Son" (*1 Apol.* 14). It is in this mention that Justin probably refers to the baptismal renunciation of the devil and all his works.

Further, Justin makes it clear that Baptism and Eucharist mark the boundaries of the Christian community. Only those who are baptized and are led to the assembly of brethren participate in the Eucharist. Upon finishing the prayers for the illuminated (i.e., new members of the church body) and for the faithful, the president [*ho prestos* = one standing before] sends up prayer and thanksgiving over the bread and mixed wine that have been brought to him. The congregation assents to this prayer, saying "Amen." Some translate the term *ho proestos* as "Ruler" or "head"; the one who is presiding is the "head of the brethren." In Ignatius's letters, the "ruler," or "head," or "president" would have been termed a "bishop." However, Justin does not use the title "bishop," since in Rome at his time the term was not yet clearly distinguished from "elder" [*presbyteros*].

In Justin's community, the deacons are very active. First, they are assistants to the head and the main links between him and the faithful. They distribute the consecrated gifts to those present and take them to those who are absent (*1 Apol.* 65). This is the earliest reference we have to sending consecrated gifts to those absent. From Justin's mid-second century text we also learn of the "prerequisites" for partaking of the Eucharist: only one who "believes that the things which we teach are true and has received the washing for forgiveness of sins and for rebirth, and who lives as Christ handed down to us." (*1 Apol.* 66). Faith, baptism, and Christian life are necessary, for in the Eucharist we do not receive "common bread nor common drink," but as in the incarnation God's Logos was incarnate in the flesh and blood of Jesus of Nazareth for our salvation, so in the Eucharist the bread and wine by transformation [*kata metabolēn*] become the flesh and blood of the Christ (*1 Apol.* 66).

In his description of the eucharistic celebration, Justin refers to the "Memoirs of the Apostles"—"which are called Gospels (*1 Apol.* 66)." The Memoirs composed by the apostles "are read as long as time permits" (*1 Apol.* 67). He does not specify how many gospels there are or which of them are included in the "Memoirs," yet it is most likely that he meant the Synoptic Gospels (Matthew, Mark, and Luke). This is the first known reference in Christian literature to the reading of the Gospels in a liturgical setting. Such readings at the Sunday worship service contributed to their canonization. Justin's account implies that reading of the Gospels was practiced everywhere, beyond the confines of Rome as well.

TATIAN, JUSTIN'S DISCIPLE

This first serious attempt to find a common ground between faith and philosophy gave birth to other similar endeavors. Justin's disciple Tatian challenged his master's vision. Like Justin, he joined the Christian church after a long philosophical and religious search and became Justin's student in Rome. Soon after Justin's martyrdom, he organized his own school. Around AD 172, he left Rome for his native Syria, where he wrote *Oration [Discourse] to the Greeks*. His apology is an attack upon paganism rather than a defense of Christianity. In contrast to Justin, he focused on the rupture between the two worlds, pagan and Christian, and displayed no interest in finding a common ground between Greek philosophy and the Christian faith. Upon his return to Syria from Rome, Tatian came under the influence of Gnosticism, which prompted him to form his own sect, the Encratites. Its members practiced extreme asceticism, rejected marriage, and replaced the wine in the Eucharist with water. Tatian is also known as the author of *Diatessaron* (ca. AD 175), a single narrative drawn from the four Gospels and used by some churches in the East until the fifth century, when it was replaced by the "separate Gospels" familiar to us. *Diatessaron* later came to be regarded as a humanly authored document, whereas the four Gospels were a divinely inspired human account of God's final revelation. Nevertheless, *Diatessaron* remains important evidence of the knowledge and recognition of the four Gospels in gnostic circles.

ATHENAGORAS OF ATHENS AND THEOPHILUS OF ANTIOCH

About a decade after Justin's martyrdom, these two philosophers continued the debate over the Logos doctrine. Athenagoras followed Justin's teaching, whereas Theophilus was closer to Tatian's.

Athenagoras, a Christian philosopher, wrote his apology, *A Plea Regarding Christians,*[3] which was addressed to the Emperors Marcus Aurelius and Lucius Aurelius Commodus. The major reason for Athenagoras to write his *Plea* was to answer specific accusations against Christians: atheism, cannibalism (related to "Thyestean feasts"), and Oedipean incest. To charge Christians with atheism is sheer "madness," he protested. Christian teaching affirms "one God who made the universe, being himself uncreated, and who made all things through his Word." And for this teaching, Christians "are treated unreasonably, by being slandered and by being persecuted" (*Plea* 4). Regarding the two other charges, Athenagoras believes that they are brought against Christians for no other reason than to convince their accusers that they have grounds for hating Christians. They are "fiction." The apologist attacks accusers for their own way of life. They live like fish, "for they gulp down whatever comes their way" (*Plea* 34). Then Athenagoras makes the observation: "Moreover, we have slaves, some more, others fewer. We cannot hide anything from them, yet not one of them has made up such tall stories against us" (*Plea* 35). The charges against Christians are raised and formulated by badly informed pagans, the apologist insists.

Athenagoras maintained the Logos Christology, and in his *Plea,* we find a highly developed doctrine of the Trinity. Christians acknowledge one God, whom Athenagoras describes with apophatic terms: uncreated, invisible, impassible, incomprehensible, and illimitable. He created the universe by his Word. Moreover, the Son of God is his Word "in idea and in actuality." The Son was not created, "for, since God is eternal mind, he had his Word within himself from the beginning." The Son, who is the eternal Word of the eternal God, came forth from God "to give form and actuality to all material things." The Holy Spirit who inspired the prophets is "flowing from God and returning like a ray of the sun." Those who hear that Christians are charged with atheism would be astonished to hear that Christians acknowledge and profess "God the Father, God the Son, and the Holy Spirit, and teach their unity in power and their distinction in ranks." Athenagoras emphasizes the oneness of the Father and the Son, and their mutual dwelling: "The Son is in the Father and the Father in the Son by the unity and power of the Spirit"

---

[3]For the text of Athenogoras' *Plea,* see Cyril C. Richardson, ed., *Early Christian Fathers,* Library of Christian Classics, vol. I (Philadelphia, PA: The Westminster Press, 1953), pp. 300–340.

(*Plea* 10). Here he overcomes Justin's ambiguity regarding the subordination of the Son.

Theophilus of Antioch is another spokesperson for the "Golden Age" of Christian apology. He was born into a pagan family, received a Greek education, and after study of the Hebrew Scriptures, particularly the Prophets, he was converted to Christianity. From Eusebius we learn (*H.E.* 4.20) that he became the sixth bishop of Antioch. His apology, *To Autolycus* (written about 180) was addressed to a pagan friend whom he wished to convert. In it, he argues that paganism, and its literature and philosophy, are futile. Plato, he charges, contradicts himself and "talks nonsense." This is in sharp contrast to Justin. Christianity, Theophilus contends, is superior to pagan religions as the truth that leads to salvation. Using Greek learning, he develops and clarifies the Logos doctrine of his predecessors. He distinguishes between God's internal Word [*logos endiathetos*] and His uttered Word [*logos prophorikos*].[4]

In Antioch, where Theophilus lived and worked, contacts between Jews and Christians contributed to friendlier relations between these two groups than in other Christian centers; they avoided conflicts with each other. The interpretative passages on Genesis contained in *To Autolycus* reveal Theophilus to be "the forerunner of the later Antiochian School" of biblical interpretation.[5] In their exegetical method, the Antiochians paid more attention to the literal and historical sense than the Alexandrians, who used an allegorical method. This does not mean that the Antiochians limited themselves to the literal meaning. They did not reject reasonable speculation and they did admit spiritual meaning of the text, beyond the literal or historical meanings. As an example, the Antiochians borrowed from the platonic tradition the term *theōria* to designate the sublime sense of a text, the meaning that is not obvious from the letter; yet, unlike allegory, it takes for granted the literal meaning as well.[6] Thus, according to the Antiochian method, biblical prophecy could only be partly understood as referring to its own time, for it also pointed to the future. Further, Antiochians differed from Alexandrians regarding the relationship between the Hebrew Scripture and the New

[4]Robert Grant has noted that the Stoics made this distinction and used these two terms, "reason" and "word or voice." To Philo, a transcendent logos would be analogous to the *logos endiathetos* and an immanent logos in the world to the *logos prophorikos*. See Robert Grant, *After the New Testament* (Philadelphia, PA: Fortress Press: Philadelphia, 1967), p. 146.
[5]R. Grant, *After the New Testament*, p. 134.
[6]See A. Vaccari, "La *Theoria* nella scuola esegetica di Antiochias," *Bib* vol. 1 (Rome, 1920): 1–30.

Testament. The Antiochians regarded the Old Testament as a preparation for the New: as a sketch is to a finished picture. This preparation implied a promise to be fulfilled. In contrast, the Alexandrians emphasized the prophesies as prefiguration, not necessarily preparation, of the new event: the future reality prefigured in the Old Testament text is already present.[7]

TERTULLIAN

Near the end of the second century, Tertullian (ca. AD 160–220), a Roman jurist attracted by the willingness of Christians to suffer for their faith, left paganism and joined the Christian community in Rome. After his conversion around AD 193, he returned to Carthage, the place of his birth, and started writing his apology, *To the Nations* (published around AD 197). It was a vigorous and brilliant response to the Roman charges against Christianity. In his apology, he asks that if Christians are "the most wicked of people, why do you treat us so differently from those who are on a par with us, from all other criminals?" In court, although criminals are given full liberty "to answer the charge and to cross-question, since it is unlawful for people to be condemned without defense or without a hearing," Christians are not given this same opportunity. "No matter what false charge is made against us, we must be made to confess it; for example, how many murdered babies one has devoured, how many deeds of incest one has committed under cover of darkness" (*A.N.* 2). To the charge that Christians do not worship the gods, Tertullian's answer is firm and direct: "We cease worshipping your gods when we find out that they are non-existent" (*A.N.* 10): the object of "our worship" is "the one God who is invisible, although he may be seen, intangible, although manifested by grace; immeasurable, although he may be measured by human senses" (*A.N.* 17). Christians, Tertullian complains, are blamed "if the Tiber floods, if the Nile fails to rise, if there is an earthquake, a famine, a plague— the cry is heard: 'Toss the Christians to the lions!'" (*A.N.* 40). Tertullian challenges the Roman officials: "Crucify us—torture us—destroy us! Your iniquity is the proof of our innocence. The more you torture us, the more numerous we are every time . . . The blood of Christians is seed" (*A.N.* 50).[8]

---

[7]See our article, "The Antiocheans and the Temptation Story," StPatr Vol. VII, ed. F.L. Cross (Berlin, 1966): 496–502.

[8]From Tertullian's *Apologetical Works*, in The Fathers of the Church, Vol. 10 (2d ed., Washington D.C.: Catholic University Press, 1971). Extensive selections from Tertullian's *Apology* are given in B. D. Ehrman, *After the New Testament*, pp. 75–82.

The Debate between Celsus and Origen

Justin's apologies, addressed to the emperors, reverberated through Roman official circles. His works were known to some friends of the Roman rulers, one of these being Celsus, a respected philosopher and "established intellectual," whose examination of Christianity, *True Doctrine* (ca. AD 178)[9]—the most serious attack on the Christian religion in the second century—could have been a response to Justin. The original text of *True Doctrine* has not survived, but substantial quotations from it appear in Origen's *Contra Celsum*. There were other hostile pagan criticisms of Christianity written during the second century, usually based on unsubstantiated rumors and general gossip, but Celsus' attack was based on his reading and interpretation of Hebrew Scripture and basic Christian beliefs known by him.

Celsus pointed out inconsistencies in the Hebrew Scriptures, criticizing the anthropomorphism attributed to God, especially in the book of Genesis. Furthermore, he protested, the Jews were totally uneducated and had composed an improbable and crude story. Celsus accuses both Christians and Jews of ignorance and want of education. The more reasonable Jews and Christians "are ashamed of these things and try to allegorize them," but neither the use of allegorical interpretation nor any other intellectual device could, in his opinion, save Genesis as a respectable religious document (*C.C.* 4.36, 48).

It fell to a representative of the next generation of apologists, Origen, to answer Celsus' analysis. Origen was born in Alexandria around AD 185, and by AD 203, before he was twenty years of age, he was head of the Christian catechetical school there. In this intellectual center of the ancient world, he was in constant dispute with educated pagans. In his mature years, around AD 248, he assumed the task of answering Celsus' *True Doctrine*, the most serious attack upon Christian belief thus far. Origen was a man of great erudition as well as knowledge and devotion to the Biblical tradition, an expert in Greek mythology and philosophy. Genesis, he pointed out, in its literal meaning, could hardly be regarded as more shameful than the outrageous stories about the gods of the pagan Greeks, "obviously shameful even if they are to be interpreted allegorically" (*C.C.* 4.48).

Celsus had turned directly to the basic beliefs of the Christians, which he had learned of from disputes with Christians and from observing their

[9]Also known as *True Discourse* or *True Reason*—Author's note.

lives. He attacked the very core of their faith: Jesus, his incarnation, and resurrection. Celsus appeared to have been rather frustrated with Christian obstinacy in worshipping Jesus: "in fact they worship to an extraordinary degree this man who appeared recently" (*C.C.* 8.12). If you teach them that Jesus is not the Son of God, Celsus complained, that worshipping him is inconsistent with monotheism, and that they ought to worship God alone, "they would no longer be willing to listen to you unless you included Jesus as well" (*C.C.* 8.14). Origen retorts that Celsus did not consider the saying in the Gospel of John: "I and my Father are one" (John 10:30; 14:10–11; 17:21–22), and insists that Christians worship but the one God. In worshipping Jesus, they do not worship "a man who appeared recently, as though he had not existed previously, for we believe him who says, 'Before Abraham I was' and who affirms 'I am the truth'" (John 8:58, 14:6). Christians therefore are monotheists, who "worship the Father of the truth and the Son who is the truth" (*C.C.* 8.12).

Celsus had not seen the purpose of an incarnation, a descent on the part of God, and had asked mockingly: "Was it in order to learn what was going on among men?" (*C.C.* 4.3) Then he took up the argument against Christians by using "ancient doctrines," which are platonic: God is good and beautiful, and if he comes down to men, "He must undergo change, a change from good to bad, from beautiful to shameful, from happiness to misfortune, and from what is best to what is most wicked" (*C.C.* 4.14). In his reply, Origen first discussed God's descent to human affairs, as it is given in the Bible: "While remaining unchanged in essence, he comes down in his providence and care over human affairs. He who was originally 'in the form of God' came down because of his love, 'emptied himself' that men might be able to receive him." He who came down "underwent no change from what is best to what is most wicked; for in what way is goodness and love to man most wicked?" (*C.C.* 4.15). Discussing the Incarnation, Celsus and Origen presented and contrasted the platonic and Biblical views of God.

They clashed again over the doctrine of the Resurrection. Origen bluntly states that Celsus did not understand the Christian teaching regarding the Resurrection. Celsus had imagined that Christians talk about bodily resurrection because "they misunderstood the doctrine of reincarnation" (*C.C.* 7.32). Celsus had asked: "For what sort of body, after being entirely corrupted, could return to its original nature and that same condition which it had before it was dissolved?" He conceded that God "might be able to provide an everlasting life; but, as Heraclitus says, 'Corpses ought to be thrown away as worse than dung'" (C.C. 5.14). Origen answers that Celsus misinterpreted the Christian teaching of the bodily resurrection, and then falsely accused Christians. Christian doctrine does not maintain that the dead would live in the same body after their resurrection. To answer the question, "How are the dead raised? In what kind of body do they come?" Origen cites Paul's Letter to the Corinthians (1 Cor 15:35–38), and observes: "There is a difference between the body that is, as it were, sown, and that which is, as it were, raised from it." A natural body is raised as a spiritual body (C.C. 5.18, 19), he concludes.

Among the other accusations Celsus had made against Christians were the performance of rites and the conducting of doctrinal teaching "in secret." They do so "to escape the death penalty that hangs over them," Celsus had explained (C.C. 1.3). Secret gatherings were illegal, yet Christians met at night and at daybreak for their sacred meals. It was a common belief among Greeks and Romans that magic practices require the cover of darkness; therefore, they believed that Christians relegated magical practices to nightly meetings.[10] Christians were driven by some unknown powers, which they got "by pronouncing the name of certain daemons and incantations." Origen was quick to correct this interpretation, stressing that Christians get their power not "by incantations but by the name of Jesus." He accused Celsus of using the charge of practicing magic to justify persecution of Christians. Celsus, however, could actually have known some gnostic groups that practiced magic and claimed to be Christian.

Origen, like other apologists before him, rejected the charge that Christians practiced magic. Jesus was not a magician but an exorcist, who "by the finger of God cast out demons" (Luke 11:20). The disciples and followers of Jesus exorcised demons in the name of Jesus Christ. Christian missionaries likewise exorcised the demonic powers in the world in which they were active. They did not introduce new gods, Tertullian insisted, but exorcised old demons (De Anima 1). Actually, Justin Martyr had previously recorded that Christians prayed to be saved from demons by the power of the name of Jesus Christ (Dial. 30ff). In addition to the name of Jesus, said Justin Mar-

---

[10]See S. Benko, Pagan Rome, p. 126.

tyr, Christians used the sign of the cross in their exorcisms, as Tertullian also recounted.[11] By making the sign of the cross, Christians protect themselves. They also used the Lord's Prayer as a prayer of exorcism.

Celsus had reiterated the official Roman position that Christians belonged to a new movement; they appeared without a tradition. To strengthen his accusations, he drew upon Jewish objections and attacks upon their Christian opponents. Celsus appeared to have been well informed about the Jewish-Christian disputes. Both groups believe that "a certain savior was prophesied to be coming to dwell among mankind, but they do not agree as to whether the prophesied one has come or not" (*C.C.* 3.1). He also had known that Jews often criticized Christians for neglecting Jewish laws (circumcision, keeping of the Sabbath, food laws) and yet, at the same time, Christians claimed to have origins in the Jewish tradition. As to their claims to this ancient tradition, Celsus had pointed to two contradictory laws, one given to Moses and another to Jesus, and he asked: "Who is wrong, Moses or Jesus?" Origen, in response, argued that here Celsus "has fallen into a very vulgar error concerning the meaning of the Bible" (*C.C.* 7.18). By contrasting two laws on the basis of their literal sense, Celsus intended to present Christians as people without roots, that is, people of a new religion, without traditions and therefore without legitimacy.[12]

Celsus had been no friend to Jews. He had disliked both Jews and Christians, but Judaism was a legally and religiously "acceptable" belief system, both for him and for the Roman authorities. The Jews had become a particular ethnic group within the empire, and proudly traced their origin to the distant past. They had ancient laws that they had maintained up to that present time and Celsus had noted that they "observe a worship which may be very peculiar but is at least traditional" (*C.C.* 5.25). Further, after the Second Roman-Jewish War (AD 132–35) and their suppression under Hadrian, the Jews presented no danger to internal peace.

The Christian religion, on the other hand, was unacceptable, and the Christians were perceived as politically dangerous. For their refusal to swear by the "genius" of the emperor, they could expect probable punishment. (*C.C.* 8.67–8). Celsus had exhorted Christians to "help" the emperor, to

---

[11]S. Benko, *Pagan Rome*, p. 118f.
[12]See R.L. Wilken, *Christians as the Romans Saw Them*, pp. 112–7.

"cooperate" with him and "fight" for him. Origen answered that Christians render the emperor "divine help," which is expressed and made effective through piety (*C.C.* 8.73). We find a similar defense in Justin's writings (*1 Apol.* 12). Celsus in *True Doctrine*, however, had provided the "ideological" justification for continued general persecution of Christians into the third century.

Nevertheless, Origen's reply to Celsus sums up the promotion and defense of the Christian movement by the apologists.[13] Justin and the other second-century apologists had "constructed a platform" for Origen's monumental *Contra Celsum,* which was composed in his mature age with great care and which abounded with proofs of the widest scholarship of that age.

Conclusion

The second century apologists went beyond the defense of Christianity. They contributed to Christian theological development and struggled to express the Christian faith in new terms. Justin Martyr pointed the way, convinced that faithfulness to the gospel and openness to the world and its needs were indispensable for the mission and expansion of the church in the universal empire. Later theologians would attack him for some of his statements about the incarnate Logos when judged by subsequent theological developments and standards; but to evaluate Justin and all the apologists, properly, we must judge them in the context of their time, their apologetic interest, and their evolving theological language. A well-known modern theologian has rightly noted: "People like Justin and Origen unhesitatingly gave their life for a christological or Trinitarian faith which they could not formulate adequately."[14] L. N. Barnard, a recent interpreter of Justin's apologies, hails Justin as "the first thinker after Saint Paul to grasp the universalistic element in Christianity and to sum up, in one bold stroke, the whole history of civilization as finding its consummation in Christ." His accomplishment "was the seedbed of the later church."[15]

---

[13]See Henry Chadwick, "Introduction" to *Origen,* Contra Celsum (Cambridge University Press: Cambridge, England, 1953), p. ix.

[14]Yves Congar, *Diversity and Communion* (Mystic, CT: Twenty-Third Publications, 1985), p. 13.

[15]Leslie W. Barnard, *St. Justin Martyr: The First and Second Apologies* (New York: Paulist Press, 1997), p. 245; translated with introduction and notes.

CHAPTER ELEVEN

ST IRENAEUS: THE CHURCH'S CONFLICT WITH GNOSTICISM

The Rise of Gnosticism

Gnosticism was a syncretistic movement, influenced by Hellenistic philosophical systems and religious traditions. Elements from Platonism, Stoicism, Zoroastrianism, Judaism, Christianity, and other religions can be detected in gnostic speculations. Yet, the actual origin of Gnosticism has eluded the historians.[1]

The Christian Fathers considered Simon Magus of Acts 8:9–24 the one "from whom all heresies got their start" (*A.H.* 1.23.2). St Irenaeus, bishop of Lyons, noted "that all those who in any way adulterate the truth and do injury to the preaching of the church are the disciples and successors of Simon, the magician of Samaria" (*A.H.* 1.27.4). One difficulty of these statements historically, however, is that the Simon we meet in Luke 8 belonged to the first century and the developed Gnosticism ascribed to or taught by him did not exist until the middle of the second century, certainly after his death. D.J. Unger records that some resolved this difficulty by arguing that Simon Magus was deified following his death, and in the second century he "became an object" of gnostic speculation, so much so that "a system was built around him, that was known by his name, although he did not originate it."[2] Or, equally probable, Justin Martyr assigned the role of archheretic to Simon, "a Samaritan from the village of Gitta" (*1 Apol.* 26.1–3). It

---

[1]Although now more than forty years old, the proceedings of the 1966 Messina conference on the origins of Gnosticism are still worth consulting: see *Le origini dello gnosticismo. Colloquio di Messina 13–18 Aprile 1966*, ed. Ugo Bianchi (Leiden, 1967).

[2]See Dominic J. Unger, *St. Irenaeus, Bishop of Lyons: Against the Heresies* (Ancient Christian Writers I; Mahwah, NJ: Paulist Press, 1992), p. 227f; translated and annotated.

is possible that Simon of Gitta lived in the second century and should not be identified with Simon Magus of Acts.

At the close of the nineteenth century and the start of the twentieth, many scholars had assumed that Gnosticism was a Christian heresy, the product of an "acute hellenization of Christianity." The gnostic documents discovered at Nag Hammadi now indicate a gradual development of Gnosticism, with roots that reach into the period roughly contemporaneous with Christianity but developed independently of it.[3]

There were conflicts and contacts between early gnostics and Christians in the first century. The Apostle Paul, for instance, argued with those members of his churches who accepted ideas that reflected disdain for the body, immorality, and "proud tolerance" of conduct which even the pagans did not accept (1 Cor 5:1–2). The apostle warned that those who had toyed with these ideas [pneumatikoi] were in danger of losing their freedom in Christ and adopting a way of life that leads to slavery. These so-called "spirit-people" live without regard for others or for the community of which they are members. They disregard any moral restraint. They behave as if they were above ordinary mortals, professing that "all things are lawful for [them]" (1 Cor 6:12).

The principle that underlines such conduct in the church in Corinth is spelled out in the second-century gnostic Gospel of Philip:

> Light and darkness, life and death, right and left, are brothers of one another. They are inseparable. Because of this, neither are the good good, nor the evil evil, nor is life life, nor death death. For this reason each one will dissolve into its earliest origin. But those who are exalted above the world are indissoluble, eternal.[4]

The historical Jesus was of no interest to the "spirit people." Only the heavenly Christ was important to them. By separating Christ from Jesus, gnostics denied the Incarnation, bodily resurrection, and the Eucharist. Refuting the gnostic claims that Paul was one of their own, Irenaeus simply referred to Paul's Christology, which does not know any other Christ but the

---

[3] Pheme Perkins, "Gnosticism," *NJBC* 80:79.

[4] See George W. MacRae, *Studies in the New Testament and Gnosticism* (Good News Studies; Wilmington, DE: Michael Glazier, Inc., 1987), p. 256. C.K. Barrett, *Commentary on the First Epistle to the Corinthians* (Black's New Testament Commentaries; London: Adam & Charles Black, 1968), 6:8, 12; James M. Robinson, ed., *Coptic Gnostic Library: A Complete Edition of the Nag Hammadi Codices* (Leiden: E.J. Brill, 2000), p. 142.

one who suffered, was buried, and rose again. For Paul, "an impassible Christ did not come down into Jesus, but Jesus, since he was Christ, suffered for us, slept and rose again, descended and ascended, the Son of God became Son of Man" (*A.H.* 3.18.3).

After Paul's martyrdom, the church remembered and praised him as the missionary and teacher of the Christian way of believing and living. He had urged his co-workers not to be occupied "with myth and endless genealogies which promote speculations rather than the divine training that is in faith" (1 Tim 1:4). He had also advised Timothy to "guard what has been entrusted" to him, and to "avoid the godless chatter and contradictions of what is falsely called knowledge" (1 Tim 6:20). The Evangelist Luke, the author of Acts, attributed to Paul a farewell speech to the Ephesian elders, in which he warned them of impending danger after his death: "I know that after my departure fierce wolves will come in among you, not sparing the flock, and from among your own selves will arise men speaking perverse things, to draw away the disciples after them" (Acts 20:29–30). In the closing decade of the second century, the memory of Paul was "liberated" from the gnostic embrace and fully rehabilitated.

The struggle against incipient Gnosticism is reflected in the Fourth Gospel as well. Irenaeus claims that John wrote his Gospel against a gnostic named Cerinthus, who was active at the close of the first century (*A.H.* 3.11.1). Irenaeus identified him as a syncretist of Jewish origin, who for a certain period lived in Alexandria. Here, in the capital of Egypt, he tried to harmonize Judaism with Platonism and Christianity. Cerinthus' teaching about Christ and Jesus is recognizably gnostic. He maintains that at the baptism of Jesus,

> the Christ came down into Jesus in the form of a dove from the Principality which is over all. And then he proclaimed the unknown Father and worked miracles. At the end the Christ left Jesus, who suffered and was raised, but the Christ remained impassible, being spiritual (*A.H.* 1.26.1).

The Christ of the Fourth Gospel hardly fits into such a docetic-gnostic scheme. Jesus was the Word "become flesh." God, who created and loved the world, sent his Son into the world to save it by means of the cross (John 12:31–36; 17). The Evangelist John focuses upon the death on the cross, resurrection, and ascension of Jesus Christ. The crucified Jesus is clearly the glorified Son. Yet, his Gospel, like Paul's letters, was twisted and used by gnostics in the second century for their own purposes.

BASIC GNOSTIC TENETS

By the middle of the second century, the church encountered full-grown Gnosticism. This term covers numerous sects, all of whom differ in their speculations, moral teachings, and ritual practices; but they had in common the doctrine of salvation through acquisition of knowledge [gnosis]. They regarded the God of the Hebrew Scripture, who had created this evil world, as an inferior divine being. It was impossible, they believed, for the true God, who is superior to the god of the Bible, to enter into contact with matter. Commenting on *Eugnostos the Blessed*–a gnostic text free of Christian dressing or influence–C. K. Barrett writes: "The chief problem in gnosis is not to evolve a doctrine of salvation but to explain how creation can have taken place . . . If spirit (deity, immortality) and matter are absolute opposites, unable to have contact with each other, how could the latter be produced by the former?"[5] The Gnostics denied the Incarnation of God in Christ and proclaimed a doctrine of salvation that had nothing to do with the death of Christ, but rather depended on knowledge [gnosis] of the truth of human existence, and of true human origin and eventual return to the world of light. They regarded themselves as "spiritual," and all others as either "psychics" or "somatics."[6]

Our knowledge of Gnosticism was much enlarged by the discovery of some gnostic texts at Nag Hammadi, Egypt, about three hundred miles south of Cairo, in 1945. An English translation of thirteen codices including fifty-two texts appeared in 1977. Modern scholars suppose that the documents were

---

[5]See C.K. Barrett, *New Testament Background*, p. 107.

[6]The use of "Gnosticism" as a blanket term to cover a multitude of different belief systems belonging to the second century is a scholarly convention of barely two centuries standing. This chapter is mostly concerned with "Gnosticism" insofar as it was regarded as constituting a serious threat to the emerging Orthodox Christian consensus as represented by such churchmen as St Irenaeus of Lyons, though informed by the light shed on these second-century movements by the discovery of the library at Nag Hammadi. For a discussion of modern doubts about the use of such a category as "Gnosticism," see Michael Allen Williams, *Rethinking "Gnosticism": An Argument for Dismantling a Dubious Category* (Princeton, NJ: Princeton University Press, 1996). A book that gives a good account of how Gnosticism and Christianity may have related is Alastair H.B. Logan's *Gnostic Truth and Christian Heresy: A Study in the History of Gnosticism* (Edinburgh: T&T Clark, 1996). An older book that raises many doubts about the traditional account is Simone Pétrement's *A Separate God: The Christian Origins of Gnosticism* (San Francisco: HarperSanFrancisco, 1990; first published in French as *Le dieu séparé: les origines du gnosticisme* in 1984).

translated from second- or third-century Greek texts into the Coptic language of the fourth century. In imitation of early Christian literature, the gnostic sects produced books of diverse literary forms: gospels, letters, acts, and apocalypses. Some are expressions of Christian-oriented gnostics, while others witness to the existence of gnostic movements outside Christianity altogether.

A central document of Gnosticism is *The Apocryphon [Secret Book] of John*, written around AD 180. Irenaeus, who drew on it when he wrote *Against the Heresies* in AD 185–90, was familiar with some version of this text. Basilides and Valentinus, two leading gnostics, also were familiar with the myth of the *Apocryphon of John*. It includes a vision of the Highest Deity, the Unknown God, who is above the God of Creation. The supreme Deity is defined in strictly non-anthropomorphic terms: "He is the invisible Spirit of whom it not right to think of as a God, or something similar. For he is more than a god, since there is nothing above him, for no one lords it over him."[7] He is total perfection, described in negative [*apophatic*] terms: He is unsearchable, immeasurable, invisible, un-nameable, and ineffable. "He is not in perfection, nor in blessedness, nor in divinity, but he is far superior." Then, in positive terms, He is an aeon-giving aeon, life-giving life, knowledge-giving knowledge, mercy-giving mercy, and grace-giving grace.

The Highest Deity is the head of all the aeons or entities. They emanate from Him. The last aeon is the Sophia, who "conceives a thought from herself," the desire to bring forth "a likeness out of herself without the consent of the Spirit." What she desired was born of her "which was imperfect and different from her in appearance." Thus, her own desire created a monster, and Sophia called him Yaltabaoth (the Yahweh of the Bible). He was responsible for the creation of our world, and he appointed angels to rule over his creation. To the angels around him, which had their source in him, he said: "I am a jealous god, and there is no other god beside me." This saying implies that there exists another God, "for if there were no other one, of whom would he be jealous?"[8]

Yaltabaoth creates man in his image and likeness, to whom he gives a material body. He planted in woman sexual desire to produce "copies of the bodies," which he inspired "with his counterfeit spirit."[9] This tragic combi-

---

[7]2; 3 *A.J.* in J.M. Robinson, ed., *Nag Hammadi Codices*, p. 105f; p. 107.
[8]Ibid., p. 112.
[9]Ibid., p. 119.

nation of man imprisoned in the body and woman with her sexual desire, perpetuate human slavery, according to the gnostics.[10]

Ignorance of Sophia, therefore, is the origin of the demiurge (Yaltabaoth) and the creation of his world. Yaltabaoth took great power from his mother and then removed himself from her. Sophia clearly saw the consequence of her desire, but she could not prevent Yaltabaoth from moving away from the places where he was born and creating for himself other entities "with a flame of luminous fire which still exists now."[11] Only a redeemer from above could remove the original ignorance with saving knowledge. In *The Apocryphon of John*, Jesus is this Redeemer, who came to impart the saving knowledge [gnosis] and to remind those in the realm of darkness about their heavenly origin.

There are variations on the gnostic myth, but the *Apocryphon of John* contains the main parts. The Unknown God, the monster creator God, and the coming of the Redeemer characterize second-century gnostic sects. The true God did not and could not create this hostile world, which was the creation of an inferior God, the demiurge, or Yahweh. In the gnostic view, human beings belong to this evil world. Gnostics go beyond the philosophical vision of the fall of the soul into matter, and its redemption through gnosis. They do not necessarily regard the soul as the human's true being, which needs liberation. What is worthy of salvation is apparently the "spark of the divine," the human's self, the human's true being, imprisoned in his material body. As Irenaeus has noted, some gnostic myths offered salvation to the soul, but the body was definitely excluded (*A.H.* 5.19.2). The Redeemer from above rescues the divine spark of light imprisoned in the world of matter, but not the whole human being. Awakened by gnosis, knowledge from God and of God brought by the Redeemer, the divine spark separates from darkness and yearns to go back to the divine realm of light. Gnosis liberates human beings from the rule of the world and the oppressive authority of its creator.

Some gnostics adopted the person of Christ as the one who brought knowledge of liberation. The Supreme Deity, the True God, raised him from the realm of the dead to transmit his secret teaching to his disciples. In *The Apocryphon of John*, the resurrected Jesus reveals the mysteries to John, the son of Zebedee. Nevertheless, in spite of its "Christian" opening, *The Apocryphon of John* contains no other significant Christian element.

[10]Ibid., p. 119.
[11]Ibid., p. 110.

JEWISH AND CHRISTIAN GNOSTICS

After the Jewish-Roman Wars of AD 70 and 135, a mood of despair spread through the Jewish diaspora, and rabbis were complaining about the strange teachings of certain Jews, about the existence of two Gods. These heretical Jews insisted that the lower God, the creator of the world, was expressed in anthropomorphic images, which were not suitable for the higher God.[12] They insisted there was no image of the Unknown God. Those who accepted this dualistic view of the gnostics abandoned the apocalyptic hope for the immediate coming of the Messiah.

Basilides, a well-known gnostic teacher and a hellenized Jew, was a member of the church in Alexandria around AD 130–155. He taught about the need for liberation from Yahweh and all the evil that belongs to his creation. The transcendent God, according to Basilides, was the Supreme Deity. Basilides thus rebelled against Yahweh, whom he considered an "aggressive" deity, confessed a kind of spiritual Christ, and rejected the crucifixion.[13]

Valentinus, to whom we shall refer in the following pages, was widely recognized as "the greatest gnostic of all time." He was a Christian gnostic, influenced by the Gospel of John, whose images contributed to second-century gnostic developments. Valentinians, among whom the Fourth Gospel was widely circulated, used terms such as Truth, Logos, and Life, which have a "Johannine ring." They also were attracted to John's Christology of the divine descent and ascent. In "I am," a revelatory proclamation of Christ, they visualized the figure of the gnostic redeemer, which appeared in later gnostic sources. In sources that can be demonstrated chronologically to be pre-Christian, we find no evidence of a gnostic redeemer myth.[14] There is, on the other hand, support for post-Christian development of a gnostic redeemer myth, "in which Christian belief regarding Jesus was one of the crucial building blocks."[15]

Although there were Jewish and Christian gnostics, Gnosticism was neither the product of the synagogue nor of the church. Jews or Christians who accepted and professed the basic teachings of the gnostics put themselves

---

[12]Gilles Quispel, "Gnosticism from Its Origins to the Middle Ages," *Encyclopedia of Religion*, V: 567ff.

[13]W.H.C. Frend, *Rise of Christianity*, p. 205f.

[14]See M. Hengel, *The Son of God*, p. 33.

[15]See J.D.G. Dunn, *Partings of the Ways*, p. 9.

outside the boundary lines of Judaism and Christianity. Gnosticism emerged as a syncretistic religion, with a new spiritual principle.[16] A radical dualism, despair over the power of evil, and revolt against the creator of the universe characterize the founding vision of this new movement. By rejecting the first article of the Christian creed: "I believe in one God, Father Almighty, maker of heaven and earth, and all things visible and invisible," gnostics laid the basis for a new religion.[17]

St Irenaeus' Doctrinal Debates

Our major source of information about the second-century gnostic teachers and their speculations, before the discovery of the Nag Hammadi gnostic library in 1945, was Bishop Irenaeus of Lyons (ca. AD 130–200). Even after that discovery, the predominant opinion among scholars has been that Irenaeus was "most reliable." The well-known Biblical scholar Raymond E. Brown, in reviewing Elaine Pagels's book, *Gnostic Gospels,* firmly defends Irenaeus' anti-gnostic writings as the "key" to the meaning of the very obscure gnostic texts.[18] Brown considers Irenaeus a trustworthy guide in interpreting gnostic teachings.

Irenaeus was well acquainted with gnostic sources, as well as with Christ-ian anti-gnostic literature. Two major works by him have survived: *Refutation and Overthrow of Knowledge Falsely So-Called* (usually referred to as *Against Heresies,* AD 185–90), and *Proof of the Apostolic Preaching,* "a synthesis of ortho-dox teaching at the end of the second century," written shortly after *Against Heresies.*[19]

Irenaeus was born in Asia Minor, probably Smyrna, and died in Lyons, Gaul. As a boy of fifteen or so, he had seen Polycarp (ca. AD 70–156), the Bishop of Smyrna. Much later, in his letter to Florinus, whom he tried to dis-suade from embracing the teachings of the gnostic Valentinus, Irenaeus men-tioned Polycarp. "When I was still a boy, I saw you in Lower Asia in Polycarp's company, when . . . you wanted to be in favor with him." Refer-

---

[16]Hans Jonas, *Gnostic Religion* (2d ed.; Boston, MA: Beacon Press, 1985), p. 33ff.

[17]See Gedaliahu G. Stroumsa, "Gnostic Temptation," *Numen* XXVII.2 (1980): 280f.

[18]*NY Times Book Review* (Jan. 20, 1980): 3. Brown cites approvingly Pheme Perkins, known for her contribution to gnostic research. Perkins characterized Pagel's study as marred by "hasty generaliza-tions, over-interpretation of the text to fit a predetermined scheme, and lack of sympathetic balance."

[19]Carolyn Osiek, "Second-Century Church Centers," *NJBC* 80:61.

ring to his childhood, Irenaeus continued, "I have a clearer recollection of events at that time than of recent happenings–what we learn in childhood develops along with the mind and becomes a part of it–so that I can describe the place where blessed Polycarp sat and talked, his goings out and comings in, the character of his life, his personal appearance, his addresses to crowded congregations." He remembers how Polycarp spoke of his relations with John and with the others who had seen the Lord, "how he repeated their words from memory." What he had heard from the eyewitnesses of "the Word of life" (1 John 1:1), Polycarp proclaimed "in complete harmony with Scripture." Irenaeus adds that he listened eagerly at that time, not committing what had been said to writing, but "learning them by heart" (*H.E.* 5.20.4–8). In the letter, he takes for granted that Christian tradition is in conflict with gnostic teachings. The tradition committed to the churches has been open, public, not the secret tradition of the gnostic sects. It is open to historical investigation and serves as the basis of religious authority.

Irenaeus left Asia Minor for Rome, where he studied in the school of Justin Martyr. From Rome, he went to Lyons, Gaul, where he was ordained presbyter in AD 164. After serving the church as presbyter for about twelve years, he was sent in AD 177 to Rome with a letter to Eleutherius, the bishop of Rome, to plead for a tolerant attitude toward Montanists, and probably to acquaint the church in the capital with the dangers of persecution of the churches in Gaul.

MONTANISM

This anti-gnostic, charismatic movement originated around AD 157, when Montanus, a native of Phrygia and a recent convert to Christianity, proclaimed himself a prophet of a new gospel.[20] He criticized the church for its decline in prophecy, ethical standards, and the immediate expectation of the end. He warned Christians to be ready, to prepare themselves with fasting and continence for the coming of the "New Jerusalem." Prisca and Maximilla, who claimed to be prophetesses, joined Montanus. The Montanists attracted attention by reviving the gift of glossolalia, or speaking in tongues. In the beginning of its appearance and proclamation of the "new gospel," Montanism spread rather rapidly and reached Rome. By the end of the sec-

---

[20]On Montanism, see, most recently, Christine Trevett, *Montanism: Gender, Authority and the New Prophecy* (Cambridge: Cambridge University Press, 1996).

ond century, it became a challenge to the church. Among its converts, the best known was Tertullian, who joined this charismatic movement in AD 207. Maximilla's prophecy, that after her "there will be no further prophets but only the end," was not fulfilled, and Montanism displayed signs of spiritual exhaustion.[21] The Parousia, the second coming of Christ, did not come, and glossolalia disappeared. Already in the first century Christians were warned about "the postponement of the end." Paul had written to the Thessalonians: "The Lord will come unexpectedly, like a thief in the night." The author of 2 Peter warned that scoffers would come, saying, "Where is the promise of his coming? For ever since the fathers fell asleep, all things have continued as they were from the beginning of creation." These scoffers ignore one fact, the author adds, "that with the Lord one day is as a thousand years, and a thousand years as one day. The Lord is not slow about this promise, as some count slowness, but is forbearing towards you, not wishing that any should perish, but that all should reach repentance" (2 Pet 3:4, 9).

What Irenaeus thought about the Montanists and their claims is not found in his extant writings. He pleaded for a tolerant attitude toward them, but undoubtedly rejected their claims that ecstatic outbursts and utterances were manifestations of a new age. He would not dispute their emphasis on spiritual gifts, but would reject the "disorderly character"[22] of Montanism.

After his Roman mission, Irenaeus returned to Gaul to succeed Pontinus, the bishop of Lyons, who had been martyred during the persecution of AD 177. During his tenure as the main pastor of the church (AD 177/8–ca. 200) Christianity was spreading and taking root in Gaul.

THE QUARTODECIMAN CONTROVERSY

A decade after Irenaeus' return to Gaul, there was a change of leadership in the church of Rome. Victor (AD 189–98), who succeeded Eleutherius, was a North African bishop of Latin stock. He became involved in disputes with the churches of Asia Minor, and this is known as the Quartodeciman controversy. For the second time in the second century, Rome and Asia Minor came into conflict over the dates of the celebration of Easter. The churches of Asia Minor celebrated the Pascal feast on the 14 of Nisan, which was not necessar-

---

[21]Kurt Aland, "Montanus" and "Montanism," *Encyclopedia of Religion*, X: 81ff.
[22]See Robert M. Grant, *Irenaeus of Lyons* (New York: Routledge, 1997), p. 6. He based his remarks on *H.E.* 5.16–19.

ily on a Sunday. Victor, the bishop of Rome, threatened to excommunicate them. Irenaeus, bishop of Lyons, urged peace and unity in the church. In a letter, he reminded Victor that his predecessors had lived in peace with Christians who followed a different tradition from their own. "No one was ever expelled because of this calendar, but the presbyters before you who did not observe [the Quartodeciman tradition] sent Eucharist to those from the churches that did observe it." Then Irenaeus reminded him of Polycarp's visit to Rome around AD 155, when Anicetus (ca. AD 154–166) was bishop presbyter. They had "modest disagreements," but "no desire for strife on this topic." Without persuading one another regarding the celebration of the Pascal feast, "they had fellowship with each other and in the church and parted in peace" (*H.E.* 5.24.12–17). As his name indicates, Irenaeus was a man of peace. He was eager to overcome distrust and hostility among individuals and groups and was involved both in the Montanist crisis and the Quartodeciman controversy in the ministry of peacemaking. "Blessed are the peacemakers [*eirenopoioi*], for they shall be called sons of God" (Matt 5:9). In the controversy over the celebration of Easter, Irenaeus stood for unity, *koinonia*, fellowship within the church, which could not be achieved by the submission of one local church to another. The "modest disagreements" between the Asian churches and the church in Rome, he thought, should be solved in love and freedom. Thus, the unity of the church would be preserved, the very faith of Christians proclaimed, and false teachings avoided.

In confronting and refuting gnostic teachings and speculations that had been also spreading in Gaul, however, Irenaeus was adamant as the voice of Christian tradition and theology. He was particularly occupied with the systems of Valentinus and Marcion as major oppositions to Christianity.

VALENTINUS' GNOSTIC SYSTEM

On the evidence of Tertullian, Valentinus, whom we have already introduced, was born in Egypt of Greek origin around AD 100. After conversion to Christianity and study in Alexandria, he moved to Rome, where he distinguished himself as a very influential and gifted teacher. While in Rome he was so popular, he was almost chosen to be a bishop in AD 143. After being rejected, Valentinus turned against Christianity.

Our knowledge of Valentinus' gnostic system comes primarily from Irenaeus' *Against Heresies*. *The Gospel of Truth*, discovered at Nag Hammadi, presumably represents the teaching of Valentinus at an early stage. It does not have the literary form of the New Testament Gospels, but is rather a homily or meditation. In his theological musing, Valentinus created a complicated system regarding the emanation of *aeons* from the Supreme Being. The word *aeon* [age] in the Hellenic period meant "time," or "endless time"; in the Hellenistic Age it received a further religious meaning, "to designate the deities of the mystery religions at Alexandria, where *Aeon* was identified with Osiris and Serapis." In the Valentinian system, God, the Supreme Being, was "the perfect *Aeon*."[23] His disciples expounded Valentinus' speculations (*A.H.* 1.1–8), which included the idea that the lowest of the *Aeons* [gods] was Sophia [Wisdom]. As already noted, Sophia was believed to have given life to the Demiurge, the creator of this universe. The mission of Jesus of Nazareth was to restore Sophia to the fullness of being [*plērōma*]. Valentinus used the Gospel of John (*A.H.* 3.11.7) as a source for his system; and Heracleon, one of his leading disciples, wrote a commentary on this text, which Origen criticized in his own commentary on John. Based on fragments preserved by Origen, Heracleon employed an extreme form of allegorical interpretation and transformed the historical events of Jesus' life into allegories. The miracles of Jesus were thoroughly allegorized.

Gnostics, apparently, were involved in the interpretation of the church's Scriptures. Some of them used the literal meaning of the texts to reject them as not worthy of any further interpretation. Influential gnostic teachers were exegetes of Christian non-gnostic writings (i.e., the Fourth Gospel and the Epistles of Paul) that would later be included in the canon of the New Testament. The Gospel of John, which was already circulating in Egypt in the first quarter of the second century, was particularly the subject of gnostic exegesis and speculation, without the constraint of the living tradition.

Gnostics would misinterpret Jesus' words and adjust any text to support their doctrines. A telling example is Valentinus' absurd interpretation of Jesus' parable "the laborers in the vineyard" (Matt 20:1–16). A householder hired some laborers at the first hour, some at the third, some others at the sixth, then at the ninth, and others at the eleventh hour. In this parable gnostics discovered thirty *aeons* simply by adding "together these hours, 1+3+6+9+11, giving a total of thirty" (*A.H.* 1.1.3). In adapting this parable to their pre-

---

[23] See D.J. Unger, *St. Irenaeus*, p. 131, n. 2.

conceived theological system, they found the *aeons,* but missed the meaning of the parable, the householder's generosity. When evening came, each laborer received a denarius, the last with the first. Irenaeus complained that the gnostics "transfer passages and rearrange them; and, making one thing out of another, they deceive many by the badly composed fantasy of the Lord's words that they adapt." To illustrate, Irenaeus takes the image of a king made out of precious stones, and supposes someone would destroy the features of the man, rearranging the jewels and making the image "of a dog or of a fox" out of them. This is how gnostics dealt with Christian texts. Valentinians "pluck words and sayings and parables from here and there and wish to adopt these words of God to their fables," making every effort to deceive the inexperienced "that this picture of a fox is that beautiful image of the King" (*A.H.* 1.8.1).

MARCION'S GNOSTIC SYSTEM

Justin Martyr had already warned that Marcion and his followers blasphemed and denied "God the Maker of the universe, professing that there is another who is greater and has done greater things than he" (*1 Apol.* 26.3–8). Marcion was born in Sinope, a city in Pontus on the coast of the Black Sea, where his father was a leading member of the Christian community. A ship owner and a very rich man, Marcion left Pontus. When he reached Rome, he became an active member of the church to which he gave a large sum of money as a gift. In Rome, Irenaeus writes, he came under the influence of Cerdo, a Christian gnostic from Asia Minor, who taught "that the God announced by the Law and the Prophets was not the Father of our Lord Jesus Christ, for the former was known, but the latter was unknown; again, the former was just, whereas the latter was benevolent" (*A.H.* 1.27.1–3). Marcion followed Cerdo and developed his doctrine, insisting "that the God who was proclaimed by the Law and the Prophets was the author of evil." He was excommunicated in AD 144 and his gift of money returned. After his expulsion, he founded his own church, with a hierarchy of bishops, priests, and deacons. The sect spread throughout the Roman world, surviving up to the fifth century.

Marcion's system was much simpler than the gnostic teachings of Valentinus and his followers. He did not share their love for speculation. Prone to radical divisions and sharp definitions, Marcion expressed some gnostic views "but of his own making." In his work, known as *Antitheses,* of which only fragments and allusions survive in the writings of his opponents, Marcion contrasted the law and the gospel. They are in his view so radically different that they proclaimed two different gods, the just (i.e., evil) god and the good god. This good god, the previously unknown God, without wrath or judgment, sent Christ into the world.

Marcion rejected the Hebrew Scriptures; he maintained that Christianity had nothing to do with Judaism. While other gnostics rejected the Old Testament by using extreme allegory and fanciful speculations, Marcion applied radical literal-mindedness, pointing out the contradictions, instead of "esoteric exegesis." Although he did not engage in allegorical speculation or claim special insight [gnosis], Marcion professed the unknown Foreign God and preached deliverance from the god who created the world. For expressing these views, he "must be considered a gnostic, although he was an exception among them."[24]

Both Valentinus and Marcion distorted the message and historical character of the gospel, Valentinus by allegory and Marcion with "the knife, not the pen," as Tertullian observed (*Praescr. 38*). Irenaeus writes that Marcion "mutilated the Gospel according to Luke, discarding all that is written about the birth of the Lord, and eliminating also many of the Lord's discourses containing teachings in which it is most clearly written that the Lord confessed his Father as the Maker of the universe" (*A.H.* 1.27.6–7). He omitted the first two chapters of Luke, which recount the birth of Christ, as not worthy of the Savior. This is consistent with Marcion's Docetism and denial of the Incarnation.

While the mutilated version of Luke's Gospel was Marcion's *Evangelium,* the mutilated letters of Paul were his *Apostolikon.* Like many modern scholars, he rejected the pastoral letters and the Letter to the Hebrews as not authored by Paul. Marcion handed down to his disciples only "a portion of the Gospel," not the whole. Then, from the ten letters of Paul he removed the texts in which the apostle spoke of the God who made the world as "the Father of our Lord Jesus Christ." From Tertullian's *Against Marcion,* we learn how extensively Marcion mutilated Christian Scriptures in making his own New Testament.

Despite the general belief that Marcion initiated the collection of Paul's letters, there is evidence that by the turn of the first century Paul's letters were

---

[24]See H. Jonas, "Gnostic Allegory," in *Gnostic Religion,* pp. 91–97.

being read in other churches, not only in those to which they had been addressed. According to 2 Peter 3:16, Christians acknowledged Paul's letters as authoritative, "which the ignorant and unstable twist to their own destruction, as they do other Scriptures." Second Peter is tentatively dated ca. AD 100, around the time of Marcion's birth, and long before he started his theological work.[25]

ST IRENAEUS AS BIBLICAL THEOLOGIAN

In the struggle with the gnostics, Irenaeus refuted "the knowledge falsely so called" with true gnosis, which he defined as "the teaching of the apostles and ancient institutions of the church" (*A.H.* 4.33.8). He opposed the gnostic tradition of a secret body of knowledge transmitted to the chosen few with the public apostolic tradition handed over to many. This tradition originated with Christ's public ministry, his post-resurrection appearances, and the Spirit's activity, which declares to each coming generation what Jesus said and did (John 16:14–15). For Irenaeus, Christ is both the origin and the very content of the tradition,[26] and "the church is the continuation of Christ."[27]

Like Ignatius at the beginning of the second century, Irenaeus at the end of the century was the theologian of the church's unity of faith, which he contrasted with the multiplicity of gnostic sects and beliefs. "Where the Church is, there is the Spirit of God, and where the Spirit of God is there is the Church and all grace" (*A.H.* 3:24.1). Docetics, according to Ignatius and gnostics, according to Irenaeus, separate themselves from the church and cut themselves off from the divine life, from uninterrupted communion with Christ. Only in the church, the body of Christ, which is "the Spirit's field of activity," is union with Christ accomplished.

Unlike Justin Martyr, who wrote in the previous generation, Irenaeus displayed no particular interest in philosophy. Without denying the value of human reason, he insisted that only "through faith in what God had revealed"

---

[25]Nonetheless, it is widely held that Marcion was instrumental in causing the Church to produce a list of "canonical" books, i.e. writings that had passed the Apostolic rule or canon and were thus regarded as constituting the New Testament (the list itself came very much later to be called the "canon"): see Hans von Campenhausen, *The Formation of the Christian Bible* (London; Philadelphia, PA: Fortress Press: 1972).

[26]Jaroslav Pelikan, *The Emergence of the Catholic Tradition, 100–600,* The Christian Tradition: A History of the Development of Doctrine, Volume 1 (Chicago: University of Chicago Press, 1971), p. 115.

[27]Emile Mersch, *The Whole Christ: Historical Development of the Doctrine of the Mystical Body in Scripture and Tradition* (Milwaukee, WI: Bruce Publishing, 1938), p. 235ff.

and "in what he had done" is salvation accomplished. The human quest for truth cannot be substituted for revelation, nor can revelation be reduced to the level of human thinking. The task of a Christian theologian or philosopher, as Irenaeus saw it, "is just that of bringing to bear on the content of Christian faith whatever intellectual equipment he may be endowed with."[28] Irenaeus' attitude toward the place of philosophy in Christian theological development is neither Justin's nor Tertullian's. Thus, by the end of the second century, Irenaeus pointed to the third Christian approach to the relation of faith and reason, an approach generally subsequently adopted by church fathers of the East and of the West.

Irenaeus was a biblical theologian, and the heart of his theology is the doctrine of recapitulation [anakephalaiōsis]: God created all things through his Word, his Son, the same Word that became flesh (John 1:14); recapitulation begins with the Incarnation and is completed by the glorification of Christ's body. In other terms, Jesus Christ recapitulates in himself the history of the human race, so human beings might receive again what they had lost in Adam (A.H. 4.38.1). Christ went through experiences parallel to those of Adam but with the opposite results: by being obedient, he was victorious. "By the obedience of one many will be justified and receive salvation" (A.H. 3.18.7).

Together with the theme of recapitulation, Irenaeus developed the doctrine of the deification of man (which was later called "theosis"): the Word of God in the fullness of time became a human being in order to restore the union between God and humanity, that human beings might become "sons of God," and what was lost in Adam might be recovered in Christ. In the Eucharist, notes Irenaeus, the faithful receive Christ; but turning to the gnostics, he asks how they could celebrate the Eucharist when they deny the Incarnation and bodily Resurrection. For them, he observes, there is no salvation of the flesh. "If the flesh were not to be saved, the Word of God would not become flesh" (A.H. 5.14.1).[29]

Irenaeus' work Against the Heresies refuted "false knowledge" with "true gnosis." Only one God is the Creator and the Redeemer of the world. He reproached his gnostic opponents, asserting that the true gnostic is the "spir-

---

[28]A.H. Armstrong and R.A. Markus, *Christian Faith and Greek Philosophy*, pp. 144–7.

[29]For God's creative energy, extended in the Eucharist, see George L. Prestige, *God in Patristic Thought* (Heinemann: Toronto, 1952), p. 13f.

itual man" who is growing in a true knowledge of God and the love of God and who immerses himself in the living apostolic tradition of the church.[30] With these convictions, Irenaeus drew the boundary line between Gnosticism and Christianity, excluding the gnostic teachers from the church. Three elements of Irenaeus: his "Biblical way of thinking," his response to the docetic and gnostic teachings, and his vision of recapitulation, made him the most influential theologian of second century Christianity. He was a man of great authority and peace. Nevertheless, the controversy continues as to what he said about the Roman church's claim to primacy. Through the centuries, exegetes have been arguing over the meaning of *Against Heresies* 3.3.1–2, a passage used to support early Roman claims to primacy. Modern scholars find the text open to more than one interpretation, and the fact that his major work, *Against Heresies,* survives only in Latin translation and not in the Greek original, complicates the issue.

Without doubt, Irenaeus, as an influential theologian, was the unifying force of his time, and remains so in ours. "Roman Catholics have cited Irenaeus on authority, Protestants on the Bible," and "Eastern theology adopted his *Christus Victor* motif" and his teaching of the deification of human nature.[31] In his own time, he worked for Christian tolerance and unity, and his writings continue to do so in ours.

St Clement of Alexandria

Irenaeus' contemporary, Clement of Alexandria (ca. AD 150–215), expresses a similar view regarding the identity of the true gnostic. After a long search for truth, parallel to the search of Justin Martyr, Clement joined the Christian church, and became the first great teacher of the catechetical school in Alexandria (AD 190–202).[32] In confronting gnostics, he described the qualities of the "true gnostic, one who worships the true God," referring to the God of the Bible, not the supreme Deity of the gnostics.

As a teacher, Clement succeeded Pantaenus, founder of a school in Alexandria. He saw as his major task the building up of a strong and united

[30]For Irenaeus on gnosis, see Louis Bouyer, *Spirituality of the New Testament and the Fathers* (vol. 1 of *A History of Christian Spirituality*; Paris: Desclée De Brouwer, 1960), pp. 252–255.

[31]See E. Glenn Hinson, "Irenaeus," *Encyclopedia of Religion*, VII:283.

[32]He was a prolific writer. His major works are *Paedagogos* ="Guide" or "Tutor"; *Protrepticus* = "Exhortation to the Greeks"; and *Stromata* = "Miscellanies."

community, capable of meeting challenges from aggressive paganism and influential gnostic teachers. There was diversity in the Christian community of Alexandria: one group of believers read and understood Scripture in a literal sense; a second group desired more theological reflection and the use of classical culture in interpreting texts. Clement himself had a positive attitude toward philosophy, and might almost be thought to have believed that Christianity had two Old Testaments: one belonging to the Hebrew people and another that expresses the best yearning of the Greek mind. Both "Old Testaments" are the tutors who lead to Christ: "The law is for the Jew what philosophy is for the Greek, a schoolmaster to bring them to Christ" (*Strom.* 1.5.28).[33] A third group were the followers of Valentinus and Basilides, who considered themselves to be Christians but were not so recognized by Clement. The life work of true Christian gnostics, according to Clement, is to hold communion with God through his Great High Priest, Jesus, the Son of God, and to achieve knowledge of the facts of the Christian religion (*Strom.* 7.3). Clement left Alexandria during the persecution of the Roman Emperor Severus (AD 202), taking refuge in Cappadocia, where he probably died.

While Clement was searching for Truth in sometimes unpromising sources, Irenaeus immersed himself in the living apostolic tradition of the church. Nevertheless, by these two seemingly converse paths, both contributed to the riches of the apostolic tradition.

[33]Greek philosophy for Clement was the word of the Lord: "For, by giving to the Jews commandments and to the Greeks philosophy . . . he leads men by both ways of advance, whether Greek or barbarian, to the perfection which is through faith" (*Strom.* 7.1.11).

CONCLUSION

Irenaeus summed up Christian development in the second century, but Gnosticism did not end with Irenaeus' arguments. It continued throughout the third century and beyond. Hippolytus of Rome (ca. AD 170–254), Tertullian (AD 160–225), Origen (AD 180–254), and Epiphanius (AD 350) all are recognized as anti-gnostic writers. By the turn of the second century, however, Gnosticism thought and practice was moving further from Christianity, and because of the figure, Mani (AD 216–277), this theological system developed into what became known as the "Gnostic World Religion."

The Teachings of Mani

The son of Iranian parents, Mani was born and lived in the syncretistic environment of Mesopotamia, where he appeared as a prophet of a new religion, based on Zoroastrian dualism. Light and darkness, he insisted, have nothing in common. The former is good and the latter evil. In Mani's view, the prophets who preceded him, Zoroaster, Buddha, and Jesus, were merely regional, not universal, prophets. Only he, Mani, could offer the message of salvation to the whole world. He stressed that each human being contains a spark of light, which when liberated unites with the God-above-God, Supreme Light.[1] This doctrine of salvation that comes from knowledge [gnosis] attracted Augustine and brought him originally into the Manichean movement; from AD 377–382 he was a follower of the teachings of Mani. Moreover, "Manichaeism," the system of thought developed by Mani, inspired many in the later centuries, and two medieval sects, the Bogomils in the Balkans and Cathari in southern France, appeared to have been under its influence.[2]

---

[1]Gherardo Gnoli, "Mani," in *Encyclopedia of Religion*, IX:158–161; "Manichaeism," pp. 161–170. Mani maintained that there is no reason to celebrate the Eucharist. It is related to the Incarnation. God could not be united with flesh.

[2]For a discussion of the Bogomils in Bosnia, see our essay: "Bosnia: History and Religion," in *New Perspectives on Historical Theology*, ed. Bradley Nassif (Grand Rapids, MI: Wm. B. Eerdmans; Cambridge, 1996), pp. 73–79.

By dividing Christian doctrine from its historical roots, Gnosticism represented a basic danger for the church. To combat this ever-present danger, Gnostic teachers were refuted not by arguments but by the very existence of the church as a historical community, witnessing and reliving the life, death, and resurrection of Jesus. Among the religions of the Greco-Roman world, the church emerged as a distinct community, with the New Testament writings in the process of canonization and the "rule of faith"—creed-like formulas for measuring orthodoxy—expanding in length and number. Within this church of the Incarnate Lord, Scripture and creed became indelible aspects of its identity and authority.

The Process of Canonization

Papias, Bishop of Hierapolis in Phrygia, wrote *Explanation of the Sayings of the Lord* in five volumes, of which only a few fragments have survived. Around AD 125, he had learned of the gospel of Jesus Christ in oral and written form. On the evidence of Irenaeus, he was a "hearer of [the Apostle] John and colleague [friend] of Polycarp".[3] Papias was familiar with the details of the life of Christ, from the "living and abiding voice," which for him was more profitable than books. But Papias' testimony to the written Gospels, the "orderly account" (Luke 1:3), which came out of the living tradition, suggests the importance and authority of the written word as well.[4]

Public reading of the Gospels in the churches, of which Justin left such a vivid description in *1 Apol.* 66–7, clearly evidences that from the second century onward Christians recognized the authority of these books, and acknowledged that they bore trustworthy witness to Jesus and the faith of the church. "The authority of the Gospels is so great that the heretics themselves bear witness to them and each of them tries to confirm his own teaching out of them," wrote Irenaeus in AD 185. The Ebionites used Matthew's Gospel; the Marcionites "circumcised" the Gospel of Luke; the docetics, who separate Jesus from Christ, preferred Mark's Gospel; and disciples of Valentinus adopted the Gospel according to John. If they had read these gospels "with a love of truth," Irenaeus asserts, they would not have gone astray (*A.H.* 3.11).

---

[3] *A.H.* 5.33–4.

[4] Regarding the historical roots of the Synoptic Gospels Mark and Matthew, we have information from Papias (*H.E.* 3.39.1–17).

He argued that the four Gospels were one gospel, "fourfold in form but held together in one Spirit."

The Rehabilitation of St Paul's Epistles

Early on, the writings of the Apostle Paul had fallen in the esteem of the Christian communities because of the use of his letters by the gnostics. These suspicions were removed by the end of the second century.[5] While Justin Martyr avoided using Paul's letters without rejecting them, Irenaeus did not hesitate to rely on Paul's authority. To repudiate the gnostic position of separating Jesus of Nazareth from the Christ (maintaining that only Jesus suffered; Christ lived without suffering), Irenaeus gathered texts from Paul's letters (1 Cor 15:3–4, 12, 21; Rom 14:15) concluding "that Jesus, since he was Christ, suffered for us" (*A.H.* 3.18.3). By Irenaeus' witness, Paul is fully rehabilitated, and his letters recognized as indispensable for the history and spirituality of the church.

The earliest extant list of New Testament books comes to us around the end of the second century, probably originating in Rome. It is named "The Muratorian Canon," after the scholar L. A. Muratory, who discovered it in the eighteenth century. The Canon includes thirteen letters ascribed to Paul, without the Letter to the Hebrews. The Letter of James, 1 and 2 Peter, and 3 John did not make the list, which consisted of twenty-two books.

Irenaeus likewise had not accepted the Pauline authorship of the Letter to the Hebrews. Though he employed some of the general epistles, "no traces of James and Jude could be found in his work." His older contemporary, Theophilus, Bishop of Antioch, had used a similar collection.[6] In contrast, Athanasius, Bishop of Alexandria (AD 328–373), listed all twenty-seven books of the New Testament canon in his Festal Letter (AD 367), stressing that these writings "are the spring of salvation," and let "no one add anything to them or take anything away from them."

---

[5]See C.K. Barrett, "Pauline Controversies," *NTS* 20 (1973): 229–245.
[6]R. Grant, *Irenaeus of Lyons,* p. 34.

The Expansion of the Rule of Faith

As the church never existed without its Scriptures, so neither did it exist without its "rule of faith," or "rule of truth," a creed-like summary of the content of the Christian faith. The earliest Christian confessions of faith are "Jesus is the Lord" (1 Cor 12:3) and "You are the Christ, the Son of the living God" (Matt 16:16). Irenaeus cited an expanded rule: "Faith in one God the Father Almighty, who made heaven and earth and the sea and all that is in them (Ex 20:11), and in one Christ Jesus, the Son of God, incarnate for our salvation, and in the Holy Spirit who through the prophets predicted the dispensations of God: the coming, the birth from the Virgin, the Passion, the resurrection from the dead, and the ascension of the beloved Jesus Christ, our Lord in the flesh, into the heavens, and his coming from the heavens in the glory of the Father to 'recapitulate all things' (Eph 1:10) and raise up all flesh of the human race" (*A.H.* 1.10.1).

The Gnostics, who lacked the "rule of faith," taught that "which the prophets did not proclaim, the Lord did not teach, and the apostles did not transmit"(*A.H.* 1.8.1). But anyone who keeps the unchangeable "rule of truth" received through Baptism, writes Irenaeus, will not accept arbitrary teachings of the Gnostics and will accept the sayings and parables of the Lord (*A.H.* 1.9.4). Therefore, both canon and creed are inspired aspects of the church's identity. They are products of the inner power of Christian faith and the demands put upon the missionary church, for there is no doubt that that conflict with the Gnostics accelerated the process of canonization and formulation of creed-like statements.

The Development of Christology

With the common confession of the faith—the Word had taken flesh and had become man—the Church refuted the teachings of Ebionites, Marcionites, and gnostics. Celsus, an early opponent of Christianity, pushed the church's doctrinal development further; he had objected to the Christian teachings of the Incarnation and raised the question: "How could God, who is good and beautiful, come down to man without undergoing change?" He confronted Christians with the question: "When God became man, did he remain God?" (*C.C.* 4.14–15). Celsus left Christians with a choice: either accept Docetism or admit a change in the Godhead.

The way out of the dilemma raised by Celsus was the doctrine of "one person in two natures."[7] Rejecting the gnostic concept of "double personality," Irenaeus emphasized the reality of Christ's passion; the Divine Logos was the personal subject of suffering (*A.H.* 3.18.6). The teaching of Irenaeus pointed toward the doctrine of hypostatic union, elaborated in the christological controversies in subsequent centuries: one Person shares the properties of two natures, and the experiences of both natures.[8]

The church in this formative period (AD 30–200) expanded into various regions of the empire, came into contact and conflict with diverse religious sects, and deepened its loyalty to the public apostolic tradition. The Apostolic Fathers, who were the leaders of the second-century churches, in their writings expressed the spirit of their diverse places of origin. In response to inner and outer threats, they acted to preserve the identity of the church handed down to them by a rule of faith. By the second century also, Rome had become the geographic center of Christian diversity, as the faithful from every region converged there. Justin Martyr and Irenaeus of Lyons dwelled in that city, as well as Valentinus and Marcion. Rome, by that time, thus represented "Christianity in miniature." The second-century church had struggled to prepare the ground for the Christian communities of the following centuries, and had shaped the early church by means of its ministry, canon and creed, and openness to the world.

---

[7]See A. Grillmeier, *Christ in Christian Tradition*, p. 124.

[8]For the union of two natures in Christ, see our article "Hypostatic and Prosopic Union in the Exegesis of Christ's Temptation," *SVTQ* 9.3 (1965): 119–137.

SELECT BIBLIOGRAPHY

Armstrong, Arthur H. and Robert A. Markus. *Christian Faith and Greek Philosophy.* New York: Sheed & Ward, 1960.

Barnard, Leslie W. *St. Justin Martyr: The First and Second Apologies.* New York: Paulist Press, 1997.

Barrett, C. K. *Luke the Historian.* Peterborough, UK: Epworth, 1961.

—————. *Commentary on the First Epistle to the Corinthians.* Black's New Testament Commentaries. London: Adam & Charles Black, 1968.

—————. *New Testament Background: Selected Documents.* Rev. ed. New York: HarperCollins, 1989.

Bauckham, Richard. *Jude and the Relatives of Jesus in the Early Church.* Edinburgh: T & T Clark, 1990.

Benko, Stephen. *Pagan Rome and the Early Christians.* Bloomington, IN: Indiana University Press, 1986.

Benoît, Pierre. *Jesus and the Gospel.* 1st ed. New York: Herder & Herder, 1973.

Bouyer, Louis. *Spirituality of the New Testament and the Fathers.* Vol. 1 of *A History of Christian Spirituality.* Paris: Desclée De Brouwer, 1960.

Brown, Raymond E. *A Crucified Christ in Holy Week: Essays on the Four Gospel Passion Narratives.* Collegeville, MN: Liturgical Press, 1986.

—————. *Introduction to New Testament Christology.* New York: Paulist Press, 1994.

—————— and John Meier. *Antioch and Rome: New Cradles of Catholic Christianity.* New York: Paulist Press, 1983.

——————, Joseph A. Fitzmyer, and Roland E. Murphy, eds. *The New Jerome Biblical Commentary.* Englewood Cliff, NJ: Prentice-Hall, 1990.

Bruce, F. F. *Philippians.* New York: Harper & Row, 1983.

Campenhausen, Hans von. *The Formation of the Christian Bible.* London; Philadelphia, PA: Fortress Press, 1972.

Carroll, James. *Constantine's Sword: The Church and the Jews.* New York: Houghton Mifflin Co., 2001.

Chadwick, Henry. *History and Thought of the Early Christian Church.* London: Variorum Reprints, 1982.

Charlesworth, J.H. *Jesus within Judaism: New Light from Exciting Archeological Discoveries.* New York: Doubleday, 1988.

Congar, Yves. *Diversity and Communion.* Mystic, CT: Twenty-Third Publications, 1985.

Conzelmann, Hans. *History of Primitive Christianity.* Nashville, TN: Abingdon Press, 1973.

Cross, Frank Leslie. *The Early Christian Fathers.* Studies in Theology. London: G. Duckworth, 1960.

Deissmann, Gustav Adolf. *Paul: A Study in Social and Religious History.* 2d ed. New York: Doran (Doubleday), 1926.

Dodd, C.H. *The Interpretation of the Fourth Gospel.* Cambridge: Cambridge University Press, 1953.

Dunn, James D.G. *Christology in the Making.* London: SCM Press, Ltd., 1980.

———. *The Evidence for Jesus.* Philadelphia, PA: Westminster Press, 1985.

———. *Jesus and the Spirit.* Philadelphia, PA: Westminster Press, 1975.

———. *The Partings of the Ways: Between Christianity and Judaism and Their Significance for the Character of Christianity.* London: SCM Press, Ltd; Philadelphia, PA: Trinity Press International, 1991.

———. *Unity and Diversity in the New Testament.* Philadelphia, PA: Westminster Press, 1977.

Ehrman, Bart D. *After the New Testament: A Reader in Early Christianity.* Oxford: Oxford University Press, 1999.

Eliade, Mircea, ed. *Encyclopedia of Religion,* 16 vols. New York: Macmillan Publishing Company, 1987.

Finegan, Jack. *Myth and Mystery: An Introduction to the Pagan Religions of the Biblical World.* Grand Rapids, MI: Baker Academic, 1997.

Finkelstein, Louis. *Akiba: Scholar, Saint and Martyr.* New York: Atheneum, 1975.

Fitzmyer, J.A. "Jewish Christianity in Acts in Light of the Qumran Scrolls," in *Studies in Luke-Acts.* L. E. Keck and J. L. Martyn, eds. Philadelphia, PA: Fortress Press, 1980.

Flusser, David. *Judaism and the Origins of Christianity.* Jerusalem, Hebrew University: Magnee Press, 1988.

Frend, W.H.C. *The Rise of Christianity.* Minneapolis: MN, Augsburg Fortress Publishers, 1986.

———. *Martyrdom and Persecution in the Early Church: A Study of Conflict from the Maccabees to Donatus.* New York: New York University Press, 1967.

Gartner, Bertil. *The Areopagus Speech and Natural Revelation.* Uppsala: C.W.K. Gleerup, 1955.

Grant, Frederick C. *Ancient Roman Religion.* New York: Macmillan Publishing Company, 1957.

———, ed. *Hellenistic Religions: The Age of Syncretism.* New York: Macmillan Publishing Company, 1953.

Grant, Robert M. *After the New Testament.* Philadelphia, PA: Fortress Press, 1967.

———. *Ignatius of Antioch.* Vol. 4 of *The Apostolic Fathers: A New Translation and Commentary.* Edited by Robert M. Grant. New York: Thomas Nelson and Sons, 1964–1968.

———. *Irenaeus of Lyons.* New York: Routledge, 1997.

———, ed. *Second Century Christianity: A Collection of Fragments.* Translations of Christian Literature. Series VI: Select Passages. London: SPCK, 1957.

Grillmeier, Aloys. *Christ in Christian Tradition: From the Apostolic Age to Chalcedon 451.* New York: Sheed & Ward, 1965.

Harnack, Adolph. *The Mission and Expansion of Christianity in the First Three Centuries.* Translated and edited by James Moffatt. New York: Harper Torchbooks, 1962.

Harrington, Daniel J. *The Light of All Nations: Essays on the Church in New Testament Research.* Good News Studies, 3. Wilmington, DE: Michael Glazier, Inc., 1982.

Hengel, Martin. *Acts and the History of Earliest Christianity.* Philadelphia, PA: Trinity Press, 1980.

_____. *Between Jesus and Paul: Studies in the Earliest History of Christianity.* Minneapolis, MN: Augsburg Fortress Publishers, 1983.

_____. *The Charismatic Leader and His Followers.* Eugene, OR: Wipf & Stock Publishers, 2005.

_____. *Crucifixion in the Ancient World and the Folly of the Message of the Cross.* Philadelphia, PA: Fortress Press, 1977.

_____. *The "Hellenization" of Judaea in the First Century after Christ.* Philadelphia, PA: Trinity Press, 1989.

_____. *Judaism and Hellenism: Studies in Their Encounter in Palestine During the Early Hellenistic Period.* Eugene, OR: Wipf & Stock Publishers, 2003.

_____. *The Pre-Christian Paul.* Philadelphia, PA: Trinity Press, 1991.

_____. *The Son of God: The Origin of Christology and the History of the Jewish-Hellenistic Religion.* Minneapolis, MN: Augsburg Fortress Publishers, 1976.

Hennecke, Edward. *New Testament Apocrypha: Volume II: Writings Related to the Apostles, Apocalypses and Related Subjects.* 2d ed. Wilhelm Schneemelcher, ed. Philadelphia, PA: Westminster Press, 1991.

Hill, Craig C. *Hellenists and Hebrews: Reappraising Division within the Earliest Church.* Minneapolis, MN: Augsburg Fortress Publishers, 1992.

Jeffers, James S. *Conflict at Rome: Social Order and Hierarchy in Early Christianity.* Philadelphia, PA: Fortress Press, 1991.

Jeremias, Joachim. *The Eucharistic Words of Jesus.* New York: Charles Scribner's Sons, 1966.

Jonas, Hans. *Gnostic Religion.* 2d ed. Boston, MA: Beacon Press, 1985.

Kesich, Veselin. *The First Day of the New Creation.* Crestwood, NY: St Vladimir's Seminary Press, 1982.

_____. *The Gospel Image of Christ,* 2d ed. Crestwood, NY: St Vladimir's Seminary Press, 1991.

_____. "Bosnia: History and Religion," in *New Perspectives on Historical Theology.* Edited by Bradley Nassif. Grand Rapids: Wm. B. Eerdmans; MI / Cambridge UK, 1996.

Kesich, Veselin and Lydia. *Treasures of the Holy Land.* Crestwood, NY: St Vladimir's Seminary Press, 1985.

Koester, Helmut. *History, Culture, and Religion of the Hellenistic Age.* Vol. 1 of *Introduction to the New Testament.* English translation. Philadelphia, PA: Fortress Press, 1982.

_____. *History and Literature of Early Christianity.* 2d ed. Vol. 2 of *Introduction to the New Testament.* Berlin / New York; Walter de Gruyter, 1982.

Kraft, Robert A. *The Didache and Barnabas.* Vol. 3 of *The Apostolic Fathers: A New Translation and Commentary.* Edited by Robert M. Grant. New York: Thomas Nelson & Sons, 1964–1968.

Lampe, Peter. *From Paul to Valentinus: Christians at Rome in the First Two Centuries.* London: T & T Clark [Continuum], 2003.

Leon-Dufour, Xavier. *Sharing the Eucharistic Bread: The Witness of the New Testament.* Mahwah, NJ: Paulist Press, 1987.

Logan, Alastair H.B. *Gnostic Truth and Christian Heresy: A Study in the History of Gnosticism.* Edinburgh: T&T Clark, 1996.

Longenecker, Richard N. *The Christology of Early Jewish Christianity.* Studies in Biblical Theology. 2d Series: 17. Naperville IL: Alec R. Allenson, Inc.

Maccoby, Hyman. *The Mythmaker: Paul and the Invention of Christianity*. New York: Harper & Row, 1986.

MacRae, George W. *Studies in the New Testament and Gnosticism*. Good News Studies. Wilmington, DE: Michael Glazier, Inc., 1987.

Malherbe, Abraham J. *Paul and the Thessalonians: The Philosophic Tradition of Pastoral Care*. Minneapolis, MN: Augsburg Fortress Publishers, 1987.

————. *Social Aspects of Early Christianity*. Minneapolis, MN: Augsburg Fortress Publishers, 1983.

Manson, T.W. *The Church's Ministry*. Philadelphia, PA: Westminster Press, 1948.

Meeks, W.A. *The First Urban Christians: The Social World of the Apostle Paul*. New Haven: Yale University Press, 1983.

Meier, John P. *Matthew*. New Testament Message, 3. Wilmington, DE: Michael Glazier, Inc., 1981.

Mersch, Emile. *The Whole Christ: Historical Development of the Doctrine of the Mystical Body in Scripture and Tradition*. Milwaukee, WI: Bruce Publishing, 1938.

Milik, Józef Tadeusz. *Ten Years of Discovery in the Wilderness of Judaea*. London: SCM Press, Ltd., 1959.

Moule, C.F.D. *The Birth of the New Testament*. London: Adam & Charles Black, 1962.

————. *The Origin of Christology*. Cambridge: Cambridge University Press, 1977.

Murphy-O'Connor, Jerome. *Becoming Human Together: The Pastoral Anthropology of St. Paul*. Wilmington, DE: Michael Glazier, Inc., 1982.

————. *Paul: A Critical Life*. Oxford: Oxford University Press, 1996.

Murray, John Courtney. *The Problem of God, Yesterday and Today*. New Haven: Yale University Press, 1965.

Musurillo, Herbert, trans. *The Acts of the Christian Martyrs*. Oxford: Oxford University Press, 1972.

O'Collins, Gerald. *Interpreting the Resurrection*. New York: Paulist Press, 1988.

O'Donovan, Oliver. *Resurrection and Moral Order: An Outline for Evangelical Ethics*. Grand Rapids: Wm. B. Eerdmans Publishing Company, 1986.

Pearson, Birger A. *Gnosticism, Judaism and Egyptian Christianity: Studies in Antiquity and Christianity*. Philadelphia, PA: Fortress Press, 1990.

Pelikan, Jaroslav. *The Emergence of the Catholic Tradition, 100–600*. Vol. 1 of *The Christian Tradition: A History of the Development of Doctrine*. Chicago: University of Chicago Press, 1971.

Perrin, Norman. *Rediscovering the Teaching of Jesus*. New York: HarperCollins, 1967.

Pétrement, Simone. *A Separate God: The Christian Origins of Gnosticism*. San Francisco: HarperSanFrancisco, 1990.

Pokorny, Petr. *Colossians: A Commentary*. Peabody MA: Hendrickson Publishers, 1991.

Prestige, George L. *God in Patristic Thought*. Toronto: W. Heinemann, 1952.

Rahner, Hugo. *Greek Myth and Christian Mystery*. New York: Harper & Row, 1963.

Reicke, Bo Ivar. *The Roots of the Synoptic Gospels*. Philadelphia, PA: Fortress Press, 1986.

Richardson, Cyril C., ed. *Early Christian Fathers*. Library of Christian Classics, 1. Philadelphia, PA: The Westminster Press, 1953.

Robinson, James M., ed. *Coptic Gnostic Library: A Complete Edition of the Nag Hammadi Codices*. Leiden: E.J. Brill, 2000.

Sanders, E.P. *Jesus and Judaism*. Minneapolis, MN: Augsburg Fortress Publishers, 1987.

Schnackenburg, Rudolf. *Baptism in the Thought of St. Paul: A Study in Pauline Theology*. New York: Herder and Herder, 1964.

_____. *The Gospel According to St. John: Volume One: Introduction and Commentary on Chapters 1–4*. Herders Theological Commentary on the New Testament. Editors J. Massingberd Ford and Kevin Smyth. New York: Herder and Herder, 1982.

Schweizer, Eduard. *Church Order in the New Testament*. Studies in Biblical Theology, 32. London: SCM Press, Ltd., 1961.

Sherwin-White, A.N. *Roman Society and Roman Law in the New Testament*. Oxford: Clarendon Press, 1963.

Smith, D. Moody. "John" in *Harper's Biblical Commentary*. Edited by James L. Mays. San Francisco: Harper & Row Publishers, 1988.

Trevett, Christine. *Montanism: Gender, Authority and the New Prophecy*. Cambridge: Cambridge University Press, 1996.

Unger, Dominic J., trans. and annotator. *St. Irenaeus, Bishop of Lyons: Against the Heresies*. Ancient Christian Writers 1. Mahwah, NJ: Paulist Press, 1992.

Whittaker, Molly. *Jews and Christians: Graeco-Roman Views*. Cambridge Commentaries on Writings of the Jewish & Christian World 200 BC to AD 200, 6. Cambridge: Cambridge University Press, 1984.

Wilken, Robert L. *The Christians as the Romans Saw Them*. New Haven, CT: Yale University Press, 1984.

Wilkinson, John, ed. *Egeria's Travels*. London: SPCK, 1971.

Williams, Michael Allen. *Rethinking "Gnosticism": An Argument for Dismantling a Dubious Category*. Princeton, NJ: Princeton University Press, 1996.

Wilson, A.N. *Paul: The Mind of the Apostle*. New York: W. W. Norton & Company, 1997.

INDEX

Available from SVS Press